PROFIT!

MAKE MONEY AS A LANDLORD
IN ANY REAL ESTATE MARKET

BRYAN M. CHAVIS

TOUCHSTONE

NEW YORK   LONDON   TORONTO   SYDNEY   NEW DELHI

New York, NY 10020

First Touchstone trade paperback edition January 2017

Touchstone and colophon are registered trademarks of Simon & Schuster, Inc.

For information about special discounts for bulk purchases, please contact Simon & Schuster Special Sales at 1-866-506-1949 or business@simonandschuster.com.

The Simon & Schuster Speakers Bureau can bring authors to your live event. For more information or to book an event contact the Simon & Schuster Speakers Bureau at 1-866-248-3049 or visit our website at www.simonspeakers.com.

Designed by Ruth Lee-Mui

Manufactured in the United States of America

1 3 5 7 9 10 8 6 4 2

Library of Congress Cataloging-in-Publication Data is available.

ISBN 978-1-5011-4582-7
ISBN 978-1-5011-4708-1 (ebook)

After facing a learning disability and a brain tumor, I now dedicate this book
to everyone who has overcome tremendous challenges in their own life.
This is for you.

CONTENTS

PART IV—BUILDING WEALTH WITH REAL ESTATE

PROLOGUE TO THE SECOND EDITION

Since *Buy It, Rent It, Profit!* was first published in 2009, much has changed in the real estate world. When I first started writing this book, my goal was to simply share my personal experience and the tools I used to achieve real estate investment success, because I truly believe that if I can achieve this, *anyone* with the same passion, conviction, determination, and perseverance can achieve this success, too. Imagine my happiness when this book became a top seller, exceeding my wildest expectations. Since the book was released, I have been fortunate enough to travel the country sharing my methods and systems with individuals and businesses. I have relaunched my website, **www.landlordacademy.com**, to offer even more information and training to those who are serious about taking their businesses to the next level. I even offer private, one-on-one coaching to those who want to fast-track their success. And along the way, my efforts continue to be validated. This book is now featured as a reading resource on Wikipedia's property management page.

But this has not been an easy journey, and with success comes survival. The difference between the first edition of this book and the one you're holding in your hands is the word "survival" in the very literal sense. Just as my book hit stores in early 2009, the financial markets (and the real estate market, specifically) imploded right before our eyes. Millions of Americans found themselves underwater and overextended on their homes. My home state of Florida had some of the highest foreclosure levels. It was a scary time. But luckily, because of the careful, rigorous formula for evaluating and maintaining properties that I laid out in this book, my business was largely able to weather the financial storm, as were so many of my Landlord Academy students.

If wading through the Florida real estate market crash wasn't bad enough, I had even more to survive—literally. In 2012, I was diagnosed with a deadly brain tumor and subsequently underwent a risky operation in a desperate bid by doctors to save my life. The tumor was so aggressive (and the surgery so risky) that many on my medical team advised me not to go forward with it because of the possibility of permanent brain damage or even death. But thankfully, due to the efforts of the great medical team at Tampa General Hospital, my brain tumor was successfully removed.

Little did I know, my journey to restoration was just beginning. Postsurgery, I had to learn to talk, walk, and even brush my teeth again through daily physical rehabilitation. It was a most difficult, exhausting, and frustrating time. Never did I think that on the cusp of turning forty years old, I would be starting all over. Slowly I relearned the basic life fundamentals, got back into a personal and professional groove, and began my return to the business that I love. I started coaching again, and then eventually giving lectures, advising hedge funds, consulting, and setting up training programs for real estate companies.

Getting back into what I enjoy doing has helped me heal tremendously, just by being with people again and collectively sharing our experiences. I learn from others as much as they learn from me because, as it is written, iron sharpens iron. I am bringing all of my experiences not only to my books but also to my website, podcasts, Periscopes, and a new feature on my interactive website where you can chat with me to get your answers in real time.

Recovering from a health crisis also has reminded me to get back to the basics in life. When things are going well, we often lose sight of our foundation and those core principles that help us weather any storm or tragedy. And I think the same is true in real estate. As the economy improves, I see that, slowly but surely, we are getting away from the basics we implemented to help us survive the worst economic downturn in our country since the Great Depression.

One of my main concerns is that most real estate books are built on the premise of a "get rich quick" philosophy. True enough, real estate has made its fair share of instant millionaires, but for the most part, those success stories are few and far between. With the very favorable economic conditions we saw during the real estate boom of the early 2000s, it seemed as though everyone had a success story, and it was easy to see why people jumped on the "get rich quick" bandwagon. The unfortunate part is that a lot of individuals got a false sense of confidence in their ability to invest in real estate and lost sight of the fundamentals. This leads me to believe that most of the success stories were spurred more by favorable economic conditions than a true understanding of the business of real estate. And as today's economic conditions continue to improve and inch toward precrash levels, I believe the same mistakes could be just around the corner.

In many real estate books, there is only very general information provided about a certain sector of real estate investing. This leaves the reader or entrepreneur with little understanding of the actual systems that he or she must implement in order to be as successful as the "expert" who wrote the book. Whatever your job may be, you understand that general theories and success stories alone are not enough to provide the success we are all seeking. The reason is that, in order to be successful, you have to learn how to run your investment like a business. Yes, that's right—a business. Real estate investing is not about jumping on the latest trends or following the latest infomercial touting the latest greatest way to make a million fast. Success in real estate investing is about learning core principles so that you can establish foundational systems in your business. And that leads me to one of the key reasons I wanted to write the revision of this book: to get back to the fundamentals.

The good news is that, even though my book continued to sell during the Great Recession, if you decide to start investing in real estate today, your path will likely be much less difficult than it would have been had you started seven or eight years ago. And the great news is that if you implement the systems in this book, you can practically put your success on autopilot. That's not to say that it will be easy—because nothing worth having ever comes without hard work—but I can guarantee you that you will not experience the frustration of not knowing what to do, which can be the most crippling part of starting a new business.

> "Success is neither magical nor mysterious. Success is the natural consequence of consistently applying the basic fundamentals."
>
> JIM ROHN

This book has been updated throughout, but there is also some entirely new material in this edition, including a chapter on the technological advancements that will make running your business more efficient than you ever thought possible—even if you're a one-man show. I'll be honest: technology and the millions of apps available to smartphone users are not exactly in my comfort zone. And if you would prefer to use paper systems, those are in this book, too. But I also have to admit that the apps I tout here have drastically changed the way I do business—for the better. Technology—which includes the time—and money-saving apps that I now cannot live without—has reduced my administrative workload by 80 percent. I am not a techie by any stretch of the imagination, but I have become one of the biggest ambassadors for proven technology that will help you as a landlord and real estate investor.

I also added a Q&A based on frequent questions and feedback from readers who read the first edition of *Buy It, Rent It, Profit!* and had specific questions for me about how to implement these systems in their own investments. Because you are holding this book, I want you to know that you are one of my biggest inspirations and motivations, so please keep your questions and comments coming! The positive feedback from the readers who utilized the forms in the first book was overwhelming. It is my hope that these forms, along with the new chapters, will help you by giving you the tools you need to be successful in real estate investing.

I cannot close this intro without more great news. During this time of great uncertainty, I met my soul mate and in 2014 married her: Dr. Lacy (Hiltbrand) Chavis, a child psychologist who specializes in pediatric trauma at the Johns Hopkins All Children's Hospital in St. Petersburg, Florida. Lacy stood by my side through thick and thin, and in 2015 we welcomed into the world our pride, joy, and biggest blessing, Naomi Grace Chavis.

In the interest of our shared desire to continue to live the best life we have been blessed with—especially when we are all put through the fire—it is my sincere hope that I can help you not only to survive but to actually thrive in the real estate investment world. I am living proof it can be done.

Sincerely,
Bryan Chavis (2017)

PART I

YOU CAN BUILD WEALTH
THROUGH REAL ESTATE

ONE

INVEST IN YOUR FUTURE

How You Can Become Wealthy as a Landlord

Gold slippeth away from the man who invests it in businesses or purposes with which he is not familiar or which are not approved by those who are skilled in its keep.

—*The Richest Man in Babylon*

We are all looking for ways to get wealthy. Some people might not state this so bluntly, but let's face it—we all crave the security that money can bring. But it's important to note that wealth doesn't have to mean *greed*. Wealth can buy you more time off to spend with your family, good education for your children, better health care, and the freedom to live the life you want to live.

Wealth to me means freedom. I want to have enough money to take time off to travel with my wife. I want to be able to help my parents live out their retirement years in comfort. And I want to give back to my community, particularly to help at-risk children have opportunities to make something out of their lives. All this takes time and money. Money buys me this time, and it provides me with these things that are so important to me.

The bookstore shelves are lined with titles that promise to reveal the "secrets to success." I was once one of those staring at a wall of titles and wondering which one would help get me to the place I wanted to be. If you're anything like me, you've probably already learned what makes the "millionaire next door" tick and how to "think and grow rich." These are great motivational books—they help you figure out what path you want to take toward building your own life of financial security and freedom. But if you've picked up this book, you probably want something more . . . specific advice on how to build that wealth through one of the smartest methods around: real estate.

I've been working in the apartment industry, where I received my Certified Apartment Manager (CAM) designation, for more than twenty years, first as a manager of large rental complexes and later as an owner. I've worked on every type of property—from single-family homes to thousand-unit apartment buildings, and just about everything in between. Several years ago, before the first edition of *Buy It, Rent It, Profit!* was published, I decided to put all the advice, systems, and "best practices" I've developed over the years into a book and seminar series called The Landlord Academy (**www.landlordacademy.com**). After working in real estate for so long, I had grown really dissatisfied by what I'd seen in the marketplace and by all of these speakers blowing into town to host seminars on how to get rich in real estate. Typically, they had a line out the door of people looking for advice, but I knew that those so-called experts were just opportunists who were taking advantage of people who legitimately wanted to create wealth through real estate. Almost everything they were teaching people about successfully investing in real estate was wrong, and I made it my mission to show people the *right* way.

I was going around to real estate associations and sharing my information with their members. At one of them, I met a guy who was a manager at Kinko's. He let me use his store's broom closet to host my own small meetings, and that was the beginning of my company, which came to be called The Landlord Academy. Meanwhile, I had also written a manual that would guide real estate professionals through every step of the investment process, including how to run their properties on a day-to-day basis and treat every investment like a business. It was called the Landlord's Operations Manual, and I was selling it directly from that Kinko's broom closet and out of the trunk of my car.

That manual ultimately became the basis for the book you now hold in your hands. When Touchstone (part of Simon & Schuster) first agreed to publish *Buy It, Rent It, Profit!*, they started with just a tiny printing. It was 2009, the world was in the throes of an economic crisis, and of course the real estate sector had been hit especially hard. The good people at Simon & Schuster were probably more than a little apprehensive about how well a book on real estate investing would sell during the Great Recession (in fact, my editor later confessed as much!). But I knew the answer: The principles, strategies, and systems I teach in this book are time tested, and they work in any economy. And sure enough, that small first printing turned into a dozen more reprints, and *Buy It, Rent It, Profit!* became a category bestseller on Amazon. Since then, through the book, my website, and many, many speaking engagements (in rooms much larger than a broom closet, thankfully), I've trained hundreds of thousands of would-be rental property owners, some of whom have gone on to be property moguls in their own right. Our academy has become one of the industry's leading consulting and coaching programs.

And the good news is that, in order to be successful, you don't have to have a hundred units—a single-family home or a duplex is just as viable for your first move as a rental investor. And, as I'll show you, it's a heck of a lot safer to hang on to property for the long term than to try to work the market with risky "fix-it-and-flip-it" schemes. That's part of the reason so many investors got in trouble in 2008. The beauty of rental investing is that you can choose the steps you want to take and decide when you are ready to take them. The key, of course, is performing your SEOTA (my own method for evaluating the right rental properties, which you'll learn in this book) and allowing this process to help you choose wisely. I'll give you all the tools, checklists, and operating systems you will need to make that first choice with confidence. That is my commitment to you. And I also promise that these principles will work every time, no matter what the current economic state is. Read on to learn how Mitchell and Thelma, two of my Landlord Academy success-story clients, put these systems into practice and used them to succeed even in the midst of the market crash.

MITCHELL AND THELMA'S STORY

Mitchell and his wife, Thelma, attended several of my Landlord Academy training courses around 2004. They were recently married with two young children, and were looking for a way to build wealth. Their financial state was OK (but not perfect) when they came to me. They both had steady jobs (though neither was pulling in the big bucks) and they had decent credit (with some outstanding credit card debt). But they also had a dream for the future: They wanted their kids to go to college (something neither of them had done), they wanted to be able to offer some security to their parents, and they had decided the 401(k)s they contributed to at work weren't going to get them where they wanted to go fast enough. They wanted to take their financial destiny into their own hands.

Mitchell and Thelma were living in an apartment and needed more space for their growing family. As a two-income family, they decided they were ready to buy a home. However, after attending some of my classes, they were excited to start their rental investment portfolio and were unsure if they should use their limited funds to buy a new home for their family, or continue to live in their apartment and buy a home to rent out.

I get questions like this all the time. I usually suggest this: Why not do both? Why don't you buy a rental property in which you can live and rent out the other units to help pay down the debt you'll be taking on?

Mitchell and Thelma had been looking at single-family homes in the $240,000 price range. I suggested that they explore buying a duplex for the same amount. They could live in one apartment and rent out the other apartment in the building to help defray the cost of the mortgage. The rental income would get them started on their journey to real estate wealth, and the family would have a larger place to live in.

Mitchell called me a few months later to report that while the lure of that bigger, more expensive home had been powerful, they'd resisted the temptation. They thought about their long-term plans and realized that this first investment move needed to be a wise one. Buying a more expensive home would be okay. It would appreciate in value, and they would have some equity to use in the future for college or a real estate investment. But by buying a duplex instead, they would advance two moves, rather than one. They might not have some of the upgrades found in the more expensive home, but they would have more space to live in and an income-producing rental unit. If they had bought the single-family home to live in, they would have had to save up more money or wait a few years for the equity to build up to use to buy a rental property. Mitchell and Thelma had just accelerated their journey to wealth.

They were smart in another sense as well. Now that they had a rental property, they used The Landlord Academy as a resource to get the training, operations manuals, and forms they needed to manage this rental profitably and legally. They took their first step seriously. It always amazes me when I see people put their entire savings at risk by buying a rental property without getting some training on how to run that property. The time and money you spend in training to be a landlord and researching the best property-management systems (whether you take a class, or you use the guidance offered in this book) will pay off tenfold. For Mitchell and Thelma, the price of enrolling in my Landlord Academy was far less than the cost of one eviction! You can use the same methods Mitchell learned in class by using the processes and forms you find in this book to purchase and operate your own rental property. Mitchell and Thelma found that by using tried and true methods of operation, they were spending less time running the place than they once did worrying about their financial future.

Mitchell and Thelma knew why their goal of wealth was so important to them. They wanted to be able to pay for their kids' educations. They didn't want to work second jobs to earn more, because they wanted to remain actively engaged in their kids' lives. And they wanted to have enough of a financial cushion to assist family members who might need assistance down the line. They wisely chose real estate as their method of achieving wealth. Then they were smart enough to find a step-by-step system to follow. This book will give you the tools to do the same thing.

WHAT ABOUT MY CREDIT?

Are you thinking that you might as well put this book down now, because you don't have good enough credit to get a loan? Don't do it! When I started my real estate journey, my credit score was a shaky 582! One of the smartest things I did was immediately get some advice on improving my credit. As I was planning my path to wealth and educating myself on real estate investing, I was also taking small but steady steps to improve my credit. By the time I was ready to make an investment move, my credit had improved dramatically.

The worst thing you can do if you have less than desirable credit is wait to do something about it. There are many companies that can help you improve your credit, as well as some simple steps you can take on your own. I'll talk more about improving your credit in chapter 6. So, don't be discouraged if your credit isn't stellar right at this moment—you can still become a successful real estate investor. For a list of creditable credit repair services, visit **landlordacademy.com**.

YOU CAN HAVE IT ALL—WITHIN REASON

Mitchell and Thelma decided that purchasing a single-family home wasn't the be-all and end-all for them at that moment. While that remained a desire, they were willing to put off realizing that dream for a while. They knew that if they acted strategically, eventually they'd be able to own a much nicer single-family home.

What really convinced them that buying the duplex and renting the other unit was the wisest choice for them was that they understood and put to use the basic principle of *leverage*—using other people's money to purchase an asset. We will talk more about the power and potential drawbacks of leverage later on, but for now you need to understand only that their down payment entitled them to own an investment valued at $240,000. In other words, they put a small percentage down and got to own a much more valuable property because the bank loaned them the rest of the value of that property. If you were going to make your riches in the stock market, to buy $240,000 of stock, you would have to write a check for $240,000! In real estate, you have to have only a portion of the purchase price in cash. The rest is loaned to you by a bank. Real estate is one of the few investment paths you can take that allows average people like you and me (who don't have huge trust funds to get started with) in the door. In addition, your property will also appreciate in value. Let's look again at Mitchell and Thelma to see several benefits of investing in rental properties.

The Benefits of Mitchell and Thelma's Investment

- The monthly mortgage of $1,350 that Mitchell and Thelma assumed with their first property was more than they had been paying before, but they had a tenant who was paying $850 a month to lease the smaller two-bedroom unit in the duplex. So, in effect, they were paying only $500 a month of their own money on the mortgage. That was far less than they had paid previously in rent. They were actually again using other people's money—in this case, their tenant's rent payments—to pay down the debt on the property.
- As the mortgage balance decreases over time, they can refinance to have lower payments—until eventually the property is paid off. The rent Mitchell and Thelma collect (which has risen, and is likely to continue to rise over time) will eventually be equal to or greater than their monthly mortgage payment. Eventually, once that balance is paid off, they will be making a profit each month in addition to being free and clear of that original debt.
- The appraised value of Mitchell and Thelma's property will also continue to increase. Whenever they decide to sell the place, they will see an increase in their investment, which they can use to reinvest in other properties.
- Perhaps just as important, they will benefit from 3-D tax advantages—deductible, depreciable, and deferrable. I'll address each of these in more depth later on, but for now, keep in mind all these benefits of investing in rental property.

MITCHELL AND THELMA TODAY

Because Mitchell and Thelma followed my Strategic Evaluation of a Target Area (SEOTA) process to pick the right investment property (which we'll learn about later in the book), they were able to locate the right rental investment for themselves in a desirable neighborhood. As the value of the property increased, so did the rents in the area. (If they'd bought a single-family home, all they would have gotten was the theoretical increase in value of the property and no actual increase in cash flow.) After a year, they were able to get an additional fifty dollars a month for the unit. Over time, that $850 two-bedroom unit was able to command a nice, even $1,000 a month: That meant only $350 of their monthly mortgage had to come from their own income.

Mitchell and Thelma decided the benefits of rental property ownership were so great, they bought a small apartment complex with the money they had saved by renting out the second unit in their first building and using some of the equity that had built up.

When they began eyeing other investments, they reached out to me again because they noticed a new trend in the market: Everyone was buying properties with "no money down." I had noticed it, too.

Right before the housing market crashed, the U.S. economy looked incredibly robust, but something just didn't feel right. I believed it was all falsified, just an illusion created by Wall Street. It was funny money. They were packaging loans and products, and giving people money who really couldn't afford it, and I was seeing it firsthand. I had a tenant who worked as a cashier at my local grocery store—a woman who could barely make rent every month—invite me to a barbecue at her new house after she secured financing from a lender.

I saw this game of shells and knew that at some point it all had to come crashing down. So when Mitchell and Thelma asked me how they should go into their next investment, I said to be smart and put a little more money down. I told them things wouldn't always be as rosy as they seemed now, so they needed to think about the future. Even though the downturn hadn't hit when we were having that discussion, the truth is that the possibility of a downturn *always* exists. Real estate markets are cyclical—there are highs and lows—and I told them that the best thing they could do as investors was to prepare for the lows, even when things were going well. I told them to give themselves some wiggle room, just in case.

Even though they didn't want to do that, Mitchell and Thelma had trusted my teachings up to that point, so they decided to follow my advice. They put a little bit more money down, so just in case rents went from $1,000 to $700, they wouldn't have to fold and foreclose. And that is exactly what happened. When people couldn't afford to pay their rent on time, all the investors started going to foreclosure because their "zero-money-down" financing had sent their mortgage payments sky high. But not Thelma and Mitchell. They were able to survive by allowing the rent to go from $1,000 to $750 and still stay afloat. Sure, they had to cut some things and they had to lean up a little bit. But they didn't have to turn their property back over to the bank like the rest of the nation did.

The best part? Because Mitchell and Thelma leveraged that deal properly, they were in a position to weather the financial storm, and when the sun came back out they were able to look around and make a careful assessment. They saw all the foreclosures going up right in their own neighborhood, and they were able to pull equity out of some of their investments to buy some of those distressed properties on the cheap.

Mitchell and Thelma already knew their neighborhood, so they recognized the good deals when they saw them. And even though rents were still around $750, their overall profits were high because they were picking up properties for less than half of what they had been priced the year before. Because they continued to follow the systems in this book, there were opportunities all around them.

Today, more than ten years after they first became Landlord Academy students, Mitchell and Thelma have sold that first duplex, purchased a six-unit apartment complex, and are in negotiation to purchase a twenty-four-unit property. Mitchell has left his job with the parks and recreation department to oversee the operations at their mini real estate empire. By thinking strategically about their goals and the path to achieve them, today Mitchell and Thelma have a net worth of $1.2 million. Not bad!

Mitchell and Thelma's story is not unique. I've worked with hundreds of individuals who have achieved similar kinds of results by using the methods and practices I've employed myself and teach regularly. Not only have they learned about the importance of evaluating an investment properly before buying it to avoid costly mistakes, but more important, they have learned the arts of landlording and running these properties efficiently and profitably through my innovative landlording systems.

While I've been fortunate to assist celebrity clients with significant capital to invest—guys like baseball superstar Gary Sheffield, boxing champion Winky Wright, and basketball's great Chucky Atkins—the vast majority of my students don't have lots of cash to invest. I've helped thousands of regular folks purchase a modest single-family home as a rental property, and just like in the game of Monopoly, these individuals and couples have gone on to purchase other properties with the proceeds from their initial investments! When you think about the whole idea behind Monopoly—to take a little green house and cash it in for a much larger red hotel with more cash flow—you realize that Milton Bradley had it right! And so can you.

SINGLE FAMILY HOMES VS. MULTIFAMILY RESIDENCES

I am often asked if it's better to buy single-family homes to rent out, or multifamily residences. Most people are shocked when I say my preference is multifamily. They've usually been told by many people to steer clear of apartments, that they are a management nightmare.

This is the voice of inexperience talking. By eventually upgrading their investment portfolio to apartment units, Mitchell and Thelma benefited from something called economies of scale.

What does that mean? It simply means a single-family home will generate only one source of income because you have only one tenant. If property taxes go up, which they will, or if insurance goes up, which it will, you still have only one major source to control these rising expenses. You can raise the rent on your one tenant only so much until what you are charging in rent is unreasonable and unrentable. This is where most investors make their mistake.

With multiunits you are benefiting from the economies of scale. You have more sources of income coming in to not only help control expenses but also to provide cash flow. You can spread your increased expenses over several renters so it's less impactful—and so you can retain the good renters and not go through the added expense of soliciting and evaluating a new tenant.

Also, multiunits are actually safer in times of economic turmoil. How? If you are renting out a single-family home and you have one vacancy, what's your vacancy rate? That's right: 100 percent. But if you have a duplex and one of your units is vacant, you have only a 50 percent vacancy rate. You're still bringing in some revenue. Clearly, the more units you have to rent, the less a single vacancy affects your bottom line.

But aren't multiunit buildings more work to manage? Actually, no. It's systematically far easier to manage one set of units than multiple single-family homes in different locations. I'd rather make a trip to one four-plex and deliver all my notices or collect all my rent than have to drive to a bunch of different single-family homes.

That said, there is nothing wrong with starting out with a single-family home as your first investment, but make sure that you are employing your SEOTA (the checklist to evaluate your property, which we'll discuss in chapter 4) before you buy. The upside with buying single-family homes is that the barrier to entry (price) is generally lower, but the downside is that the margin for error is a lot smaller, so it's important that you properly analyze the deal. We will talk about buying foreclosed properties at length later on, but I warn you that all that glitters may not be gold. Just look at the mistakes so many speculative investors made ahead of the crash. Don't make the same mistakes they did. It's easy to get caught up in the moment, but you have to think strategically. With the tools I'll give you in this book, you'll learn how.

RICH VS. WEALTHY

Mitchell and Thelma's success has allowed them to live their version of the American dream. They are not only providing for themselves and their children and their family today, but they are securing a sound financial future for themselves and for generations to come. They aren't necessarily what I would call "rich" because they learned early on that riches come and go—often going just as quickly as they came. There is a big difference between being "rich" and being "wealthy." Wealth is long-lasting and can stand the test of time. It isn't as subject to the kinds of fluctuations and factors that were dominating headlines and creating jitters in Americans of all ages and income levels when the first edition of this book was published. Wealth is a long-term, strategic plan. Riches are a onetime move to make some money. Getting rich is like checkers, one move at a time, with not a lot of thought given to the next. Acquiring wealth is like chess, a strategic plan where you always have your next three moves planned out in advance.

In many ways, Mitchell and Thelma are the epitome of *investors*—they have learned that investors can make money in any market if they learn to read market conditions and make the proper investment at the proper time. They don't get suckered into what everyone else is doing. Often by the time you hear what "everyone else is doing," that strategy is drawing to the end of its effectiveness or going to collapse because everyone will do it all at once. A great example of this is the condo craze of 2004 to 2007. Huge numbers of apartment communities "turned condo" and sold their apartment units as condominium homes. Some investors made tons of money with this strategy. Others jumped on the bandwagon only to find that the market was saturated, with too many condos for sale and not enough people to buy them. In fact, I watched the banner at an apartment complex near my house go from reading "Now Leasing" to "Condos Starting in the $260's" to "Condos in the Low $200's" to "Condos Starting in the Mid $100's" back to "Now Leasing" in the span of a year.

Smart investors learn to forecast the market and plan for where the market will be, not where it is right now, and assess economic conditions to ensure that they are working in their favor and not their detriment. They look toward the horizon, and not a few feet in front of themselves.

In 2008, the economy taught us a tough lesson about the cyclical nature of real estate. But I'm worried that people are starting to forget. And that's what Wall Street wants you to do. They want you to forget about all of the mistakes that were made. I'm telling you *not* to forget. There are opportunities to be made in recovery, as there are opportunities to be made in a downturn. But the only way to maximize in either situation is to apply basic fundamentals.

With current interest rates so low, people are beginning to advertise their get-rich-quick schemes again, and I'm beginning to see some of the same mistakes being made. Interest rates are low and the government is trying to stimulate the economy because, right now, there's not a lot to entice anyone to jump into home ownership. Now, that's beneficial from an investor's standpoint, because with low interest rates you can possibly buy yourself a duplex or a quad and take advantage of current opportunities in the real estate market. Simply put, you can get more for your money. But the problem is, as soon as you get a good, robust economy, interest rates will start rising again, and that cycle will be fed by more favorable access to capital to—again—entice people into the market. Rates will continue to rise, and then, once they peak, the government will shut it all down. Employment begins to go down, followed by the interest rates. Then you'll have another crash and recovery. It's an inevitable cycle that you must learn to recognize and navigate if you are going to be a successful investor.

True investors are not *speculators*—those whose vision is fixated on the short-term, get-rich-quick, fix-it-and-flip-it game. Speculators usually have one short-term plan and can get caught off guard if conditions change and that one plan doesn't work. You really can make money in any market. But you have to know how to recognize the market and apply the right strategy to it. In my quest for wealth, I have investigated all the strategies. My friends called me crazy when I didn't run out and buy a condo to rent during the condo craze and they called me crazy when I didn't snag up some homes to "flip" during the fire-hot real estate market of the early 2000s. I am not saying those would have been bad things to do, but they weren't a part of my long-term plan for wealth. I had my resources pointed toward the one strategy I've found that consistently, over the long term, outperforms every other real estate investing strategy (and any other type of investing for that matter) and that's rental investing.

Now, lucky for you, you don't have to roll the dice with your first investment move. This book will provide you with the steps to narrow down and select the right neighborhood to invest in, and then to evaluate a specific investment property. I'll help you navigate the tricky waters of securing financing and closing on your deal. Then, once you are officially a "landlord," this book will provide you with day-to-day systems to manage your property efficiently.

THE FIVE CONTROLS OF REAL ESTATE INVESTING

As both Mitchell and Thelma told me, the best move they ever made was investing in real estate and not in the stock market. They both love the idea of having something tangible to show for their investment dollars, and they love having direct control over how their money works for them. Neither of them was temperamentally suited to letting someone else call most of the shots. Stocks can be a great investment, depending on what your goals are. However, one of the key benefits I like about real estate is *control*. Mitchell and Thelma enjoyed:

- Control over choosing what property to invest in
- Control over rental rates
- Control over tenant selection
- Control over expenses
- Overall control over cash flow

When you have control over each of these things, you ultimately have *control over value!* That means that you have control over profit as well. You don't get that in most investment vehicles. I know Microsoft certainly didn't call to ask me what I thought about releasing a new software program, though I had put my hard-earned money into buying their stocks. Now I control my investment dollars, and you can, too.

In this chapter, I've given you a preview of the advantages of the *Buy It, Rent It, Profit!* program. In the next chapter we'll explore why this is really a better plan in the long term than the other hot real estate trend in recent years, the "fix it, flip it" mentality. And I'll tell you a little bit about how I developed this program, so you can benefit from my hard-won wisdom and use the best practices I've developed over years of rental property investment to buy, manage, and grow your own rental empire.

> I went by the field of the lazy man, and by the vineyard of the man devoid of understanding; and there it was, all overgrown with thorns; its surface was covered with nettles; its stone wall was broken down. When I saw it, I considered it well; I looked on it and received instruction: A little sleep, a little slumber, a little folding of the hands to rest; so shall your poverty come like a prowler, and your need like an armed man.
>
> —Proverbs 24:30–34

BUY IT, RENT IT VS. FIX IT, FLIP IT

The Game of Monopoly and Its Hidden Secrets for Real Estate Riches

I had a history teacher who told me that the original drafts of the Declaration of Independence contained the sentence, "We hold these truths to be self-evident, that all men are created equal, that they are endowed by their Creator with certain inalienable Rights, that among these are Life, Liberty, and *the pursuit of Land*." That's right; Thomas Jefferson and others considered property ownership to be one of our inalienable rights.

Our forefathers later exchanged the pursuit of land for the pursuit of happiness. I find it interesting that in their minds, Land equals Happiness. I'd say that for most of our history we have a lot of evidence that home ownership is a goal for the majority of Americans. Most of us want some place we can call our own, and we'll go to great lengths to get it. That's one reason people come from all parts of the world to live in this country. Something deep in every human soul stirs at the thought of owning property.

I know that I feel an enormous sense of satisfaction in home ownership—not only in owning my own place, but also in being able to provide others with a clean, safe place to live. I'm not so naïve to believe that's the only reason you have an interest in owning and operating rental properties, but I bet that has a lot to do with it.

There's nothing else like the security and pleasure that come from being able to look at a building and say, "That is mine." I know of no better feeling than being able to have a tangible representation, something solid and substantial that you can see and touch, of hard work and savvy thinking. For me, having a piece of paper or a few pixels on a computer screen indicating my "ownership" in Imaginary Enterprises doesn't move me in the same way as having a rental property.

Of course, the rewards aren't only emotional. The material/financial rewards that come from wise investments in the rental property market can be substantial. I'll talk about this at greater length in the following pages, but you all know what kind of roller-coaster ride the stock market can be. If you're like me, the thought of sending your hard-earned cash on a roller-coaster ride you have no control over isn't all that appealing. The one word that keeps cropping up as people discuss the stock market is "volatile." I'm no English scholar, but that word doesn't sound good.

What "volatile" means for people like you and me is that from one day to the next it is downright difficult, if not impossible, to know what the markets are going to do. We just watch the TV at the end of the day to see if the market ended high or low. During the day, nothing we can do will impact that end-of-the-day result. Real estate markets fluctuate, too. But, as a real estate investor, we can make our own choice about how to deal with those market changes. And typically, we have more warning signs before a significant change occurs—that is, if we know how to forecast them. Let's take a look at some other kinds of real estate investment that took on many of the same traits as that volatile and risky stock market and learn why rental investing remains more solid than other kinds of real estate investing.

WHY FIX IT AND FLIP IT FAILS

As a short-term, step-by-step, checkers-like approach to real estate investing, the fix-it-and-flip-it method doesn't work well for most people. One advantage of real estate investing is that it is less risky than other forms of investing. But like the stock market, fix-it-and-flip-it "strategies" are subject to many economic forces that can change in an instant, making fixing and flipping a volatile investment strategy. Certainly some people have made a great deal of money in buying undervalued properties and then selling them at overvalued prices. That's the buy-low-sell-high mantra that "works" in the stock market.

What many people don't realize is that the high returns those fortunate few were earning came with a high degree of risk. Why? Because the only source of those returns is an increase in the value of those properties. The investors can make money off this strategy only if they can sell the property for more than they bought it, and sell it quickly so they don't have to pay the monthly payments for long. As long as the housing market remained robust and those properties were appreciating in value, those risks were worth taking.

But things weren't as rosy as they may have seemed.

When the whole real estate market was booming, the price of even undervalued properties increased as well. So the entry point into that market also got higher. For the average person getting started in real estate, trying to buy even one supposedly undervalued single-family home became difficult—the prices had just climbed too high. So would-be investors stretched by paying too much for dubious properties and financed those properties with riskier loans, all in the belief that those properties would continue to appreciate in value. When the rates of appreciation began to slow, or even slide in the opposite direction, what once seemed like a good deal wasn't such a bargain. Investors saw the value of a property for which they paid $150,000 (and that only a few years before had been valued at $100,000) either remain at $150,000 or fall below that value.

When they factored in whatever they'd spent on rehabbing the place, they were operating at an even greater loss. The fix-it-and-flip-it house of cards had come falling down.

So, these investors had two options with that once undervalued, now overvalued property. They could put it on the market as a rental, or they could continue trying to sell it. Both these options have serious problems. Because a lot of people overpaid for these properties, the amount of money they needed to collect in rent to cover the monthly mortgage payment was more than they could get anyone to pay. They probably didn't do a market rent analysis before they bought the property because they never planned on renting it. They'd hoped to flip it, so such a consideration didn't even enter into their decision. They're now stuck with an overpriced property and find themselves "upside down" on the deal—in other words, what they can get in monthly rent is less than their monthly mortgage payments.

The other option—keeping the house on the market at a lower price—can put them in a similar situation—if they are even able to sell it at all. At the height of the real estate boom, getting loans was almost ridiculously easy. Not so anymore. As a result of many economic factors, the money supply is much tighter. Now far fewer people are qualifying for loans to buy your fixed but not yet flipped house. So these hapless investors find themselves stuck with an overpriced house whose rent roll doesn't cover its mortgage—and a smaller pool of qualified buyers able to take that property off their hands.

See why I'm not the biggest fan of the "fix it, flip it" approach?

Flipping is volatile, and if you can't flip a property, there aren't a lot of good backup plans. But the other main reason I don't like flipping as a long-term strategy is that it isn't passive income. Passive income is income that you make without having to actively work for it. With flipping, you make more money only when you are doing a new deal. So you constantly have to be working. If I wanted to do that, I'd just get a job that offered stability and health insurance! With rental investing (hanging on to a property for the long term), you will receive passive income as your tenants continue to pay you rent, year after year. Once you acquire enough properties to make it work financially, you can outsource or hire a property manager so you don't have to do that work yourself. You just sit back and collect your monthly income. This is a really nice plan for retirement! And don't forget, your real estate also continues to appreciate. While real estate prices are volatile in the short term, the long-term returns have historically shown steady appreciation. Just like the stock market, real estate is a much safer investment over the long term than in the short term.

Now with that said, if it's a good market, if you have cash you can reasonably risk and a good deal in front of you, there is nothing wrong with flipping a house and making some cash. I just don't like it as a long-term wealth strategy. Flipping is like checkers; rental investment is like chess. Flipping works only sometimes, in some markets. Rental investing historically has outperformed any other type of investment . . . and it lets you amass a real estate empire from which you can live off the passive income. I like the idea of being on an island somewhere, playing golf, while money is being deposited in my bank account each month!

Why Not Invest in Stocks?

Many people have had success using the stock market as their investment vehicle of choice. Stocks should be an important part of any investor's portfolio. But what bothers me about the stock market is you can't control the market. Too many variables go into how and when stock prices will fluctuate—and fluctuate they will.

The market ebbs and flows, it lurches in one direction and then the other. Large-scale forces (macro economics) like gross domestic product, inflation, governmental policies worldwide, and other forces out of your control all will have an influence on how your hard-earned dollars will rise and fall in the market. How much influence do you have over those enormous market forces? How predictable are those cycles? And what about events like September 11, 2001, and the negative influence it had on stock prices? Could anyone have predicted those events? Was there anything you could have done to slow that rapid downturn?

I was working on a property management team during the September 11 tragedy. I remember the owner of a very large apartment complex (352 units) telling me, "Now you see why I chose to invest in rental property?" What he was pointing out was that during the terrorist attacks the stock market took a major hit. Investors, sophisticated and beginner alike, lost a lot of their hard-earned money, but the apartment complex I remember never skipped a beat. It was then that I could see with my own eyes how resilient, how fundamentally strong, rental property was. Even though the economy struggled during this time, the occupancy rate at that apartment complex never dropped below 93 percent (which was very good). People might stop taking vacations and cut back on going out to eat in hard times, but people always need a place to live.

Now, I know what you're thinking: September 11 was a once-in-a-lifetime tragedy that happened more than fifteen years ago. Surely the stock market is more stable today. And my response to that is, yes, I sincerely hope that our country never has to experience anything close to what we did on September 11, 2001. But I also know that, while extreme, those events merely underscored the vulnerability of our country's economy. While we have not seen a complete shutdown like we did in the days following the terrorist attacks, other events around the world have caused various ripple effects in the market that could significantly impact an investor's portfolio.

In a 2014 article on usatoday.com, Lawrence Creatura, a vice president and portfolio manager at Federated Investors, explained why the U.S. stock market is so vulnerable to outside threats. "Stock prices are derived from expectations of future earnings," he says, which essentially means that if there is any uncertainty whatsoever, stock prices will likely take a hit as stockholders begin to unload shares. He notes that another attack similar to 9/11 wouldn't lead to the same level of economic crisis as it did in 2001 because government leaders would know what to expect; it is the *unknown* that stands to have the biggest impact on the stock market at any given time. Creatura mentions the ongoing threat of the Islamic State and the ability of individual members—many of whom can gain direct entry into the United States from the Middle East—to sow feelings of economic fear and uncertainty.

But terrorist threats aren't the only factors dictating market fluctuations. Economists have shown that oil and stock prices typically move in sync, and with oil prices periodically falling due to an excess of worldwide supply and decreasing demand, stock prices have also plummeted. Meanwhile, an early 2016 market dip triggered by a crash in the Chinese stock market shows how closely the U.S. stock market is tied to the global economy and, as a result, just how little control Americans have over it.

Consumer trends, and global market fluctuations, can change overnight without warning and leave you with stock that's not worth the paper it's printed on. On the other hand, let's take a look at owning rental property. This type of investment is far less prone to consumer whim—it is driven more by *need* than *want*. People want to own a home but some can't afford one, so they rent. As the population of this country increases, so will the need for affordable housing. Florida isn't getting any bigger just because people keep moving there! Doesn't it make sense that the laws of supply and demand will prevail? As we have more and more people needing an affordable place to live, those of us providing rental homes will have a larger pool of tenants to rent to. And in most areas in this country it is cheaper to rent than it is to buy. Historically, there has always been a large segment of the population who will either need to or want to rely on rental housing. Along with being trend resistant, there are quite a few other reasons why owning rental properties is an attractive way to build your wealth.

The Advantages of Long-Term Rental Property Investment—A Review

So to summarize, investing in rental properties gives you four main advantages over other types of investment.

- **You can predict your monthly cash flow.** Rental properties generate revenue for you through, no surprise here, the collection of rent. You can predict it and budget for it, and it won't be subject to the short-term whims of economic forces and trends. If the euro begins to outpace the U.S. dollar, your tenants aren't going to suddenly panic and move out on you, leaving you holding the bag. Yet that same announcement can cause the stock market to plunge hundreds of points while you watch your hard-earned dollars going down the drain. By far and away, the predictable and consistent flow of revenue from rents is a huge advantage over the more volatile stock market.
- **You are building equity.** As you pay off your mortgage, your debt ratio decreases and your profitability increases. As you make those payments like clockwork, you're essentially paying yourself through the equity you are building in the property. The only way to own a greater portion of a company is to buy more stock in it, and if the company is doing well, you will have to pay more for those shares than you did for the previous ones. With a rental property, your debt is a fixed amount initially that decreases over time. You will be paying less while earning more.

- **Your property will appreciate.** If we have seen one trend that we can all count on, it is this: well-cared-for, solid rental properties, in a well-chosen location, will continue to increase in value, and rents will continue to rise. The days of an annual 20 percent increase in valuation may be over, but for lots of reasons (some of which I will get to in a moment) solid rental properties will continue to increase in value, and rents will continue to rise. That's the definition of a win-win.

- **You get tax benefits as a property owner.** Finally, you can enjoy additional tax breaks as a result of owning a rental property. Along with the deductions for the property taxes you pay on the building, you can also make deductions based on the depreciation in the value of the objects in the units themselves. I highly recommend that you speak with an accountant about the specifics of your financial picture, but in general the tax advantages are real and in some cases substantial. You can also visit **landlordacademy.com** and go to our Tax Advantage page for the most up-to-date information on the latest tax laws.

Be careful when you listen to reports on "the real estate market"—it's important to remember that there are several different segments of real estate, and they don't always perform the same way in any given market. There is **single-family real estate** (homeowners who buy a home for their family to live in). There is **retail real estate** (shopping centers and such). There are **office spaces** and **hotels**. And there is **rental investing**—the kind of real estate we're talking about in this book.

Now, even in the rental investment category there are different segments, like luxury rentals, vacation rentals, and affordable housing rentals. As I write this book, luxury rentals are having a tough time, but affordable housing is at an all-time high demand. Every city has its own market influences—in fact, even within a city one part of town might be in demand for rentals, while another area is oversaturated. Again, I will teach you how to read the markets, but be careful when listening to reports on TV because they often overgeneralize. The wise investor asks: How does this news affect *my* particular real estate sector?

TAKING CHARGE OF YOUR FINANCIAL DESTINY

It's hard to know who to trust when it comes to investing, which is why I always fall back on the Fifth Law of Gold from the book *The Richest Man in Babylon.*

Gold flees the man who would force it to impossible earnings or who followeth the alluring advice of tricksters and schemers or who trusts it to his own inexperience and romantic desires in investment.

The best defense against being tricked or lured into a get-rich-quick scheme is to educate yourself. Trust in yourself by investing in yourself. Set your goals, create your road map, and continue to pursue your dreams. That's what I'm going to teach you how to do in this book, by educating you in the SEOTA method of property evaluation and giving you access to The Landlord Academy forms, checklists, letters, and other property management necessities. By the time you're done with this book, you'll have all the tools you need to run your own property empire—whether it's a 100-unit apartment building or a single apartment on the top floor of your house.

But before we get into the nitty-gritty, I want to tell you a little bit about myself and explain how I became an expert in real estate investment. After all, before you can trust me to give you advice, you need to know that I know my stuff. Rest assured, I was once right where you are today.

You've probably heard the expression, "The best investment you can make is in yourself." I wholeheartedly agree with that statement, and since you've picked up this book and have begun to read it, I suspect you believe the same as I do. Investing in yourself and believing in yourself isn't always easy. There will always be doubters and naysayers in our lives. One thing I've learned in my time in the real estate business is that faith in yourself is a very powerful thing.

In the apartment industry and as an owner of my own properties, I've managed single-family homes and 1,000-unit apartment complexes and just about everything in between. I learned at the ground floor how to operate investment properties. Only then did I purchase one. You can benefit from my experience and take a shortcut to actual investing using my time-tested methods, procedures, and operating systems.

Because of my experience in the business and my confidence in the team I assembled, my first purchase was a mid-sized thirty-two-unit multifamily apartment complex. A lot of people say I took a shortcut, but trust me, my friend—there was no shortcut in the years I spent managing other people's property and seeing the profits I deposited into the bank for them, while getting paid a pittance. But I knew I was gaining the experience I needed to manage my own property, and assembling the team I would need to do so. It was like going to school and getting paid for it. I also have to credit the National Apartment Association, which helped provide me with a lot of the training and education I needed to succeed. I took all my education and on-the-job training and created a step-by-step system for landlording.

As I will say many times throughout this book, one of the great things about real estate investing is that it doesn't require that you have a specific level of education, just wisdom. I don't have a college degree. I didn't study economics, finance, or property management. I had real world experience. I didn't talk about becoming successful; I lived it. And you only have to look at what I've accomplished to see how far hard work can bring a person in this industry. I listened and I paid attention—and I asked a lot of questions. During the course of my ten years in the business, I learned a great deal—and more important, I was trained to take a systematic approach in acquiring and managing properties. It's a simple system of actions, checklists, and analyses you can perform in order to make owning and operating rental properties as headache-free as possible and to minimize expenses and maximize income.

The Importance of Systems

Truth be told, I not only like step-by-step systems, I *need* them. I not only wanted to trust in and invest in myself, I *needed* to. You see, as a kid I was diagnosed with dyslexia and severe ADD. As a result, for a long time it was hard to get others outside my family to believe in and to trust in me. In order to overcome that lack of trust and to prove to others what I was capable of, I had to do an honest and thorough assessment of myself. Before I can expect you to put your trust in me, I want you to know a little more about me and my strengths and weaknesses. My story can serve as a reminder that you don't have to be a genius and you don't have to have a ton of money to succeed in real estate investing.

I grew up in a love-rich but financially un-rich family. I knew I wouldn't be receiving an inheritance from a wealthy aunt, and I wasn't betting on winning the lottery anytime soon. I knew if I wanted to take care of my family and live the life I dreamed of, I would have to figure out a plan and achieve it on my own.

Like a lot of you, I wanted independence. I didn't want to have someone telling me all day every workday what it was I had to do. Once I achieved some success, taking $150 and turning it years later into a $1.5 million apartment complex, I realized that in one sense I was wrong about not wanting to listen to what others said. I've learned that I greatly value listening to and learning from experts. However, by being my own boss, now I can choose to listen to people I respect and who have integrity. I can build my own team of experts. I learned I didn't like having to work with and answer to people who had no pride in what they were doing and no dreams for a bigger future. I will say more later about the power of surrounding yourself not just with experts, but with people who are growth-oriented and have good values, because they support you in your growth as well.

People are an important part of your journey. In addition, you need a plan. I like to call my plans "road maps." Plans will change, but a road map is an overall guide to get you where you need to go. You can adjust it as things change, but the destination doesn't change. When I started out, I searched and searched for, but couldn't find, a time proven, step-by-step guide to making a success of myself in real estate. I hope this book will motivate and inspire you to do what I and hundreds of others have done by sharing with you our stories of success. It will also provide you with the actual proven operating systems that contributed to every single success story in this book!

The other day a friend mentioned that someone he knew had just bought his second Subway sandwich franchise. This guy had tried and failed at several other small business ventures in his life, but had made a real success with his first franchising operation. You probably know that most small businesses fail within a few years of opening, but franchises succeed at a much higher rate. Why is that? The answer is simple. When you buy into a franchise, you are provided with an easily repeatable set of processes and steps that have proven successful before. So, for example, if you buy a Subway franchise, you are given an operations manual that tells you how long to bake the bread, what toppings to offer, how to set up your store, and so on. You don't have to figure it all out on your own. You get to use the systems that other people have already developed to make your company work effectively and profitably. You don't have to repeat the same mistakes that other people made; you get to benefit from their experiences.

My Landlord Academy systems are based on the same principles as a franchise, and they will help you to run a successful real estate investing business no matter what the economy or housing market. Mitchell and Thelma are proof that my systems work, and as you read this book, you will learn about the same turnkey infrastructure and methods you will need to succeed in rental property real estate investing. From a step-by-step approach to property selection to the systematic approach to screening possible tenants to the actual lease forms you can use, this book delivers on the promise of making rental property real estate investing a profitable and easily manageable method to secure your financial future. And as part of the update of the first edition of *Buy It, Rent It, Profit!*, I have also included new information about online systems that, when combined with the paper systems and forms contained here, can make your business even more efficient and profitable. In a very real sense, reading this book provides you with a network of support and a solid infrastructure you can rely on just as a franchise does.

The Importance of Personal Determination

As I mentioned earlier, at the age of five I was diagnosed with severe learning disabilities that included dyslexia and attention deficit disorder. Now today, almost everyone I talk to has ADD. I don't know whether it's overdiagnosed now or just a result of our fast-paced lives, but I know thirty years ago, when I was a kid, having ADD was unusual and embarrassing. My teachers didn't have a lot of information or training on how to deal with a hyperactive child who had trouble paying attention. I was just one of thirty kids in a class and became labeled as a "behavior problem child." I remember one teacher at my school, Lime Street Elementary, became frustrated by my distracting behavior. One day, the school maintenance man came into class and moved my desk to the back corner. Then he asked me to be still as he placed a refrigerator box over me and my desk. It had a hole cut out in the front so I could see the teacher. The rest of me was surrounded by this box.

The teacher thought that was a good idea because it would keep my fidgeting from distracting the other students and limit my view to keep me from being distracted. The school's administrator told my parents that this was the only way I could stay in school. As an adult, I realize now that as a hyperactive child I must have been causing a distraction for other children in the class, but I still can't help thinking there must have been a better way to deal with it than to place a box over me. The box didn't keep my mind from wandering and it certainly didn't fix my dyslexic view of the words and numbers in my books. So for my elementary years I remained in that box. I felt stupid, different, and embarrassed.

My ADD caused me to fall behind in my classes, and it only got worse as I got older. From fourth grade through high school, I was placed in slow learning disability (SLD) classes away from the mainstream students. I remember Career Day when the segregation from the "normal" students seemed particularly acute. While the rest of the school had doctors, lawyers, and other professionals visit their classrooms and talk about the careers they could aspire to, my SLD class had a McDonald's manager tell us that if we worked hard, one day we might become a McDonald's team leader. When my teacher asked me why I wasn't completing the McDonald's application the manager had passed out, I told her that I didn't want to be a McDonald's team leader. She told me that because of my disabilities, college was not a realistic goal—that I should go on and fill out the McDonald's application.

Now there is nothing wrong with being a McDonald's employee, but that future didn't interest or inspire me. Not a lot did. I began to believe what the teachers told me, that maybe something was truly wrong with me. But one day, I had a realization that changed me forever. I realized that because of the limitations others were placing on me, if I wanted to live the life I dreamed of I was going to have to figure out how to get there myself. I was going to have to find the resources that worked for me to learn and figure out methods that worked for me.

My teachers were right, I did learn differently. But they were wrong, I wasn't stupid. Once I figured out how to organize my world—with systems, checklists, goals, and constant check-ins—I could accomplish just as much as anyone else. I began to think, *Maybe there's nothing wrong with me, maybe something is wrong with them!* I also understood that if I didn't believe in myself and invest in myself, the bleak future predicted for me would become my reality.

I had to learn how to learn in a way that made sense for me, that allowed for my differences but still produced the results the teachers were looking for. That I am today able to write this book, run a leading real estate education program, and successfully own and operate my own rental properties demonstrates what faith in yourself and investing time and energy in bettering yourself can do. The key for me was not buying into the limitations others placed on me. Not letting that box keep me trapped inside it. I had to learn and believe that different wasn't bad, different was just different.

The Importance of Wanting It

Part of my desire for consistency and predictability had to do with another part of my upbringing. Not only was I operating at a deficit in terms of my ability to pay attention and focus in school, I wasn't born with a silver spoon in my mouth either. While my family was generous with love, understanding, and the attention they paid to my needs and me, finances were always a concern for my family. I remember many years hearing, "It's not going to be a big Christmas this year." Which was my mother's warning not to be disappointed when the "big gift" presents I hoped for weren't under the tree.

I know what it is like to go without, and to dream of "being rich." I grew up in a small town about an hour from Disney World. One year my parents saved up enough to take my brother and me to The Magic Kingdom. I remember taking the monorail from the parking lot to the front gates. This monorail goes right through the middle of a Disney Resort hotel called the Contemporary. I remember as a ten-year-old kid gluing my face to the monorail window in awe as we went right through the hotel! You could see the lobby and the hotel guests walking to and from their rooms. I remember saying to myself, "Wow! This is where the rich people stay!" Then and there, one of my tangible goals of "being wealthy" was to grow up and stay at Disney World.

In the ten years since I began working in the real estate industry, starting at its lowest levels, I've gone on to become a pivotal member of groups making purchases of rental properties valued in the millions. I've learned you can succeed, in spite of others' small expectations of you, if you have higher expectations of yourself. It's also important to me to know what I am working for and what it really means to me. At the end of the day, money is just money. It's paper, but what does it mean? Well, to me it means that for the past seven years I can take my wife, my mother, my in-laws, my nieces, and other children I unofficially "Big Brother" to Disney World every Christmas to enjoy the vacation I dreamed of when riding that monorail as a kid. But this time I am one of those guests in the hotel!

MY SEVEN DISCIPLINES TO SUCCESS

My success was created out of my many failures—and I do mean *many* failures—but what separates me from most is that I never gave up, even with my background and my disabilities. I chose long ago to neither accept nor be afraid of failure, and not to let the limitations other people put on me define my future. That refrigerator box represents limitations to me. I now know to never allow someone else to place limitations on me, including myself.

All skilled craftsmen have disciplines that they follow to perfect their craft. No matter the craft, these disciplines must be mastered before success is achieved. The welder must master the craft of metalworking, Michael Jordan must master the craft of basketball fundamentals. Tiger Woods, Oprah Winfrey, Walt Disney . . . no matter the craft, all these individuals had to first learn to master themselves before they realized any huge amount of success in their respective fields.

I have tried to break down the formula that has worked for me into Seven Disciplines of Success. Learn to master these seven disciplines and you will begin to see dramatic changes in your life.

1. **Vision:** It has been said that many people are born with sight but what they lack is vision. It doesn't matter whether you have a lemonade stand or a multimillion-dollar real estate company—you will need to possess vision if you truly want to succeed. You have to learn to see what can be, not what is.

2. **Discipline:** Vision alone isn't enough. You have to take action to make your vision become reality, and have the discipline to keep at it. It is a fact that if you want to

beat 80 percent of the people all you have to do is just show up. If you want to beat 85 percent of the people all you have to do is just show up on time. If you want to beat 90 percent of the people all you have to do is show up on time and with a plan. And if you want to beat 95 percent of the people you have to show up on time with a plan and be willing enough to execute the plan. And if you want to beat 100 percent of the people all you have to do is be willing to show up, on time, with a plan, execute the plan, and by all means possess the self-discipline to see it all through! When you look at it that way, you can see why you don't need a master's degree or a family trust fund to win. To have confidence even when the odds are against you, use this formula that has kept me moving forward. Wake up each morning knowing you have 80 percent of people beat because you simply showed up!

3. **Diligence:** Be willing to put in the work. Work brings profit and talk brings poverty. These were the words of King Solomon, one of the richest and wisest men who ever lived. You must learn to appreciate work and develop a strong work ethic. This is so important to me that the words "Work brings profit. Talk brings poverty" are literally tattooed on my arm as a constant reminder that merely talking about something won't make my dreams come true, I must work for them. Remember, you are probably working a full-time job. If you someday want to quit that job and make real estate your full-time pursuit, then you must be willing to work for it. And remember this: You have no right to any of your dreams if you are not willing to work for them!

4. **True intelligence:** You might not be the smartest, and that's okay. In fact, I am a firm believer that if I am the smartest person on my team, my team is in trouble. As the team's leader, it's my job to find the most qualified experts in each area I need help in. My job isn't to be the smartest, but to find the smartest and provide leadership and vision. We each play our role, so our team can succeed together. It's OK to be some dumb, just don't be plum dumb!

5. **Network:** Surround yourself with wise individuals and ones who encourage you. Discouragement can come in many forms. People may try to talk you out of something, some may make negative comments, and some may just avoid you and not speak to you. You can't allow this to stop you from seeking out your dreams.

6. **Strategy:** Develop a love for the art of strategy. Strategy is in all things. Whether you are developing a marketing plan, negotiating, developing a goal, or creating a self-development plan, you must learn to possess the art of strategy. Remember, checkers versus chess. Quick, fleeting riches versus long-term stable wealth.

7. **Wisdom:** Above all things seek wisdom. Seek wisdom and not money. Trust me, making money is not going to be the difficult part, keeping it will be. The wise learn to see danger ahead and prepare for it, while fools go blindly on and suffer the consequences. Seeking wisdom—not money—will keep you out of a lot of trouble.

Please don't do what countless others have done and allow procrastination to settle in. Break that habit of delaying. Remember, talk brings poverty, work brings profit. Opportunity is knocking, my friend. Let's get to work!

> Discipline yourself to do the things you need to do when you need
> to do them, and the day will come when you will be able to do
> the things you want to do when you want to do them.
>
> —Zig Ziglar

THE MISSION OF THE LANDLORD ACADEMY

So, I've overcome obstacles. I've learned to take control of my disability and my future. Most importantly, I learned that I will always encounter obstacles, and I can either be stopped by them or learn to overcome them. People always comment on my determination, but to me, it's just normal. When I've faced a roadblock, it's just natural for me to start chipping away at it instead of stopping or thinking about giving up. That's a powerful lesson to have learned, for we all are faced with obstacles. Think of how much time and energy people waste being frustrated by obstacles, when they could be putting that energy into getting past them.

In establishing The Landlord Academy, I devised a mission statement that reflected my experiences: "My goal is to empower individuals through providing the right information and training so that they can break through any barriers to enjoy the kind of life they envision for themselves and their loved ones." I've spoken with thousands of people from varied backgrounds and the one constant in all their stories is financial independence. This book provides you with step-by-step instruction on how to achieve that goal, and we are excited to be launching our new interactive website to bring together landlords all over the world. I can't make you decide to take control of your future and tackle whatever obstacles you face in your life. But if you have made that decision, I can help you get there not just quicker than most, but by building a stable investment foundation, so once you get there, you stay there!

> There are no obstacles, only opportunities.
>
> —Albert Einstein

THE SEVEN KEYS TO BECOMING A SUCCESSFUL LANDLORD

And the Ten Most Common Pitfalls to Avoid

Theodore Roosevelt said, "The only man who never makes a mistake is the one who never does anything." I've shared with you some of the challenges I faced as a child and as an adult trying to find my path to success. I share this story and this book with you for two reasons. The first is obvious. I hope that by sharing what it has taken me over a decade to learn, including my mistakes, you can achieve success even faster.

The second reason is the hope that hearing my story will encourage you. Maybe you've tried your hand at investing and made some mistakes. Maybe you're worse off now than when you started. Don't give up. Maybe you haven't begun your journey yet. You're not sure where to begin and you're afraid of losing your limited resources. Maybe you are doing well, but want to continue to further your success. Maybe you feel you have waited too long to get started, and don't have enough time or money to become wealthy. Wherever you are in your journey, remember, if I can do it, it can be done! Teddy Roosevelt also said, "Never throughout history has a man who lived a life of ease left a name worth remembering." Perhaps, like me, the struggles you are facing will one day allow you to inspire others to not give up.

In this chapter, I will share with you my Seven Keys to Becoming a Successful Landlord. Throughout this book, I will give you procedures, step-by-step instructions, and helpful tips for successfully buying and managing rental property. In chapter 2, I shared with you my seven disciplines of success. These are areas, or arts, you should work to master to become empowered as a person. These seven keys to becoming a successful landlord are the fundamental principles to building a successful rental investing empire. Think of them as your North Star. They are the principles that have helped me learn from failure and become successful—not just as a landlord, but as a businessperson. For that's what you are building, a business.

In the chapters to come, we will deal with some complicated scenarios and talk about some of the risks involved with investing, as well as the benefits. If it seems overwhelming, remember—this book is here to serve as an operating system for you to refer to. But there is a lot of work to be done, and you have to be willing to get started, and stick with it. Remember, to beat 100 percent of the people, you have to show up, on time, with a plan, execute the plan, and finish what you start! Now, before we get into the nitty-gritty details of buying and renting property, let me share with you those Seven Keys to Becoming a Successful Landlord and the Top Ten Pitfalls I see landlords deal with. Be encouraged and learn from these pitfalls. And ask yourself, Isn't success worth the risk of occasional failure?

THE SEVEN KEYS TO BECOMING A SUCCESSFUL LANDLORD

1. **Get educated.** You are already taking the first step to getting an education by reading and studying this book. But it doesn't stop here. Always keep learning. I am a recognized trainer and literally wrote the book on property management, but every week I continue my education. I keep reading, I keep asking questions, I keep learning. All the wisdom you need to succeed already exists. All you need to do is expose yourself to it.

2. **Always be professional.** You will learn later in this book how your professionalism has a direct impact on your cash flow. Not being professional hurts your ability to lease a unit and hurts your renewal rate. I'll teach you how to be firm, but professional. Professionalism also extends to your team and you, as the leader, must set the example and establish the standards for professionalism. This includes your team's personal appearance and attire, how they answer the phone, and the expected response time to tenant requests.

3. **Develop effective systems.** The third key to becoming a successful landlord is to put systems in place and follow them. Systems allow things to be done consistently, correctly, and in less time. This will increase your profitability and decrease your mistakes. Once you have systems, follow them! One of my all-star students, Michael, now owns a thirty-unit apartment complex valued at over $2 million. He is also now an instructor at The Landlord Academy, teaching other students how to achieve the success he has. When he bought his property, he used the same Buy It, Rent It, Profit operations manual systems you'll find in this book to manage it. But each time a situation cropped up, he would put his own spin on how to handle it. For example, when a tenant was late on rent, he decided it would be nicer to send a nice note reminding the tenant to pay rent before issuing a Notice to Pay or Quit, which might scare them. He ended up increasing his collection times significantly. He learned that every time he deviated from the system, things went wrong. I'll share the same sys-

tems Michael uses with you later in this book. They are designed from years of experience managing rental property.

4. **Build a team.** A key to your success will be your team. You will need experts in various fields to help you invest and manage profitably. Look for team members that have the same values, work ethics, and goals you do. Review the Seven Disciplines of Success shared with you in chapter 2 and see if they meet your criteria. Remember, as you proceed on your journey to success, you can't take everyone with you. You need productive team members who will help you move forward in your journey, not ones who will be like stones in your pockets weighing you down. Each team member should contribute, either in his or her field of expertise, or by providing encouragement or inspiration. Assemble your "Dream Team" and you'll be unstoppable. A team that works together wins.

5. **Manage your time.** Time management is key to any business, but none more so than rental investing. You have only a certain number of hours in any day. It's what you choose to focus on during those hours that will determine your success. When many of us start our journey, we still have full-time jobs, so our time is even more precious. Time management doesn't mean working more and sacrificing your family or your health. That is not a long-term strategy for success and won't get you far. I always organized my time by prioritizing. Cash flow activities come first, actions to minimize my expenses come a close second. I balance activities that bring in cash flow today and will pay the bills, but also carve out time to work on projects that will increase my wealth down the road. You always want to keep moving forward.

   As the leader of your team, it's also important to help your team members manage their time. I use a Weekly Focuser checklist to list out the top five things each team member must accomplish each week for the team to collectively meet its goals. This allows us to all be on the same page and also allows me to check up on each person's progress.

6. **Maximize income, minimize expenses.** You will hear me repeat this mantra again and again in this book, for it is key to your success. Later you will learn how to maximize your income, by setting proper rental amounts and handling late rent decisively. You will also learn how to minimize expenses, by reducing turnover, implementing preventive maintenance to avoid avoidable repairs, and more.

7. **Set goals and achieve them.** In property management, goals will provide benchmarks for achievement, like 97 percent occupancy or 90 percent on-time rent collections. Setting these goals and using them to measure your performance provides you critical foresight about areas you need to improve before disasters occur. For example, measuring your occupancy rate and seeing that it is below your goal lets you know that your cash flow will be lower than expected. Now you know that leasing

should be on the top of the priority list, and perhaps that you should hold off doing new landscaping until occupancy is higher. Goals should be specific and measurable, not vague. "Make more money" isn't a goal. How do you specifically measure that? Increasing rents by 10 percent on your property as leases come up for renewal is specific and measurable.

Goals also allow us to set our sights on major projects and break them down into smaller steps we can work on. They provide a compass point we can chip away at each week. Goals also allow us to measure our progress and celebrate our successes. Many of us who are ambitious never stop to celebrate our accomplishments. By the time we reach a goal, we have already set our sights on something bigger. Ambition is great. It keeps you moving forward. But don't overlook the importance of stopping and celebrating your achievements. This helps increase your confidence and gives you courage to take on bigger goals. Stopping to enjoy your success for a moment energizes you to take on the next mountain. Acknowledging goals met is especially important for your team. They need to know they are recognized and rewarded. For instance, when I closed on my first apartment complex I never stopped to celebrate. I was already headlong into the next deal I wanted to close. I never stopped to celebrate our accomplishment with my team. I let a great opportunity go by to increase all of our confidence and get the most motivation possible from our accomplishment before jumping into the next deal. A celebration doesn't have to take a long time or be expensive. A dinner together can suffice. Think of it as putting money in the bank for the next time you need some encouragement to draw on. Now, I make a habit of stopping and celebrating my team's and my own success.

Always return to these Seven Keys to Becoming a Successful Landlord as you proceed on your journey to wealth. They will serve to keep you on the right path.

GETTING A GOOD DEAL

Now that we have learned and begun to implement some of the disciplines learned in chapter 2, we can begin to focus on perfecting the craft of real estate investing. Let's begin by turning our attention to the Seven Keys to a Good Deal:

1. **Target the net operating income (NOI) of the property.** Understand the rental market to determine the net operating income long term. The net operating income of a property is the amount of revenue it will generate for you. Knowing what the present NOI is, knowing what you can do to increase it, and projecting what that num-

ber of dollars will be in the future is absolutely essential to being a successful landlord. You will learn in chapter 4 about NOI and what it means to you as an investor.

2. **Target the middle income demographic.** Why do I say middle income? They are typically the largest sector of employed individuals in an area. There are far more middle-income jobs in any area than there are low-income or high-income jobs. Middle-income jobs produce enough income for a person to pay rent, but not always enough for the person to buy a home. These people make up a large portion of the rental market. According to 2015 data from the Pew Research Center, middle-income Americans are defined as having an annual household income of between $42,000 and $126,000 for a household of three. And according to these statistics, 50 percent of the U.S. adult population falls into this category.

   Targeting this group makes sense because those individuals and households tend to remain within that income zone. The Pew Research Center also reports that because of the housing market crash, middle-income households took the biggest hit to overall wealth and have had a much harder time rebuilding than upper-income households. Middle-income earners statistically don't move to lower or higher income brackets. As a result, they are often long-term renters and will provide you with a stable tenant base. Generally, as the cost of living increases (and therefore their rent), their salary will just keep pace with those increases, again ensuring a stable tenant base for you. Typically this demographic is locked in wages and buried in debt, leaving them with a very fixed income. With the middle-income class growing, demand will only increase for affordable rental housing. Generally speaking the middle-income group is the most stable one to target.

3. **Target the correct unit mix.** As above, knowing the key demographics is crucial. If you are targeting middle-income families, it is important to know not just what those families earn and are likely to spend on housing, but how many people live in their household. For the area you are considering purchasing in, you will need to find a building that can best offer the correct mix of units (studio, one bedroom, two bedroom, etc.) for the type of households in that area.

4. **Target added-value properties.** In chapter 1, I stated that this book is not about fixing and flipping. That doesn't mean that you shouldn't buy a building with an eye toward upgrading it or renovating it at some point. Added-value properties are those in which it is possible, with sometimes a little and sometimes a lot of effort and money, to increase their value through renovations. Why target added-value properties? The simple answer is that if you do the right kind of analysis you can come up with a property that is undervalued—whether because the current owners don't understand the trend in the rental market in that area and are not collecting the maximum rents they possibly could, or because some aspect of the building has

fallen into disrepair and you could restore that building to its optimal level and increase the net operating income.

5. **Target expenses:** The easiest and most effective way to target expenses is to control not only what cash comes into the property but also to control what costs go out. The easiest and most effective way to do this is by having a good maintenance plan, as well as educating yourself in the subject of preventive maintenance techniques. We will discuss this in depth in chapter 12. Remember, when it comes to preventive maintenance on your rental property you must inspect what you expect!

6. **Target economies of scale.** Economies of scale means, for our purposes, that the more units you have, the less expensive and time consuming certain things become. For example, if you ask a painter to paint the exterior of two single-family homes you have he might charge you $2,500 per home. If you have a duplex, he might charge you $3,500 to do the whole thing. That equals $1,750 per unit, which is much less than the price for single-family homes. This is economies of scale. It takes the painter less time and material to paint one duplex than two single-family homes, so the cost per unit is less. Savings such as this are common with vendors.

7. **Target the right team.** We talked already about how important your team is. Among the members of the team you will need:

- Small business/asset protection attorney
- Eviction attorney
- CPA with experience in taxes for rental investors
- Title company
- Lender
- Maintenance team
- Realtor or broker
- Education and resources personnel

This book and my Landlord Academy can help you with the last item. If you can't find an answer in this book or on our website, you can always call or email The Landlord Academy with any questions you might have.

In the pages ahead, you will get more specific advice about why you need each of these people on your team, how you can locate them, and what to look for in each.

THE TOP TEN PITFALLS ALL LANDLORDS FACE

So far, we've been talking a lot about what you should do to be an effective landlord. Another way to look at this is by talking about what you should *avoid*. I've been in this business for a while now, and I've seen good owners/landlords/property managers and I've seen bad ones. Even the good ones make mistakes, but the key is learning from them. Here are what I consider the top ten pitfalls all landlords face:

1. **Not continuing to educate yourself.** You must continue to educate yourself about the real estate market. Education keeps you out of trouble in many ways. When I first started in the property management business, I found out quickly that ignorance was costly. There is a legal and proper way to do everything in this business. For example, not understanding how to properly deliver a tenant notice under the local or state laws can cost you, when the tenant you are trying to remove gets to stay an extra couple of days and sometimes weeks. This all adds up. Each day the tenant stays without paying rent costs you money. Most of the mistakes that I see landlords make over the years can be attributed to them not continuing to educate themselves in an ever-changing profession.

2. **Not following the proper landlord systems.** Having proper landlord operating systems, like systems in any other business, is extremely important. They are the backbone of your operation, allowing you to be efficient, productive, and consistent. You will need these operating systems through every landlording phase, from dealing with a prospective tenant to moving out. You run your systems, and your systems will run your business.

3. **Not following Fair Housing laws as they apply to landlords.** Many landlord lawsuits are a result of a Fair Housing violation by the landlord—and the crazy thing is, many landlords don't even know they are violating these laws. Fair Housing is federal legislation you must comply with, and violations can be costly. We will talk about this subject in more detail later to make sure you are equipped to comply with the Fair Housing Act.

4. **Not understanding how to screen tenants.** Tenant screening is one of the most important processes in the landlord business, and it is also one of the most overlooked. The most common mistake I see is to move a tenant—any tenant—into a rental simply to fill a vacancy. Often the landlord has to evict the tenant a few months later because she chose to overlook issues on the prospective tenant's application, or it will cost the landlord extra time and money to deal with other unforeseen tenant issues. When you factor in the eviction fees as well as the fees associated with getting the rental rerented, these costs far exceed the cost of allowing the unit to stay vacant for an extra month. Not properly screening tenants always ends up costing the landlord more money in the long run. Trust me, you soon learn that it is far easier to stick to your qualifying criteria and wait to get a good tenant in the rental versus moving someone in just to fill a vacancy.

5. **Not using a well-written lease.** Your lease is your first major line of defense. It pains

me to see investors work so hard to purchase their first rental investment, only to watch the investment's wheels fall off soon afterward. If you have a very small child who needs a car seat, and you found out that the car seat you have was recalled, I know that you would get rid of that seat and get a new one—one that would protect your child. The same holds true with an investment property. Why would you trust your most valuable investment to a poorly written lease? Your lease is the contract that binds you and the tenant, spelling out all the rules and regulations as well as clearly outlining the terms of that agreement.

6. **Not conducting a market survey (see Form 2 on page 215 of the Appendix) every one to three months.** Rental market surveys are just what they sound like—a look at what other comparable apartments or properties are renting for in your area. Charging the proper rent for your property is probably the single most important thing an investor needs to do—and you don't just do this once. It's a number you should be constantly monitoring. This is where a lot of investors make their first costly mistake. The more units you have, the more often you'll have new vacancies and the more often leases will come up for renewal. If rental income makes up 99 percent of net operating income that a property can produce, which you will learn about in depth in the next chapter, then you as an investor must do your homework to make sure you are charging the right rent amount. If you are undercharging, you are just throwing money away. Later in chapter 4, you will learn how to conduct a rental market survey in your property's area to keep your rent on target.

7. **Not properly maintaining your property.** When it comes to maintenance, the old saying "an ounce of prevention is worth more than a pound of cure" holds true. With investment properties it helps to be very proactive with maintenance. You will learn in this book to perform routine maintenance checks on your rental units. Most investors/landlords pay attention to the building only when there is a problem—like a leaky faucet or a toilet that is not flushing correctly. Being proactive and addressing these items when they are an acorn and not an oak tree will help maximize income and minimize expense.

8. **Not building the proper team and network infrastructure.** A wise man once told me that "If you're the smartest person on your team then your team is in trouble." In real estate we talk a lot about leveraging. Most of us think of leveraging as a financial term but it doesn't just apply to financing. You have to learn to leverage relationships that you develop. I see so many would-be investors and would-be entrepreneurs stop short of their goals because of their lack of understanding of how to leverage relationships. You will always be just one contact person away from your goals. Understand that someone close to you may be holding the key that will unlock the door to your success! I will stress the importance of team again and again in this book. Remember, if you want to go fast, go alone. If you want to go far, go with others.

9. **Not enforcing your rules and regulations.** As a landlord performing day-to-day operations this should be your call to arms. A lot of landlords make critical mistakes by allowing the tenants to dictate the business relationship. Remember that this is a business; there is no place for weakness. You must be professional and you must also stay in control of the tenant relationship as well as your property. Routinely ask yourself: Are you running the property or is the property running you? Stay in control.

10. **Not treating landlording as a business.** This is a business; more important, it's *your* business. And it should be treated like a business. You wouldn't show up late for work at someone else's business or miss deadlines. You wouldn't throw away someone else's money by not reducing expenses. Why would you do anything less for your own business, the one that can provide you long-term wealth and financial freedom?

I've shared with you some of the keys, both to bettering myself and to conducting my business, that guide me in any market and under any conditions. Part of the key to my success is that I've always followed these principles no matter how down on my luck I was or—sometimes even more tempting—no matter how much money someone offered me. If a person is not guided by wisdom or principles, then I'd rather not waste my time with them. I know in the long run I will save myself major headaches down the road.

I've chosen to spend a lot of time in the first three chapters on self-development to prepare you mentally for your success. In the chapters that follow, we will focus on locating target areas and evaluating rental properties—how to pick the properties that will be the key to your financial success as a landlord.

If we don't start, it's certain we can't arrive.

—Zig Ziglar

PART II

INVESTING IN RENTAL PROPERTIES

FOUR

WHERE SHOULD I BUY A RENTAL PROPERTY?

The SEOTA Method of Evaluating Properties

In real estate investing, you will hear constantly "buy undervalued properties." This makes a lot of sense, but there is more to it than just buying an inexpensive house (assuming you can even find one!). Unfortunately I have too many students who come to my Landlord Academy after the property they bought at 30 percent below market value turned quickly from a dream deal into a nightmare.

I remember one student, Anthony, in particular. He came to my class sweating bullets. He was one step away from foreclosure on his first investment property. He had done what all the books he read had advised—he "jumped in and got his feet wet." Eager to become a landlord, he had heard about a small eight-unit property for sale at a too-good-to-be-true price. When he saw the line of prospective buyers lined up to make a bid, he quickly wrote out a deposit check. After all, everyone else was clamoring to make a bid; he didn't want to miss this great deal. And it was "undervalued" just like all the books said to look for. Right?

Well, the unit Anthony purchased consisted of studio and one-bedroom apartments. That would have been great if they were near a college or university—someplace with a high percentage of young singles. Instead, the area in which the units were located had an average household size of 4.3 persons. And families with four-plus people don't live in studios and one-bedroom apartments. Anthony had a very small pool of prospective tenants from which to draw, and ultimately the majority of his units sat empty.

A proverb attributed to King Solomon, considered one of the wisest and richest men to have ever lived, says, "An empty stable stays clean . . . but there is no income in an empty stable." This applies to rental units as well. They might stay clean, but unless you have a tenant in there, you have no income.

The 30 percent equity that Anthony had when he purchased the undervalued property was quickly lost to vacancy costs, as he had to make mortgage payments with no income coming in. Needless to say, the property was unprofitable. You might think he should have questioned more diligently why that property was so undervalued and done some additional digging to determine why the previous owner was willing to make such a great deal. You'd be right! Unfortunately for Anthony, he had read a book on rental property investing that strongly advocated the "buy undervalued" advice. Only once he dug a little deeper did he realize that there are many other important considerations when evaluating the potential profitability of rental property.

Anthony was playing checkers. He saw an opportunity and he jumped on it. But then he was able to advance only one square—from being a prospective owner to an owner. That was as far as he got. Instead, he should have been looking several moves in advance. He should have already done his research and learned not just how to be an owner, but how to be a *landlord*.

This is unfortunately a true story, and I see it happen to first-time investors all the time. There is more to buying rental investments than buying cheap. "Undervalued" does not necessarily mean "a good investment."

LEARN ABOUT YOUR PROSPECTIVE TENANTS

Most books, like the one Anthony read, teach the reader to look for the investment property. All they focus on is the building itself, but the truth is that in the time I have been in the rental investing business, bricks and mortar have never paid me rent. By that I mean the building does not pay the rent; *people pay the rent*. That is why most investors have trouble filling vacancies on their rental property and their cash flow suffers. I want you to think about rental properties in the way a big business like Wal-Mart thinks about their customers. You have customers, just like Wal-Mart does. Yours are your tenants.

Have you ever been to a Wal-Mart and noticed there were different items on the shelves—particularly in the front display areas—than in the last Wal-Mart you visited? In one part of my city, before you even get in the doors at Wal-Mart, the outdoor area is lined with plants, gardening tools, and patio furniture. Fifteen minutes away, in another part of town, the outside is lined with children's plastic swimming pools and portable grills. Wal-Mart will not stock any items that the demographic in each particular area will not purchase. The first Wal-Mart I mentioned is in a part of town where the demographic is homeowners, who buy items to landscape their homes. Most of the homes in this area have in-ground pools, so they don't buy a lot of plastic pools.

The second Wal-Mart is in an area with a large percentage of renters. There aren't a lot of in-ground pools in this area, and research shows the demographic purchases a lot of plastic pools and portable grills. Wal-Mart understands the importance of knowing each store's demographic needs, and then filling those needs. If big businesses like Wal-Mart pay attention to demographics, shouldn't we? After all, Wal-Mart has deeper pockets to absorb mistakes than you or I do!

That's thinking several moves in advance. I can't just look at a property, I have to look at the people in that area and determine if it's a product they will rent.

That's what my method of property selection allows you to do—think further ahead and anticipate your renter's needs in advance. As the first of my Seven Disciplines of Success from chapter 2 told you, you have to have a vision. Only when you know what you're looking for will you find it. Employing my Strategic Evaluation of a Target Area will allow you to do that consistently to avoid the kind of surprises that had Anthony backed into a wall.

KNOW YOUR ASSET CLASSES

In addition to understanding the prospective tenants you plan to attract, you must also understand the types of properties you can invest in. And, ultimately, that decision will play a large role in determining your future tenants.

Many real estate books and media outlets make very general statements about real estate markets and their current economic conditions. Statements like "Vacancy rates are extremely high" or "Rental rates are softening" are confusing because they're too general and don't apply to any specific segment of the market. The key for real estate investors is to drill down to the specific segment of the market the individuals are speaking about, and determine whether it applies to the class of property they own.

There are several different classes of properties that a real estate investor can own, and each one will have different opportunities and challenges, and rarely will those opportunities and challenges be the same as those of a different property class. Here are a few examples:

1. **Class A and B:** These classes are typically associated with luxury condos, luxury rentals, high-end single-family homes or high-end luxury multifamily buildings located in high-end areas. The demographics and psychographics of tenants in these classes will be completely different from the demographic and psychographic profile of middle- and low-income tenants. What affects the rich does not affect the middle- and low-income tenant, so you have to be very conscientious when making investment decisions. Typically, these properties are going to be priced at market or over market. As a result, the investor has to understand that he is not necessarily buying for high returns, but for the anticipation of appreciation of their assets over time. A break-even cash flow and above-modest appreciation typically makes paying at market or slightly over market more justifiable depending on the forecast conditions. This is a costly but sound investment when you consider that high-end properties typically are more stable when it comes to income-producing assets. Delinquencies as well as costly turnovers can railroad the net operating income on other asset

classes fairly quickly, making it difficult to achieve positive cash flow, even on properties that were priced at below-market value. This is generally not the case for Class A and B properties.

2. **Class C:** Class C properties typically cater to the middle-income demographic. When investing in Class C properties, the investor again must pay attention to the demographics and psychographics. Understanding employment factors are key in this segment because middle-income is considered to be stable but fixed, meaning that the household income typically grows at a moderate pace depending on various economic cycles. That is why it is very important for you to do your historical due diligence process before investing in this asset class. When you understand this demographic's employment conditions and short- and long-term forecast, it makes investing in this product type a little easier. Personally, I like this asset class because tenants are typically more likely to be long-term renters, especially with today's economic conditions, and have access to capital, which means they can keep up with rent payments. However, transition and turnover will occur more often than with high-end properties, and issues like delinquencies increase a bit more in this asset class as well.

3. **Class D:** One reason that many investors—especially those who are just starting out—are attracted to this asset class is because of the acquisition price. The generally low price of Class D properties allows for individuals with limited access to capital to participate in real estate investing and typically make their first purchase. On its own, that's a good reason to invest in some of these properties in low-income, sometimes blighted neighborhoods. But please keep in mind that this particular demographic and asset type is extremely volatile. The tenants who rent these properties are typically at or near the poverty line, so their income and their ability to generate income is extremely volatile. It's also important to remember that when there are economic downturns, the low-income demographic is the first to take a hit. Their wages are the first to be cut and their hours are the first to be slashed. A reduction in hours and wages renders these individuals unable to pay rent, resulting in high evictions and a high turnover rate. This ultimately erodes the net operating income and may require the investor to spend his own money to cover the mortgage. I also know from personal experience that Class D properties require much more involvement from the investor than other classes. Simply put, a small Class D duplex can require the same amount of manpower as a ten-unit Class B apartment building. It is possible to make these properties work for you, but you have to be particularly savvy in property management when dealing with Class D assets.

SEOTA DEFINED

SEOTA stands for the Strategic Evaluation of a Target Area, a step-by-step process for evaluating a property and determining if it's a good investment for you. Notice that we're going to be thinking strategically. Unlike Anthony, we're not going to make those "one jump at a time" moves that may result in us getting boxed into a corner or jumped by economic circumstances. Instead, we're going to very carefully consider all aspects of an investment before we purchase anything. Now, I know you might be worried about a process involving research and analysis—will it slow you down? Not necessarily. The SEOTA method is simply a system to follow. In fact, I find that once I've *identified* exactly what I am looking for, I can *find* it a lot faster.

Notice that the last words in our process are "Target Area." The first phase of this is to select the general area you are looking for investment properties in. We are not ready to target specific properties yet. Let's not put the cart before the horse. We should have some sense of where the most profitable locations are within a region before we waste time running numbers and visiting specific properties. I know, even if you are a beginner in real estate, you've heard the cliché location, location, location. Well, yes and no. Location is obviously key, but with rental property be careful whose opinion you are listening to. A nice neighborhood with rising home values may be a good location to buy a home in, but may not be an attractive rental area.

When we perform our SEOTA analysis, we will be taking a look at key demographic and economic indicators that reveal whether or not an area is worth investing in. These indicators are:

- Building permits
- Employment
- Average household size
- Demographics
- Psychographics
- Mortgage interest rates
- Rental market rates
- Occupancy rates

We'll examine each of these individually, and I'll give you suggestions on how you can collect this data.

Whether your goal is to own one or one hundred properties, the basic principles of SEOTA remain the same and will serve you well.

BUILDINGS DON'T PAY RENT, PEOPLE DO!

Most real estate books talk only about the building, how to evaluate it, buy it, and fix it up. The building is the second part of the equation. Remember my Wal-Mart story? You must first understand what the demographics and psychographics show the renters in your target area want. Then you can find a building that fits those needs. When you learn to anticipate your target demographics needs in advance, you will be less likely to find yourself with a vacant rental unit.

STEP ONE: FIND YOUR TARGET AREA

The first goal of the SEOTA process is to identify areas that are good rental markets to invest in. Once you've done that, the information you assemble in your SEOTA will provide you a clear picture of who your potential tenants are and what they need. Will you be selling patio furniture or plastic pools?

YOUR MOST EXTRAVAGANT EXPENSE

Here's a little secret I'll share with you. I'm kind of lazy. Not in a bad way—things usually don't come easy to me, so I know I have to put my work in to achieve results. But I'll be honest, I'd rather spend my day playing golf than working. So, I've learned to not just work hard but to work smart.

I heard once that the Army always gives the laziest soldier the new task, because they know he will find the fastest, easiest way to get it done. Then that becomes their system. That's my kind of plan. I like to find the fastest, easiest way to do something. Of course, you can't be sloppy in your work, but there is nothing wrong with getting something done in the most efficient, quickest way possible. That's good business, because in business your most costly and extravagant expense, and the one that doesn't show up on any financial sheet, is your time! Learn to work smart!

The first step to locating a target area is to evaluate the key indicators of an area. These key indicators will have a positive or negative effect on the supply and demand of housing. Evaluating them will identify the areas with the strongest rental markets.

1. **Building permits.** We look at building permits to help track growth. We evaluate the various types of building permits, from single-family homes, multifamily, office space, and retail to paint a much clearer picture of the health and stability of the local economy at the micro level. This also helps you forecast supply and demand. Building permits help you see growth in advance because they are pulled before building begins so you can get an idea of what's coming.

2. **Employment.** Where there is employment, the need for affordable housing is sure to follow. Strong employment also increases the demand for affordable housing. Over time, this can be a key indicator of who your target demographic is. A strong demand for housing can positively impact your occupancy rates and give you the ability to increase your rents steadily over time, which in turn increases the value of your property.

3. **Average household size.** This is used to help determine the proper unit mix. If you learn the average household size is 3.7 persons per household, then pursuing a building with a mix of studio and one bedroom apartments won't work. Remember Anthony and his mistake? Identifying average household size helps you avoid a pitfall like Anthony's.

4. **Demographics.** Demographics determine who will rent from you. It gives you the age, gender, and income level, and helps you get a picture of who your prospective tenant will be. When searching for demographics also note the total population of the area and how fast it is growing. Growth means more people looking for a place to live.

5. **Psychographics.** Psychographics determines why someone will rent from you, or why they will not. Demographics tells you who they are, psychographics tells you what they want. Knowing who the typical renter is and anticipating his needs in advance, and what amenities he will want (garages, covered parking, pools, in-unit washers and dryers, walk-in closets, proximity to highways, bus transportation) will also help you focus on the right kind of building for your market and dramatically reduce the likelihood of vacancies.

6. **Mortgage interest rates.** These help to evaluate and determine market cycles. If rates are at an all-time low, more people will be qualifying for mortgages and are therefore less likely to be in the rental market. When the money supply is tight and lenders are cautious and interest rates are high, that's when you're in the best position as a rental property owner. And when rates are low but lending standards are tight for the middle to moderate income demographic, this demographic will typically be forced to rent.

7. **Rental market rates.** A survey is a vital tool that will identify the base rental rates in the area according to the respective unit size. Looking at the rental rate history in an area helps you determine where rents are currently and where they will be in the fu-

ture. Sophisticated investors don't buy property based just on where rents are now, but also where they are headed. Harvard University's Joint Center for Housing Studies estimates that, depending on the pace of immigration, the number of renters in the United States will likely increase by between 4 and 4.7 million households from 2013 to 2023. It's a slowdown from the growth seen immediately after the housing market crash, but it's still far greater than the gains seen in the 1960s and 1990s. More stringent lending practices have kept some families out of the housing market, while younger professionals tend to prefer renting because of the flexibility it provides. But no matter what the reason, more renters means higher rents. It's a simple matter of supply and demand. The sky-high rates in markets like San Francisco and New York are a direct result of the limited supply of rentals.

Based on this information, plus more detailed statistics in your local market, you can identify certain trends in the marketplace, and predict what will happen in the upcoming years. And in combination with the other factors listed above and below, you can see why the SEOTA process is so valuable. It gives you the ability to forecast into the future. A farmer will plant his seeds in fertile soil only after he forecasts the best time to plant his seeds to produce the most crops. Rental investing is the same. You want to forecast the conditions and then plant your seed in a property that will produce maximum results.

8. **Occupancy rates.** This is the percentage of currently rented units. This helps you forecast how many vacant units to average in your numbers so your financial calculations are based on accurate vacancy estimates. If you are significantly off in this estimate, it can have a serious, negative impact on your expected cash flow.

Where Do I Get This Information?

This is where you will like the fact that I am a bit lazy. Previously, I made it a point to find the fastest, easiest places to get all the information you'd need as a real estate investor. That worked shortly after this book was first published, but after a time, I started getting calls from people telling me that many of the sites I mentioned were no longer in existence or didn't have the same resources I'd mentioned in the book. So this time around, I've compiled everything you need to know on my site, **www.landlordacademy.com**. Sign up for the free email newsletter and you can be sure that we'll keep you updated on everything you need to know in the world of real estate investing.

Using Your SEOTA Information

You now understand how important it is to look to the future trends that will determine whether an area is worth investing in. But now that you know what to include in your SEOTA report, and where to look for it, what exactly do you do with this information? It is, after all, a lot of data to take in and evaluate.

Let's say that you have done some initial due diligence work to determine that a place is worth investigating. For example, let's say you're intrigued by the reports about San Francisco's housing market growth, and you learn that the city's 2015 population hovers around 850,000—its highest ever and over 45,000 more than the 2010 population. You also learn that the city has added more than 480,000 private sector jobs since 2010, but only 50,000 housing units. One of the most obvious questions then is: Where are all these people going to live?

With this information about San Francisco's population growth, the second step in our process is to identify the demographics of the target area of San Francisco. Silicon Valley continues to recruit and employ some of the nation's brightest minds with salaries that are much higher than the national average. The 2015 median household income in San Francisco is $83,222—an increase of nearly 3 percent over 2014, and 26 percent and 36 percent higher than the median in California and the entire United States, respectively.

With that data in hand, you can envision a little more clearly what the demographic group is going to be able to afford for housing. By thinking a few moves ahead (forecasting) instead of just looking at current market trends, you can determine that interest rates will rise, construction costs will continue to rise, and those new arrivals, based on our analysis of the largest employment segments, will not be able to afford San Francisco homes. They will be entering the rental market. Our SEOTA analysis indicates this could be a strong rental market. By doing a rental market survey, we can see that rents are rising each year steadily. So, we can predict that we will be able to raise rents periodically to keep pace with changes in the cost of living and keep our profits rising.

We also have to consider what kind of units will best suit this future market. By doing our SEOTA due diligence, we can make educated, strategic decisions. We won't be responding to unanticipated changes, but riding ahead of the curve.

Additional factors can also be important to middle-income families. Remember, you have to think like your prospective tenants, and their needs may be different from your needs.

- Close to transportation, highways, etc.
- Close to public transportation (bus lines, subways, etc.)
- Close to retail and shopping
- Close to large employment centers

Here is a checklist you can use as you begin your evaluation of a target area. I like to organize my SEOTA information into a three-ring binder. I use this checklist as a table of contents that also serves as a quick reference summary of the SEOTA details.

SEOTA CHECKLIST (FORM 1)

Target Area: _____

Preparation Date: _____

1. **Basic Area Information & Map**
2. **Building Permits (i.e., single family, multifamily, commercial)**

   # of Single Family _____   # of Multifamily _____   # of Commercial _____

3. **Employment**

   Largest Employment Class _____   Average Income _____

   Second Employment Class _____   Average Income _____

   Has employment been stable in the local area? _____

   Any impact from national employment anticipated? _____

   Comments: _____

4. **Average Household Size & Income**

   Average Household Size _____   Average Household Income _____

5. **Demographics & Psychographics**

   Annual Medium Income: _____

   Summary/Comments: _____

6. **Mortgage Interest Rates**

   Current Mortgage Interest Rates: _____

7. **Market Survey**

   Studio Average Rent: _____

   1 Bedroom Average Rent: _____

   2 Bedroom Average Rent: _____

8. **Occupancy Rates**

   Current Average Occupancy Rates _____

When I first started developing this system and reviewing the areas around me to find a target area, I did what seemed natural to me. Because I am dyslexic, I tend to prefer pictures and visual information versus written. In fact, when I put together anything that needs assembly, I skip the written directions and just look for the picture—that just makes more sense to me.

So when I started analyzing areas to find my target, I got a big map of my city and hung it on the wall. Then I took stickpins with colored ends and began to place them, by color, where building permits were being pulled. I used different colors for single-family, multifamily, and retail developments. I also knew that renter income was another key aspect of my strategic evaluation, so, with more colors, I marked areas with middle-level average incomes and high population density.

I suspected that I was looking for strong, middle-income rental units in areas with a high population density and middle-class incomes. When I stood back and looked at the wall, it didn't take a genius to see that the pins tended to bunch in certain areas. By stepping back to look at the

BRYAN'S TIP

Just before the first edition of *Buy It, Rent It, Profit!* was published, speculative investors made many major mistakes in the housing market. Speculative investors are people who invest in real estate based on appreciation speculations alone. If these investors had paid close attention to the wages in their target areas of investing, they would have seen the major variances between wages and the appreciation that caused the average person to be unable to afford to buy a home. These speculative investors were left with many properties they overpaid for and couldn't sell. When the market crashed, they were left holding the bag, and many ended up in foreclosure. This is why your SEOTA is so important. It allows you to consider all factors that impact a rental investment, not just appreciation, and it allows you to avoid making the same mistakes from nearly a decade ago.

big picture, I could see areas that looked promising and start to predict where the areas of future growth would be.

Then I looked for opportunity. Now, opportunity, like beauty, is in the eye of the beholder. Generally opportunity is going to show up as something inconsistent on that map. To me, opportunity showed up in lots of middle-income employment growth in an area, like a warehouse and hospitals, paired with an overabundance of single-family homes and a lack of multifamily complexes. Doctors aren't the only people who work at hospitals. You have technicians, janitors, administrative staff, and more. These middle-income jobs are in that demographic that finds it difficult to buy a home. If affordable housing is lacking in the area, that spells opportunity to me. It's simple supply and demand. Even if you plan to buy a single-family home and rent it, as long as the rent is affordable for the middle income, it's going to be in demand. These areas became my target areas.

HOW DO I AFFORD MY TARGET AREA?

Don't get too discouraged if you locate a "perfect" target area, only to find when you start looking for properties that everything is overpriced. That simply means the institutional investors may have beaten you to the area—and once word got out they were buying up property, prices went up. That happened to me, too. I found a perfect part of town, only to find I was a day late and a dollar short. Just keep looking. Be diligent. Don't give up. The SEOTA process will lead you to a target area.

STEP TWO: NARROWING YOUR FOCUS TO FIND THE RIGHT PROPERTY

The SEOTA process helps you to determine whether or not a particular area is one in which you should consider finding an investment property. Once you've taken that preliminary step, it is time to look at specific rental properties that are for sale.

Doing your research on an area before you start looking at specific properties serves as protection against getting sidetracked into looking at every "great deal" someone wants to pitch you. And I promise you, once people find out you are a real estate investor, you will be pitched deals left and right. Knowing the area will save you tons of time and endless aggravation.

A mortgage broker can help you determine what you can afford to purchase based on the amount of money you have available for a down payment. I'll talk later about ways you can get started if you don't have any money of your own to invest. Then your professional team—that is, your broker or Realtor—can start feeding you deals that fit your budget and are in your target area.

Again, if you have done your SEOTA work well, you will have a checklist you can quickly consult to determine if a property in a particular area is worth pursuing and evaluating in detail. For example, if the unit mix doesn't match the average household size of the area, it might not be worth your time.

If a property passes your initial SEOTA check, the next thing to look for is if the property generates cash flow. Does it produce enough income to cover the expenses? Now, this can take a little more investigating. One of the biggest opportunities you have is that now, by reading this book and understanding how to correctly evaluate a property, you will see a lot of opportunities that other investors overlook. Many investors, even successful and sophisticated ones, look at the financial bottom line of a property, which usually provides a calculation called capitalization rate (cap rate) or cash-on-cash return. If the rate isn't high enough for them, they discard the property and move on. However, we are going to look further at what makes up these calculations and see how often diamonds in the rough are overlooked.

Let's continue down our step-by-step approach to evaluating a property and stay organized. You have all your SEOTA information on your target area—demographics, employment information, and so on—organized in a three-ring binder with your SEOTA Checklist summarizing those findings at the front. Now, as you look at properties for sale in your target area, I recommend you complete a Property Snapshot Form to summarize the basic property information you need to know.

PROPERTY SNAPSHOT FORM (FORM 3)

Use this form to collect initial information on a property you would like to explore further.

Subject Property Address: _____

City: _____ County: _____

Area of Town: _____

Listing Realtor:_____ Phone #: _____

Single Family _____ Multifamily _____ (# of buildings: _____ # of Units: _____)

1 story _____ 2 story _____ 3 story _____

Type of Construction (circle): wood frame brick cement block stucco

Other: _____

Type of Roof (circle): flat pitched wooden shingles asphalt
rubber membrane fiberglass shingles

Amenities:

Garage: _____ Fence: _____ Pool: _____ Patio/Porch: _____

Other: _____

Condition of Structure: Poor Average Good

Repairs/Rehab: Minor Average Major

Occupied?: Yes No

Current Rent: _____ Market Rent: _____

Notable Problem Areas:_____

Notable Advantages: _____

Notes: _____

Any Nearby Rental Properties or Apartment Complexes for Comparison Due Diligence—Note Name and
Contact Number: _____

STEP THREE: EXAMINING THE DNA STRAND OF A PROPERTY

The next thing we will evaluate is the financial makeup of the property. Now, science never was my best class, but most of us have watched *CSI* and the Discovery Channel, so if I know what DNA is, I'm sure you do, too. It's a person's genetic makeup—what makes you who you are. I am now going to teach you the financial DNA of an investment property—the fundamental makeup of a property's financial performance. First, let's learn what the DNA is. Then, I'll teach you how to inspect each component of the DNA to see if you can make this property produce more than it currently does. Understanding how the DNA is calculated also greatly reduces your risk of getting "one put over on you."

BEGINNER'S SAFETY NET

1. **Look for add-value properties.** An add-value property is one for which the current owner does not realize its full potential. This potential is realized through the rental rates. Typically these add-value properties are located in areas where there is a greater demand for rental units than there are units currently available.
2. **Look for properties that are at most fifteen years old.** Anything older than that, unless it has been recently renovated, will be costly in repairs and upkeep. Older properties typically require more extensive repairs to major systems like roofs, electrical, plumbing and heating, and cooling.
3. **Look for properties with pitched rather than flat roofs.** As a general rule, flat roofs collect moisture. Moisture causes rotting. Rotting requires repair or replacement.
4. **Depending on your geographic location, look for homes that are masonry block or brick.** Wood-framed buildings and wood-sided buildings are more costly to maintain, are susceptible to termite and other damage, and are a higher fire risk.

So, let's move on into the DNA calculation. But don't worry, you don't have to have a background in calculus. All we're going to be doing is some simple adding, subtracting, multiplying, and dividing. I promise you, if I can do it, you can do it! Remember, I am highly dyslexic and numbers don't come easy to me, so I've broken down this section in a format that's easy to learn and execute.

First we'll go over all the DNA key terms and formulas. Then we'll put these definitions and formulas to work in a practical application.

GPI (Gross Potential Income)

Your main source of income is the rents you take in. The GPI is the maximum possible rental income you will collect if all of the units are being rented. You calculate it on an annual basis. So, you would add up the rent on each unit and multiply the amount by 12, to calculate twelve months of collections. If you have a duplex with each side renting at $950 a month, you take the total rents you will collect each month ($950 x 2) which would equal $1,900. Multiplying the $1,900 by 12 gives you the annual total, $22,800. That's your gross potential income.

VAC (Vacancy Loss)

In a perfect world, all of your units would be rented all the time. That's not always going to be the case, so we have to allow for some vacancies when we are putting together a financial forecast for the property. This is known as your **vacancy loss**. We also have to assume that not everyone will pay all the rent all the time. We call this loss of income **collection loss**. The average vacancy rate used by investors is 5 percent. It's more accurate to determine the average vacancy rate in your specific target area, which is a step of your SEOTA. You don't want to be surprised with a higher vacancy rate than you expected. Now, to determine what vacancy loss means to your property evaluation in dollars and cents, take your GPI (the total yearly rent of all units added together) and multiply that figure by your vacancy rate.

$$GPI \times \text{estimated vacancy rate} = VAC \text{ (vacancy loss)}$$

So, continuing with our duplex example, let's assume an average vacancy rate of 5 percent. We would multiply our GPI of $22,800 x .05, which would equal $1,140. This is our expected vacancy loss for the year.

Effective Gross Income (EGI)

$$GPI - VAC = EGI$$

Effective gross income is defined as your total income from possible rents minus VAC and collection loss. Again continuing with our duplex example, our GPI of $22,800 minus our VAC of $1,140 gives us an EGI of $21,660. This is the amount we can expect to collect on the property per year from the rent roll.

OI (Other Income)

Other income (OI) is defined as money received from sources other than rent. Washing machines and dryers, vending machines, parking fees, application fees, and other sources of income are examples. When you add your OI to your EGI you get your gross operating income (GOI).

$$EGI + OI = GOI$$

The GOI is the total amount of cash the property has available to pay expenses.

$$GPI - OE \text{ (operating expenses)} = NOI \text{ (net operating income)}$$

Any expense incurred in operating the property is considered an operating expense. Some of these are fixed and others are variable. An example of a fixed operating expense is property taxes. You know what that dollar amount will be. A variable operating expense is something like eviction costs. You know you will pay them but you don't know how often you will have this cost or what the total will be. Typically a seller will provide you with the total operating expenses of the property. However, I always add 3–5 percent onto their total. You can also have a home inspector or maintenance technician take a look at the expense total and see if it's in the ballpark of reasonable. Later when we inspect the property in more detail, we will go over expenses with a fine-tooth comb.

$$GOI - OE = NOI$$

When you take your gross operating income and subtract your operating expenses, you get your net operating income. Think of this as the difference between your before-taxes income and your actual take-home pay. NOI is the income remaining after all expenses are paid, except for your mortgage payment. NOI is a key figure in all the calculations of a property's value from here on out.

Net operating income is like blood to the body. Without blood, the body dies. Rents make up 99.9 percent of your net operating income, so if you take away rents from the property, the property dies. One of the biggest mistakes I see investors make is taking the NOI of a property at face value. If 99.9 percent of the NOI is made up of rents, doesn't a property's rent schedule warrant a closer look?

You will be amazed at how many properties are underperforming because the rents charged are too low. This is where my background as an apartment complex manager is worth its weight in gold. It's commonplace in the apartment industry to do monthly market rent surveys. You call nearby complexes and check out what their rental rates are to make sure you are not too high and not too low. It seems so easy, but I promise you that you will see again and again properties for sale where the rents are not in line with the current market rents. This is a great tip for you to know. Many investors will pass right over a deal, because the cap rate or cash-on-cash return looks too low. You, as an educated investor, know to take a closer look at what makes up all those fancy formulas, and that, my friend, is the rent. Understand what you can charge for rent and you are on your way to understanding the value of a rental property.

NOI – RRA (Replacement Reserves Account)

An RRA is intended to be used for replacement costs of items that wear out, such as roofing, boilers, exterior paint, and parking areas.

NOI – RRA – DS (Debt Service)

Debt Service is defined as or better known as your mortgage payment.

$$GPI - VAC = EGI + OI = GOI - OE = NOI - RRA - DS = BTCF$$

When we put this all together, we get **Before Tax Cash Flow (BTCF).** This is the cash flow the property will produce, before considering taxes.

REVIEW EXERCISES

There are several formulas used to estimate a property's value. Let's review the most important ones.

Capitalization Rate (Cap Rate)

$$NOI / Value = Cap\ Rate$$

Cap rates are primarily used to help estimate the value of income properties. The cap rate is a measure of the absolute return on dollars invested. It does not consider the use of borrowed funds (i.e., leverage); it considers only the return on investment as if you paid all cash for the investment.

For example, if a property has an NOI of $100,000 and the price of the property is $1,000,000 then the cap rate is 10 percent.

Rule of Thumb: Typically, the lower the cap, the higher the price. Bryan's Tip: Keep in mind that a cap rate is like beauty: it's in the eye of the beholder. So is a cap rate when you consider the formula used to calculate it: NOI, which is verifiable, divided by value, which is debatable. Everyone can have an opinion on value—the bank, the seller, the appraiser, and you, the investor. Just keep that in mind when you think about cap rates.

Cash-on-Cash Return

The cash-on-cash return is the ratio of annual before-tax cash flow divided by the total amount of cash invested, expressed as a percentage. In other words, cash-on-cash return differs from the cap rate when the investor considers that the investor has used leverage, i.e., has acquired a mortgage. Remember, the cap rate is the return on investment when the investor has paid all cash for an investment, cash-on-cash return factors in the use of leverage (borrowed funds). With that said, the investor surely will want the cash-on-cash return to be higher than the cap rate. If the cap rate is higher than the cash-on-cash return, the investor has borrowed money with a negative repayment rate.

The cash-on-cash return formula is extremely important because it allows the investor to determine returns after using other people's money (i.e., leverage) to help purchase the investment. This is why the wise investor chooses real estate. The use of borrowed funds to increase your returns is hard for any other investment vehicle to beat.

$$\text{Annual before-tax Cash Flow} = \text{Cash-on-Cash Return \% Equity}$$

The Da Vinci Code of Rental Investing

After reading this chapter, I can most certainly understand why you may find yourself scratching your head. It took me a long time to grasp all of these formulas and apply them. This chapter should be read more than once to fully grasp all the concepts. To help you, I have created what I call the Da Vinci Code of Rental Investing. This code examines the three most important formulas used by investors, appraisers, and banks to determine a property's value. These formulas are:

$$\text{CAP RATE} = \text{NOI}/\text{Value}$$
$$\text{Cash-on-Cash Return} = \text{NOI-Debt Service} = \text{BTCF}/\text{Owner's Equity}$$
$$\text{DCR} = \text{NOI}/\text{Annual Mortgage Payment}$$

What do all these formulas have in common???
NOI
Remember that rent makes up 99 percent of NOI!

No matter what formula an investor chooses to interpret the value of an investment property, he or she must understand the root of all income—and that root is employment. In all my years of real estate investing and property management, brick-and-mortar buildings have never paid rent. People pay rent. And for the most part, no one is teaching real estate investing from a standpoint of understanding the demographics and psychographics of future tenants, which will *then* help you accurately forecast value. As I have stated, 99.9 percent of an investment property's net operating income will be derived from rents, especially in the case of single-family homes and small apartment buildings. Once you identify rent, you can gain a better understanding of potential NOI and interpret current and future values of the investment property.

EXERCISE #1: KNOW YOUR REAL ESTATE TERMS

Before you continue, complete the quick exercises that follow. If you have trouble completing them, review this chapter. If you don't fully grasp these terms now, you will have trouble as we begin to apply them.

Match the following terms with the correct description.

1. I provide data on the area's growth, while also providing an accurate account of building activity? Who am I?

   _____

2. If evaluated, I can provide you with an overall picture of the health of a local economy. Who am I?

   _____

3. If evaluated, I can give you a clearer picture of what types of apartment units to look for. Who am I?

   _____

4. If evaluated, I will tell you what the current apartment market conditions are in your target area. Who am I?

   _____

5. If evaluated, I can help determine valuable facts about a specific group of people, such as the income, family size, and typical job of a person. Who am I?

   _____

6. I am the process in which data is scrutinized to reveal your target area. Who am I?

   _____

Terms to Use:
Average household size
Demographics and psychographics
Building permits
Market survey
Due diligence process
Employment

EXERCISE #2: COMPLETE THE DNA STRAND

___ – ___ = ___ + ___ = ___ – ___ = ___ – ___ – ___ = BTCF

Let's practice a little and take a look at a hypothetical case that shows how all these numbers and concepts work together. Use a setup sheet similar to the one on the next page to outline your calculations.

For the purpose of this example, and because I already confessed to you that I'm not great at math, I'm going to use big, round numbers. The formula works the same for any deal, big or small. Let's say our purchase price was $1,000,000 and we put 20 percent down ($200,000), leaving us with a remaining debt of $800,000. For now, I'm not going to explain all the steps I went through in order to get some of the figures like garbage collection, insurance, and so on. For now, let's assume we've done our due diligence work and gotten the best deals on each of these services.

As you can see on page 59, all of our calculations were fairly straightforward arithmetic that leads us to our before-tax cash flow of $47,505. Is that figure good or bad? We'll talk more about what benchmarks to look for in property returns later. Right now, I want to make sure you understand the terminology and formulas that make up the returns. Try to work through the next two examples and determine your before-tax cash flow. If you have trouble, refer back to the DNA strand above. As a kid who barely graduated high school, I hate homework and am sorry to assign you some. But trust me, you want to make sure you understand how these formulas work backward and forward before you take on real-world deals with real-world money.

> Champions aren't made in the ring, they are merely recognized there.
> What you cheat on in the early light of morning
> will show up in the ring under the bright lights.
>
> —Joe Frazier

Sample Setup Sheet
Cash Flow Apartments
Purchase Price: $1,000,000   Mortgage: $800,000

Gross Potential Income:	
25 Units @ $425/mo.	$127,500
12 Units @ $500/mo.	$72,000
	GPI = $199,500
Less Vacancy & Collection Loss @ 5%	**VAC** = $9,975
Effective Gross Income (GPI – VAC)	**EGI** = $189,525
Plus Other Income	$0
Gross Operating Income (EGI + OI)	**GOI** = $189,525
Individual Operating Expenses	
Property Taxes	$8,700
Garbage Collection	$2,800
Pest Control	$4,500
Insurance	$9,600
Maintenance	$9,600
Management @ 5%	$9,476
Resident Manager's Apt.	$4,200
Total Operating Expenses (TOI)	**TOI** = $42,776
Net Operating Income (GOI - TOI)	**NOI** = $146,749
Reserves for Replacement Account	**RRA** = $15,000
Debt Service ($800,000 @ 10% for 30 Years)	**DS** = $84,244
Before-Tax Cash Flow NOI – RRA – DS = BTCF	**BTCF** = $47,505

EXERCISE 3: CREATE A PROPERTY SETUP SHEET

Asking Price

Unit Mix	_____ total units	Unit Breakdown
Equity / Down Payment	$	
GPI	$	
− VAC (@5%)	%	
EGI	$	
+ OI	$	
= GOI	$	
− OE	$	
= NOI	$	
− RRA	$	
− DS	$	
= CF or (BTCF)	$	
Cap Rate	_____ %	
Cash-on-Cash Return	_____ %	"Equity Divided Rate"

Property A

20 units—all 2 bedroom and rent for $650/month

Purchase price: $1,000,000

Owner's equity: $250,000

Operating expenses: 8% of GOI

Debt service payment: $40,000

Reserves for replacement deduction: $1,000

EXERCISE 4: CREATE A PROPERTY SETUP SHEET

Asking Price

Unit Mix	_____ total units	Unit Breakdown
Equity / Down Payment	$	
GPI	$	
− VAC (@5%)	%	
EGI	$	
+ OI	$	
= GOI	$	
− OE	$	
= NOI	$	
− RRA	$	
− DS	$	
= CF or (BTCF)	$	
Cap Rate	_____%	
Cash-on-Cash Return	_____%	"Equity Divided Rate"

Property B

10 units—all 1 bedroom and rent at $650/month

Purchase price: $550,000

Owner's equity: $137,500

Operating expenses: $5,928

Debt services payment: $35,000

Reserves for replacements deduction: $1,000

EXERCISE 5

Answer the questions below using the formulas you have learned in this chapter.

1. If a property generates an annual NOI of $85,600 and requires $48,865 for annual debt service, what is the property's before-tax cash flow?
   A) $132,635   C) $36,735
   B) $57,000   D) $80,000

2. What cash flow would be required if an investor wanted to receive a 12.5 percent cash-on-cash return, considering a down payment requirement of $135,000 and the closing costs were $13,500?
   A) $79,000.35   C) $9,000.00
   B) $12,000.12   D) $18,562.50

3. Which property generated the lowest capitalization (CAP) rate?
   A) Property 1 sold for $8,600,000 with an NOI of $1,504,000
   B) Property 2 sold for $86,000 with an NOI of $11,020
   C) Property 3 sold for $20,000,000 with an NOI of $2,670,000

If you take only one tip away from this chapter, remember this: You need to do your own research before embarking on any real estate deal . . . and you need to go deeper than just looking at comparative prices in the area. Using the SEOTA checklist, you'll be able to accurately evaluate how much money a rental property will actually bring in, also known as your Net Operating Income (NOI). This number is the key to successful real estate investment. It doesn't matter if all the two-family homes in a neighborhood are valued at $300,000. If the rent you can get for apartments in that building (the NOI) supports only a $225,000 mortgage, then that property is overpriced.

That's why so many homeowners and property investors got into trouble in the recent real estate crisis. They gambled that their properties would continue to appreciate in value . . . and they lost. If you follow the SEOTA checklist, evaluate a property's value with a clear head using the facts in front of you today (not the specter of financial appreciation in the future), you'll be able to build safe, strong real estate wealth in the long term—that's the *Buy It, Rent It, Profit!* way.

Now that you understand the basics of the SEOTA Method of Property Evaluation, we'll turn to the next important task of becoming a landlord: negotiating a great deal on a property in your chosen neighborhood.

HOW DO I GET THE BEST DEAL ON A PROPERTY?

Mastering the Art of Negotiation

You don't get paid what you are worth, you get paid what you negotiate.

A friend of mine, former Major League Baseball player Gary Sheffield, is a guy who knows a thing or two about the art of negotiation. Gary once negotiated a $39 million deal with the infamously tough negotiator George Steinbrenner when he played for the New York Yankees. I asked Gary if he could tell me one thing about negotiating, what would it be? He told me "Mark my words, you don't get paid what you are worth. You get paid what you negotiate." I've found that is one of the truest statements you will ever hear in real estate or any other business. If you want to get ahead, you have to understand the art of negotiations.

HOW TO BE A MASTER NEGOTIATOR

Listening Skills

Master negotiators have great listening skills. If you are doing all the talking, you can't be listening. If you let the other party do enough talking, they will reveal their agenda. Not that you should regard the person across the table from you as a fool, but it was King Solomon who said, "A fool is always identified by the multitude of his words." God gave us two ears and one mouth for a reason.

Ability to Read People

You have to be able to hear what the other person is saying, even if she doesn't say a word. You can do this by reading a person's body language. Is she present in the conversation? Is she only interested in getting her points of view across? Does she make eye contact with you and/or your team? These are things I look at when negotiating.

Understand How the Other Person Gets Paid

Before you enter into any negotiation, you need to know how the other person gets paid. Once you have figured that out, you can begin to uncover any possible agendas or angles employed during the negotiation period. As a good example, in one deal I was negotiating, the seller's broker would constantly try to get everyone on my team worked up by saying that the seller was getting frustrated and was going to walk from the deal. I noticed this happened every time we requested an extension for financing. The seller always seemed fairly reasonable to me, so by realizing that the broker just wanted to sell the property as quickly as possible and for as much as possible so he'd receive a higher commission faster, I understood that he was just yanking our chain. He didn't have our best interest at heart, or even his own client's, because his interference almost killed the deal. He was focused on a higher commission for himself, and not on making the deal work.

Remember, salespeople make money from you, advisors make money for you. Be careful, even on your own team, about whose opinion you trust, and always understand what's in it for them.

KEYS FOR NEGOTIATING

1. Never agree to anything that the other party is not willing to put into writing.
2. Don't allow others to pressure or rush you into signing a contract. "See thou a man that is hasty in his words? There is more hope a fool than of him." —King Solomon, Proverbs 29:20
3. Be careful of flattery. Don't let others charm you out of paying attention to details. Stay focused.
4. Understand that the devil is in the details. Write down all the key points brought up during meetings involving contracts.
5. Seek qualified advice and counsel to review your contracts.

So far we have used our SEOTA process to identify our target area. We've learned who our prospective tenant is and what he or she will rent. Then we evaluated a specific property in our price range using our DNA strand and formulas. Once you settle on a deal that has positive cash flow, is "rentable" to the demographic in your target area, and achieves positive leverage, the next step is to begin negotiations.

MAXIMIZE INCOME, MINIMIZE EXPENSES

Many deals you evaluate will not initially meet the cash flow or returns you are looking for. Don't throw them out yet. If you complete your DNA strand and a property isn't producing the returns you want, there are three ways to reevaluate this deal.

- First, try to obtain better financing terms. For example, a lower interest rate will positively affect your returns.
- Second, increase the NOI through maximizing income and minimizing expenses. If you know the property is undercharging rents, or you can make some improvements on the property to charge higher rents, you can increase the NOI through maximizing your property's income. If you can reduce expenses, perhaps by handling maintenance work yourself, you can increase the NOI by minimizing expenses. Increasing NOI will increase your returns.
- Third, negotiate a more favorable asking price. Before you negotiate the asking price with the seller, you need to know the maximum price you can pay for the property and still get the returns you want. You can rerun your numbers with a lower asking price until you find your maximum suggested offering price.

THE LETTER OF INTENT

Once we settle on price, the first step is to send the broker listed (or if there isn't one, the owner) a letter of intent, commonly referred to as an LOI. The LOI is not a binding contract, but it's a written communication of your intent to make an offer on the property. It outlines your offering price and other basic details. An LOI is commonly used to state your deal terms and see if the seller will accept them before preparing a lengthy, detailed contract. It allows you to negotiate the major deal terms, like price and due diligence period, before a contract is prepared to avoid constant, major contract revisions.

Key elements of an LOI are:

- Your name and contact information
- Address of property and property name, if any
- Purchase price you are offering
- Purchasing entity, "or assignees" (meaning you can assign this deal to someone else or to another entity name if you create a new LLC or trust to hold it)

- Deposit amount and time line of when you will make it. Deposit should be refundable during and up to three days after due diligence period ends
- Due diligence period, not less than thirty days
- Title contingency stating seller will deliver property free of all title claims
- Financing contingency
- Closing date. Once a deal is made and your due diligence is complete you typically want to close as soon as possible. The longer before you close the higher the possibility your financing offer can change. The property may also change: tenants may be moving out, etc.
- Who pays closing costs
- Due date and time for seller to respond to LOI
- Your signature
- Seller's signature

Here is a sample LOI for you to review:

SAMPLE LETTER OF INTENT (FORM 9)

Apartment Investment Advisors, LLC
Address
Phone/Fax/Email

April 4, 2017

Re: Letter of Intent for (Property Address)

This Letter of Intent (hereinafter referred to as the "Letter of Intent") is intended to set forth the general terms and conditions under which APARTMENT INVESTMENT ADVISORS, LLC (the "Buyer"), or its assigns, successors, subsidiaries, etc., is proposing the acquisition, as stated below, of SAMPLE APARTMENTS, a 60-unit single-story residential apartment complex located at 3315 Main Street in Tampa, Florida 33609 (the "Property") from FLORIDA APARTMENTS, INC. (the "Seller"). If the terms and conditions set forth below are acceptable to the parties, the Buyer is prepared to promptly begin its due diligence review and preparation of definitive documentation, including a Purchase and Sale Agreement (the "Purchase and Sale Agreement") under the following terms and conditions:

1. *Purchase Price*: The proposed purchase price (the "Purchase Price") to be paid by Buyer shall be Three Million Eight Hundred Thousand Dollars ($3,800,000.00) for a one hundred percent (100%) interest in the Property. The Purchase Price is based upon information provided to date to Buyer by the Seller and is subject to both the Due Diligence Review (as defined herein) and a satisfactory inspection. This offer is based upon the accuracy of any information pertinent to the Property received by Buyer as of the date of this Letter of Intent; thus, any inaccuracy may affect and alter the proposed Purchase Price.

2. *Inspection Period*: The inspection period (the "Inspection Period") shall commence with the full execution and delivery of this Letter of Intent and terminate sixty (60) days thereafter. Buyer may, in its sole discretion and with or without cause and without penalty, terminate by giving Seller notice in writing at any time prior to the end of the Inspection Period. Should Buyer not terminate, then Seller shall furnish Buyer with those items in Paragraph 4 below within ten (10) days after the later of: (a) Buyer's acceptance of the Inspection Period; or (b) execution and delivery of the long-form purchase and sale agreement for the Property.

3. *Deposit*: An initial good-faith deposit of two hundred thousand dollars ($200,000.00) (the "Initial Deposit") shall be paid to North American Title as escrow agent by Buyer following the full execution and delivery of this Letter of Intent, pursuant to mutually agreeable escrow instructions, and upon the expiration of the Inspection Period. The terms of this Letter of Intent shall be incorporated into the Purchase and Sale Agreement (the "Purchase and Sale Agreement") to be drafted by Buyer and negotiated by the parties.

4. *Seller's Duties*: Seller shall pay for and obtain (where applicable) state stamps on the deed, cost of fee title insurance policy in the full amount of the purchase price, new staked survey certified to Buyer and Buyer's lender(s), real estate commission, its attorney's fees, and acceptable new termite inspection report. Seller shall furnish Buyer with a Phase I Environmental Audit acceptable to Buyer and its lender(s). Should said updated Phase I Environmental Report dictate the necessity of a Phase II Report, then Seller shall promptly furnish same to Buyer at Seller's expense. Should Seller not be able to deliver the property free and clear from any environmental problems, Buyer may terminate the Purchase and Sale Agreement.

5. Buyer shall pay for Buyer's financing costs (including mortgage assumption, intangible tax, and transfer fee, if applicable), its attorney's fees, and recording fees.

6. Buyer and Seller shall prorate taxes, insurance, utilities, assessments, and net rents as of the date of closing.

7. Security deposits and all funds in Common Area Maintenance (CAM) account held by Seller shall be transferred to Buyer at closing.

8. WITHIN THREE (3) BUSINESS DAYS AFTER THE FULL EXECUTION AND DELIVERY OF THIS LETTER OF INTENT, SELLER SHALL DELIVER TO BUYER AND/OR BUYER'S BROKER(S) THE FOLLOWING ITEMS, AS WELL AS SUCH OTHER INFORMATION AND DOCUMENTS AS BUYER MAY REASONABLY REQUEST DURING THE INSPECTION PERIOD:

- Copies of or access to all tenant leases encumbering the Property.
- Copies of or access to all contracts of employment or consultancy affecting the Property.
- Copies of or access to all management, maintenance, service, and other agreements affecting the Property.
- An up-to-date rent roll showing the rental due under each lease, security deposits held, prepaid rentals, and the status of each tenant's rental payments.
- Copies of all plans and specifications, reports, etc., used in the construction of the Property, and "as built" plans if available.
- Copies of all insurance policies applicable to the Property.
- Operating statements for the year-to-date and two preceding years.
- Memoranda covering the terms and conditions of any unwritten leases or contracts affecting the Property.
- Copies of inspection reports, existing notices, and due dates for same from any governmental agency having jurisdiction for or an effect on the Property, including any additional notices which may be received prior to closing.
- Copies of the last three years ad valorem tax bills, and current bill, if available.
- Copies of all documents relating to litigation or other disputes affecting the Property.

- A copy of all permits and certificates applicable to the Property, including Certificates of Occupancy.
- Copies of all warranty agreements for real or personal property, including roof bonds.
- Financial statements on all tenants in the Property, if any.
- Tenant delinquency reports for the past two years, if any.
- Schedule of personal property to be transferred with the Property.
- Declarations certifying there are no tenant delinquencies (a) as of this Letter of Intent and (b) as of the date of closing.
- Copy of the Common Area Maintenance budget and ledger showing all payments and disbursements.
- All pertinent information of Seller's existing financing, if assumable.
- Copies of Seller's existing appraisals and environmental audits, if any.

9. The Purchase and Sale Agreement shall contain standard "prevailing party" language.
10. Seller shall be solely responsible for: (a) payment of any commissions with respect to leases on the Property through the closing date and for future contingent commissions for lease renewals of option periods applicable to said leases; and (b) completion, at Seller's or tenant's sole cost, for all tenant improvement work for pending or signed leases on the Property.
11. Financing shall be obtained to the satisfaction of the Buyer. **This offer is specifically conditioned, in part, upon Buyer's obtaining financing, on terms and conditions acceptable to Buyer in its sole discretion and judgment.**
12. If Buyer does not terminate during the Inspection Period, then Seller shall deliver those items described in Paragraph 4, all acceptable to Buyer in its sole discretion, within ten (10) days following the expiration of the Inspection Period.
13. Closing shall be thirty (30) days after the last item in Paragraph 4 is delivered and Buyer has obtained the financing described in Paragraph 11 (with all of the foregoing to be acceptable to Buyer in its sole discretion). Both parties confirm that time is of the essence and agree to make every effort to expedite a closing.
14. Seller shall hold Buyer harmless against all claims by brokers and agents for any real estate commissions due in this transaction.
15. Seller shall deliver to Buyer, within ten (10) days of full execution of the Purchase and Sale Agreement, an estoppel certificate, in a form and with content reasonably acceptable to Buyer, signed by each tenant in the Property.
16. In the event of Buyer's default after full execution of the Purchase and Sale Agreement and acceptance of the Property by Buyer following the Inspection Period and upon the securing of adequate and acceptable financing by Buyer, the Initial Deposit shall be forfeited by Buyer as Seller's sole remedy. In the event of Seller's default after full execution of the Purchase and Sale Agreement and acceptance of the Property by Buyer following the Inspection Period, with the exception of any change in financing by Buyer's Lender, Buyer shall have the option of: (a) having the Initial Deposit returned, including reasonable costs, expenses, and attorney's fees; or (b) pursuing specific performance of the Purchase and Sale Agreement. The Buyer's deposit will be refundable, if at any point, should Lender change any aspect of the financing of this transaction.
17. Seller shall not enter into any agreements (including any contracts of sale of the Property, or any letter of intent in connection therewith), lease amendment or extensions until the Purchase and Sale Agreement is fully executed or negotiations terminated. Should Seller enter into any such agreements without Buyer's prior written approval or should Seller not be able to deliver estoppel certificates from the tenants acceptable to Buyer and its lender, Buyer may, at its option and in its sole discretion, terminate this Letter of Intent and/or the Purchase and Sale Agreement and have any binder money paid returned.
18. Either party hereto shall have the right to treat the Property as part of a tax-deferred like-kind exchange

under Section 1031 of the Internal Revenue Code and, to that end, shall have the right to assign or otherwise alter this Letter of Intent in order to accomplish that objective; provided, however, that the net economic effect (including exposure to liability) shall be essentially the same as under the original Letter of Intent.

19. Seller and Buyer shall keep the terms of and existence of this Letter of Intent strictly confidential and shall not disclose any of its terms or its existence to any third party other than to their respective brokers, consultants, attorneys, accountants, lenders, and engineers.

20. The last signature date below shall be deemed the effective date of this Letter of Intent.

While this Letter of Intent is nonbinding, it is the intent of both parties to negotiate and execute within thirty (30) days of execution of this Letter of Intent a binding and definitive long-form Purchase and Sale Agreement along the above lines and with other terms and conditions customary for this type of transaction and mutually acceptable to both parties. The terms of this Letter of Intent shall be incorporated into the Purchase and Sale Agreement. If the general terms as outlined above are acceptable, please indicate by signing one copy of this Letter of Intent and returning it to the undersigned Buyer.

Agreed to and accepted:

BUYER

By: _____

APARTMENT INVESTMENT ADVISORS, LLC

Date: _____

SELLER

By: _____

FLORIDA APARTMENTS, INC.

Date: _____

One of three things will happen when you send out an LOI. The first and best option is that the seller will accept your offer. If this happens, you will proceed to enter into a legally binding contract. We'll talk more about key contact points in just a moment.

The second and more common thing that can happen is that the Seller will counteroffer with a price higher than your offering price. In this situation, you will need to determine if the seller is in the ballpark of what you are willing to pay, or if they are too far off. If they are too far off, you can respond with your reasoning for your offer. So for example, if the price they are asking is too high because the vacancy rate is too high to produce cash flow at their asking price, you can explain this to them. I like to be polite and always ask them if they can help me to understand how the property would work as an investment at their offering price. While normally they can't, it's important to be courteous because sometimes these deals have a way of "boomeranging." If the seller and I cannot get close on a price now, I'll put the project on a shelf. The seller may not be able to sell the property, particularly if they are asking way too much, and months or even a year or two later they may drop the price. In this case, I may consider making another offer. I don't want them to remember me as offensive or arrogant, but as professional and educated.

Now, if the seller counters my offer but is reasonably close in price to my offer, what I like to do is accept it and proceed to contract. In my contract, one of my key points is a minimum thirty-day due diligence period before any money "goes hard." This means my team and I have thirty days to evaluate the property in more depth and review the actual property records, including going on-site to inspect the property. During these thirty days we can back out of the deal and any money we have put down is fully refundable. Once money is nonrefundable it's said to have "gone hard." When the money goes hard and how much will be a key negotiation point in the contract.

Now you might wonder why I would go into a contract with a sales price higher than my financial evaluation says I should pay. If I am confident that I can prove the value of the property, not just my opinion about it, but facts and numbers that show the true value, I use this thirty-day due diligence period as time to do some more fact finding and then report back to the seller. I will explain then that based on what I've found during my due diligence I can't proceed with this sales price. I offer a lower price (usually what I initially offered or close to it) and give my facts to support why. I find this works much better than haggling over a price before contract, which can offend sellers.

- First, if you go into contract you are locking up the deal for thirty days. No one else can get in line to purchase the property in front of you.
- Second, psychologically many sellers start getting excited about selling the property and imagining what they will do with the profits. It's like test driving a car. The salesperson always wants to get you to sit in the car and drive it because you start imagining it's yours, and it's harder to turn away.
- Third, a seller can see in your due diligence process that you are educated and professional and know what you are doing. It's harder for them to keep asking for a price that is too high when you are showing them the facts and figures behind your offering price. You are telling them that 2 + 2 = 4, and even though they are asking for it to equal 5, the numbers show 2 + 2 is still 4. I call this strategy attacking the integrity of the asking price. You go past opinions and slowly pick apart the integrity of their asking price during your due diligence process. This is a much more powerful way to negotiate than to just throw numbers back and forth at each other in an LOI.

This is a powerful negotiation technique, but should be used cautiously. It's unprofessional to be overly aggressive in putting properties under contract if you are not close to making a deal or do not have the money to purchase the property. It locks up that property and if you do this too often you will get a reputation for being unreliable.

THE CONTRACT PHASE

When you proceed into contract, expect to put some money in escrow when you sign. This is like a deposit on the property, and it's a sign that you are a serious prospective buyer. Escrow means that the money will be held in a third party's account, like a title company or your broker's escrow account. A key point of your contract should be that this money is refundable within that thirty-day due diligence period if you decide not to go forward with the deal. But you should expect and be ready to write a check for this deposit money when you sign the contract.

I have prepared a contract that I use as my master template. It has all the key provisions to protect my team and me during the purchase process. Some of these points are negotiated and modified in each deal, but I like to start with my master template contract so I know nothing is accidentally left out or overlooked. It's faster and easier than starting from scratch each time.

I always have my attorney review any changes the other party wants to make to the contract to let me know how those changes will affect me. I do not try to do this myself. I am not an attorney, and even though I've helped negotiate a lot of deals, I am a big believer in letting each expert on my team play his or her role. I don't try to cut corners and deal with things I am not fully qualified to handle. It's not worth the risk to my investment deal. If you decide to grow and work on larger deals, you will probably be working with multiple investors and this becomes even more important. You won't just be putting your money in a deal, but risking other people's money if you try to take shortcuts.

Sometimes, something can go wrong on a deal through no fault of your own. A good example of this is a deal I worked on once when our financing fell through at the eleventh hour. The bank had given us a written agreement to finance the deal, but they backed out after the point at which our deposit money had gone hard, leaving us with no financing. The rest of this deal was extremely stressful and risky—we were up against our deadline to close on the deal and scrambling for financing. We couldn't very well walk from the deal because we had $25,000 hard and nonrefundable. We had done everything right so far, but the bank still backed out even though they had given us a written commitment.

Ultimately, other financing came through. Later, I took a close look at what had occurred. Could I have gone back and sued the bank? Possibly, but when I did the math, months of litigation to get a bank to be responsible just wasn't a good use of my time or energy. After all, I am in business to buy investment property, not to sue banks. So instead, I learned to build a provision into my future contracts that states that my deposit money is protected and refundable if financing falls through at no fault of my own. I'll never find myself in that position again, and thanks to my experience, neither will you.

Key Contract Points

1. **Purchase price.** Clearly state purchase price in your contract.
2. **Minimum thirty-day due diligence period.** You need at least thirty days to conduct your due diligence on the property. No money should go hard and you should be able to cancel the contract during this time period.
3. **Access to files, including leases.** Your contract should allow you to review any and

all files relating to the property. You will need to review leases, payment schedules, payment history, and the like.

4. **Access to bank deposits.** We always verify what the leases say tenants pay in rent, and compare this with what the bank shows is actually deposited. Many times a landlord has accepted lower rent-payment concessions than initially agreed to, and we don't want to purchase this property and be surprised by those lower payments.

5. **Property's rent rolls/schedule.** We always want to review the property's rent roll and schedule. This is the seller's report of each unit's rental rate and how many are vacant. The seller and seller's broker should always sign this, acknowledging it is true and accurate.

   This really saved a deal for me once. I had not been given access to the seller's bank deposit records, which I now know is a must. When I closed on the property and began collecting rent, there were five vacant units I had not been told about and three that were occupied but were paying less rent than I was told. The tenants had copies of their money order receipts for the last six months showing they paid this lower amount. Obviously, this discrepancy really impacted my NOI. I had to move quickly if I hoped to recoup any of my losses. Fortunately, I'd had the seller and her broker sign off on the rent rolls they submitted during the purchase process, so I had proof that they'd misled me on the vacancy percentage and was able to negotiate the return of some funds to compensate us for their misinformation. This got me through the first few months until I could lease up the empty units.

6. **Access to property.** Being able to get on-site and inspect a property is key. An unfortunate student of mine purchased a property without being able to get inside to inspect it. Why she did this, I will never know, but she did. And she paid for it. When she closed on the townhome and was able to get inside, it was empty. And I mean literally empty. It had no walls, just the studs. It had no stairs to the second floor, no plumbing, nothing. It was uninhabitable. She had to pay out of pocket for major renovations and could not rent the property for two months while these were being completed.

   Many times if you are purchasing a property that is already rented, sellers will give the excuse that you can't get on-site because it might upset the current tenants and cause them to move out, leaving you with an empty unit. Don't fall for this; it's a huge red flag. My father is a housing inspector and he's always told me, "Inspect what you expect." In other words, if you think you are purchasing a property in good condition, you'd better have inspected it to see if it meets your expectations. You can use the Subject Property Inspection Checklist beginning on page 220 to conduct your inspection.

7. **Security deposits.** It should be clearly spelled out if the security deposits are being

transferred to you. Ideally they should be, because if a tenant moves out you may have to refund the deposit or use it for repairs. During your due diligence process you always want to verify the security deposits listed on the leases and what is actually in the security deposit account at the bank.

8. **When does the money go hard?** You don't want to find yourself behind the eight ball as I was in that earlier example when my financing fell through. Always, always be clear in your contract how much money goes hard and when.

9. **Build in financing contingencies.** Always have language in your contract that allows you to back out of the deal if you cannot secure financing.

10. **Set aside escrow money for rent.** An often overlooked key provision is to have the seller place money in escrow for rent collections. If you are purchasing a property with tenants already in it, you want to make sure there is compensation available to you for the portion of the month you take over the property. For example, if you close on the property on the 20th of the month tenants will have already paid their rent for that month. You should negotiate in your contract for a prorated portion of that rent for the days you are the new owner. You want a sum in escrow to pay this amount to you.

11. **Equipment.** A contract should state clearly if the purchase includes any equipment on the property, such as tools, storage shed, and lawn or pool care equipment. It should also specify that anything left on property at closing is now yours. So if there is a toolshed in the back of a rental home you purchase and the seller leaves equipment there, it's now yours to keep or throw away.

12. **Existing contracts disclosure.** A contract should also require a seller to disclose any contracts they have with anyone relating to the property. Some of these contracts say that whoever purchases the property assumes the contract, so you want to be aware of them. For example, it's common for a multifamily unit to lease washers and dryers for a laundry room. You want to know if you are tied to this contract or not. Remember, expenses are key to your NOI!

SEOTA PROCESS PART II— DUE DILIGENCE PROCESS ON SUBJECT PROPERTY

The first part of the SEOTA we discussed in the last chapter was designed to help you identify a target area and learn about prospective tenants in that area: who they are, what they like, what they can afford in rent, and so on. The second phase of the SEOTA is the due diligence process. This is the in-depth review of a specific property you intend to purchase. The due diligence process includes reviewing the seller's records and actually going on-site to inspect the property. Below are key parts of the Due Diligence Action List with explanations—you'll also find this checklist in the Appendix.

Sales Comps

This is the process to compare the sales price of your subject property to similar properties in the area. You need to know what the going rate is for a similar property in the marketplace. Then you start to consider amenities and how they impact the price.

Rent Growth Forecast and Market Survey

Perform your rental market survey to see what similar units are charging for rent in the area. I also like to check the going rate for public housing, i.e., government funded rental subsidies, as a benchmark of what you can command in rent. You can find helpful tools to determine market rents in your area on our website.

Vacancy

Check the historic vacancy rate of the area for the past three years. Your local chapter of the National Apartment Association (NAA) is an excellent source for this. You can also work with a local real estate broker who specializes in rentals.

Maintenance and Home Inspection

This is a very important part of the due diligence process, and you want to have a good maintenance technician or home inspector on your team. I prefer to have someone with experience with rental properties. They understand what must be done to make a unit market ready, how to do basic improvements between tenancies, and the importance of keeping expenses within budget. They can give you a more accurate estimate of what it will cost and how long it will take to get each unit market ready. And remember, empty units stay clean but there is no income in an empty unit. Maintenance technicians with rental experience understand the delicate time line of readying a unit to rent it.

Part of this due diligence process is not just walking the units but also reviewing the last three months' maintenance expenses. Often repair bills can tell you what major repairs are coming down the pipeline. There's an entire chapter on maintenance later in this book.

Market Survey Rental Income Check

This part of the process is to verify the rent roll with actual rents collected.

- Obtain the most current rent roll from the seller.
- Check that the current rent roll matches up with the rents listed on the deal sheet.
- Check the market rents on the street or in the neighborhood—are the rents in the neighborhood consistent with the rents this building is getting?
- Check the building's financial statements for the past year—do the rents match up with the operating statements?

Lease Audit

In auditing the leases, you want to verify several things in addition to the rent amount. Check the move-out dates so you can anticipate when you may have vacancies. Be sure to verify security deposits and look for any side deals or concessions.

- Check leases to make sure the rental amounts match up with rent rolls provided.
- Check bank deposits to make sure the rent deposits match up with rent rolls and leases.
- Check all move-out dates in the lease to make sure they match up to rent rolls.
- Check tenant correspondence with current management and ownership, and make sure there are no outstanding disputes.
- Check leases for any side deals or concessions with tenants—is anyone getting a break on the rent?
- Check the cash deposits against the collected rents.

For example, one of my students came to class after having bought a property that looked like a good deal on paper. It was a duplex, with each unit renting at $995 a month. The total rent roll therefore was $1990, which was sufficient to cover the mortgage and expenses each month, with some to spare. Well, my student told me that after he closed on the property and went to collect the monthly rent, one of the rent checks was only $765. He asked the tenant why he didn't pay the full rental amount and was told that the tenant's rent was $765 a month, not $995! When my student checked the lease, sure enough, while the rental amount was $995, there was a separate agreement that as long as that tenant mowed the grass and handled the landscaping of the duplex, his rent would be reduced in compensation. My student was stuck with this arrangement for seven more months, until the tenant's lease term was up.

In a proper due diligence, as my student now knows, you should review bank deposit records to verify exactly what was deposited on a monthly basis and also perform a full tenant file review to learn of any other agreements or history you are taking on as the new landlord. I myself have been guilty of rushing through and not dotting all my "i's" and crossing all my "t's" during acquisition. And trust me, you pay for it later. When you're in the middle of assembling all this information in a short time line, it's easy to overlook something. This is why I created a Due Diligence Action List, to make sure every detail, big or small, is covered. I've included this very important form in the Appendix of this book so you don't overlook any of these important steps during acquisition.

Escrow Accounts (Security Deposits)

- Check leases to make sure security deposit amounts match up with rent rolls provided.
- Check that security deposits match up with rent rolls and leases.
- Check tenant correspondence with current management and ownership to make sure there are no disputes regarding security deposits.
- Check leases for any side deals or concessions with tenants pertaining to security deposits.
- Check the cash deposits against the collected security deposits.
- Check records to make sure security deposits were not used as rent.

Bad Debt

You want to check the delinquency reports to see how common late rent is. This definitely is important because a negligent property manager may have allowed a culture of late rent and undisciplined payment schedules.

Other Income

Review and verify reports of other income—such as extra fees for parking spaces or laundry machines on premises. A common contract for a property is a contract with laundry machine suppliers. Check to see what contracts exist, when they expire, and what the splits are. A property I just purchased was under contract with a company that placed coin-operated washers and dryers in the property and did not split any of the money collected with the landlord. This is a huge missed opportunity by someone not familiar with how the rental industry works. It's very common to get at least a 50/50 split on the washer and dryer income, and the supplying company will handle all related maintenance.

Operating Expenses

Along with verifying expenses, you want to verify service contracts to see if you have any warranties, for example. You want to have any pending litigation disclosed as well as all code violations or notices. Then you can review all these with your maintenance technician. A good maintenance tech can usually come up with ways to lower operating expenses.

Advertisement Cost

First, review all advertising contracts and make sure they can be canceled. You don't want to be obligated for any yellow page or newspaper ad. Then, based on your vacancy rate, determine what you should expect to spend initially to advertise and rent these units.

Total Payroll Costs

If the property is large enough to warrant employees, verify the pay schedules for all employees—how much they are paid, if they are under contract, and for how long.

General and Administrative Cost

Review supplies, business permits needed, and any associated transfer costs for these.

Management Fee Costs

Decide if you will handle management (bills, rent collection, and the other day-to-day operating tasks of running the property), or if you will outsource it. If you do it yourself, decide if you will pay yourself management fees or not. You may need to if you do not have other sources of income and need additional cash flow. Make sure you account for management-fee costs in your budget if you will be outsourcing it.

Landscape Cost

Review the historical cost of upkeep and the current condition for needed upgrades. Be sure to check irrigation or sprinkler systems and timers.

Unit Turnover Costs

Check the historical turnover rate and cost. Also review with your maintenance technician or home inspector what items will need to be replaced at the next turnover in tenant. For example, I have a unit with an AC that will need to be replaced before I can rerent it. It's working now, but my maintenance tech has informed me that it is outdated and it will be difficult to re-lease the unit if it isn't updated. So we can budget to replace this AC once the current tenant's lease term is up.

Repair and Maintenance Cost

Get an idea of the history of maintenance costs as well as an itemized budget for items that currently need repair or replacement.

Utilities

Obtain from the seller copies of all bills for services, and verify those bills with the individual utility providers.

- Water/sewer
- Gas
- Electricity
- Trash
- Other

Try to speak personally with utility providers to ask about forecasted rate increases.

Property Tax

Be sure to calculate your property tax based on the sales price, as it will be adjusted and increased when you buy it.

Property Insurance

Get bids for insurance and include the cost in your projections.

- Personal property and liability insurance
- Hurricane/flood insurance (where necessary)

Reserves

Most investment properties require a "reserve fund"—a rainy day fund to pay for any unexpected costs or repairs. You'll need to determine what an appropriate reserve fund will be.

- Check historical capital expenditures
- Evaluate recurring items of concern
- Determine the adequate reserves amounts

The Due Diligence Action List provides you with a comprehensive checklist of items to complete. Additional forms can be found at **landlordacademy.com**.

DUE DILIGENCE ACTION LIST (FORM 8)

Use this form once you find a subject property you wish to make an offer on to ensure that every major area of consideration (legal, tax, physical condition, and financial) is inspected and meets your approval. This form is critical to keep you organized as you execute your due diligence on a property and make sure nothing is missed.

LETTER OF INTENT
- Review and sign off by (date) _____
- Review and sign off by legal team

Make sure:
- Due diligence will expire without obligation by buyer
- Deposit release requires written action
- Sufficient time is allowed for due diligence
- Sufficient time is allowed for financing
- Pre-approval letter from lender
- Deposit goes hard on (date) _____

PURCHASE AGREEMENT
- Confirm investment commitment date
- Deposit goes hard on _____
- Sufficient time allowed for due diligence
- Sufficient time allowed for due financing
- Deposit release requires written action
- Due diligence will expire without obligation by the buyer
- Review and sign off by legal team
- Review and sign off by _____

FINANCING
- Select lender
- Send preliminary numbers to lender
- Calendar of any dates that were agreed to
- Prepare and send lender package
- Send all lender-required documents to appropriate personnel (i.e., rent rolls)
- Agree to and verify closing date and funding date

COMPARABLE PROPERTIES
- Complete economic rent comps
- Complete at least three market surveys along with shopping the target area

SALES COMPS
- Complete economic sales comps
- Tour sales comps of other like properties
- Check accuracy of market rents with third party sources (i.e., locator services)

MARKET SURVEY RENTAL INCOME CHECK
- Obtain the most current rent roll
- Verify rent-roll totals by running a tape
- Compare current rents in place match up with the deal sheet
- Verify market rents on the street match up with the deal sheet
- Verify rents match up with the operating statements

LEASE AUDIT COMPLETED
- Check leases to make sure they match up with rent rolls provided
- Check deposits to make sure they match up with rent rolls and leases
- Check all move-out dates to make sure they match up to rent rolls
- Check tenant correspondence with current management and ownership to make sure no disputes
- Check leases for any side deals or concessions with tenants
- Check the cash deposits against the collected rents

ESCROW ACCOUNTS
- Check tenants' security deposits against owner's escrow account holding deposits
- Open escrow account for security deposits to be transferred before or at closing
- Check owner's reserves for replacement account

RENT GROWTH FORECAST AND MARKET SURVEY
- Verify by third party research
- Check reliable sources for rent growth
- Check to make sure that rent-growth percent is used in financial projections for each year

VACANCY
- Check historic vacancy for the past three years
- Calculate financial projections vacancy based on market survey info

BAD DEBT
- Check history of bad debt
- Check to see if bad debt is included in cash flows

OTHER INCOME
- Receive reports showing other income generated by property
- Review other income for accuracy

Note: Do not evaluate nonrecurring items; do not evaluate forfeited deposits.

LAUNDRY CONTRACTS
- Check to see when they expire
- Check to see who they are with
- Check to see last time renewed
- Check what the vendor and landlord splits are

OPERATING EXPENSES
General
- Obtain copies of all service contracts from Seller
- Review and make sure cancelable in thirty days
- Obtain list copies of all insurance claims for past year from Seller
- Obtain list of pending litigation (if any)
- Obtain a list of any government notices or code informant claims

ADVERTISEMENT COST
- Review all advertising contracts
- Make sure all contracts are cancelable in thirty days or less upon purchase

TOTAL PAYROLL COSTS
- Verify number of office personnel and payroll

GENERAL AND ADMINISTRATION COST
- Review equipment lease
- Verify all office leases are cancelable within thirty days
- Review supply list and pricing
- Review legal expenses (i.e., evictions)
- Review business permits and the renewal date of each
- Review pool permits
- Review janitorial costs

MANAGEMENT FEE COSTS
- Select property management company, if you are outsourcing management
- Agree to the fee you will pay company or if you are managing yourself, determine the fee you will pay yourself and add to financial projections
- Review pest control cost
- Review historicals for expense
- Examine any unusual items or indication of recurring items
- Include them in financial projections

LANDSCAPE COST
- Review historical costs
- Review general condition of existing landscape
- Check condition of irrigation system, clocks, and timers
- Budget fully for landscape improvements

APARTMENT TURNOVER COSTS
- Check historical turnover rate
- Check historical turnover cost per rental unit
- Factor turnover rate into operating costs
- Factor turnover costs per unit
- Evaluate any unusual turnover expenditures (i.e., wallpaper, stoves, etc.)
- Check maintenance checklist to see what items need to be budgeted for

REPAIR AND MAINTENANCE COST
- Review maintenance checklist
- Check historical maintenance costs
- Review any unusual items that showed up on the maintenance checklist
- Pull out nonrecurring capitalized items
- Evaluate any work orders unit by unit (should show up on maintenance checklist)

UTILITIES
Evaluated historical cost
Service providers:
- Water/Sewer
- Gas
- Electricity
- Trash
- Other
- Speak personally with utility providers re: forecast rate increases (include in financial projections)

PROPERTY TAX
- Recalculate property tax based on sales price

PROPERTY INSURANCE
- Get insurance bids
- Include new bid in financial projections
- Receive personal property insurance quote
- Obtain hurricane insurance (if needed)
- Include all new quotes in financial projections

RESERVES
- Check historical capital expenditures
- Evaluate recurring items of concern
- Create adequate reserves amounts

THIRD PARTY DUE DILIGENCE
- Perform physical inspection
- Complete maintenance check on each unit performed and report reviewed. Use Subject Property Inspection Checklist (Form 6)

FINAL APPROVAL CHECKLIST
- Complete tour property by all member managers and owners
- Match executive summary with deal summary
- Complete financial review by accounting
- Complete rent growth assumptions supported and sign off on
- Review refinance option for accuracy
- Review exit strategy tax adjustment
- Check deferred maintenance numbers for accuracy
- Review annual return

CLOSING DEAL DETAILS
- Check that the closing rent roll was received and approved
- Check tax calculation
- Confirm purchase price on statement is correct
- Confirm seller credits on statement are in order
- Confirm payment of closing cost consistent with contract
- Check to see if financing amount is correct
- Check payment for points
- Check other finance cost and approve
- Check legal costs and approve
- Verify total cash due from buyer
- Transfer tenants' escrow deposits to buyer's account

KEYS TO TEAMWORK

Remember that you have a limited time period to complete this due diligence process. To meet your deadline, it's important as the project leader to keep your whole team on track and moving forward. Important members of your team are your maintenance technician or home inspector, your attorney, your mortgage broker or bank, your Realtor, your CPA, and your title company. I like to schedule a weekly meeting or teleconference that each person is required to attend every Monday. It doesn't have to be long; thirty minutes is sufficient to review the due diligence checklist, check off items that are completed, and assign deadlines for items still due. You can then schedule separate times with each team member to review their particular information and discuss its impact on the deal. This meeting is simply to touch base on progress made and keep momentum moving forward. It also makes team members accountable for completing their tasks within the time line agreed to. No one likes to show up to a team huddle without completing their assignment and let the team down. Group check-ins work well to encourage accountability.

• • •

So, in this chapter, we discussed how to negotiate, what tools are used in negotiation, and how to evaluate the subject property using the due diligence process. All of these are important keys to the purchase process. The next chapter will explore another key to securing a profitable investment property, and that's financing. Since one of the powerful tools used in real estate is financial leverage, mastering the art of financing is instrumental in building long-term wealth.

> Let us never negotiate out of fear,
> but let us never fear to negotiate.
> —JOHN F. KENNEDY

HOW DO I PAY FOR IT?

Getting the Right Financing

We've talked a lot about how powerful leveraging is in real estate. Leveraging allows you to use a small amount of your own money, and a lot of someone else's, to own a valuable asset and build wealth. Financing is the key to leveraging.

In real estate, like any other business, it's nearly impossible to achieve any lasting success without a firm understanding of finance. Before we can secure the most favorable financing available we all, as investors, must be qualified. Banks do this by reviewing our credit score. In this chapter you will learn the first basic aspects of real estate financing—including how to make yourself attractive to lenders and how to get financing at the most favorable terms possible. Trust me, you won't continue down the path to real estate wealth until you have fully mastered these skills! Financing can make or break the profitability of a deal. This chapter will discuss the different parts of the financing process and how each aspect can support your real estate deal.

So far, we've learned to take a proven, systematic approach to every step of our investment deal. This step (securing financing) should be no different. We will methodically look at the different financing options and use our team of experts to evaluate those options.

KNOW YOURSELF AND YOUR BANKERS

I once read in the book *The Art of War*, by Sun Tzu, that to know yourself and not your enemy will cause you to lose; to know your enemy and not yourself will cause you to lose; only those who know themselves *and* their enemy will find victory. This holds true in business as well. You must not only know about your rental investment, you must know the team you have assembled as well. In the case of working with lenders there are a few things you should understand.

There are two main cornerstones that a lender looks at that I discuss more in depth later in this chapter. The first is the relationship between the loan amount and market value (LTV).

The second is the relationship between annual debt payments and the property's income (NOI). You will find some lenders who prefer to lend to rental investments and will offer up very attractive loan products. Other lenders may not like to lend on rental investments. Some lenders will be more receptive to the smaller private investor, generating many loans under one million dollars. Typically this type of small investor-oriented lender is best when you're starting out. Knowing your investment and the lender will aid you in closing the deal.

IMPROVING YOUR CREDIT

Despite my war analogy, I don't want you to think of your lender as your enemy. It's not like the two of you are going to be locked in combat with the winner being the one who gets the interest rate you want. Yes, you do want to get the best terms for yourself, but lenders have a shared interest in seeing you succeed—they don't want to see you default on your loan and the property go into foreclosure. That's not good for you and it's not good for them, because banks are in the business of lending money, not handling property management for a foreclosed property they inherit.

You are allies. Now, with that said, you still must keep your guard up for possible **lender land mines** that could go off during your deal. We will talk more about these later.

Let's learn first what you need to understand about working with a lender. Some lenders' main focus will be on your credit worthiness as an investor, and the rental investment will be a secondary item of focus. Others will look first and foremost at the rental investment's numbers. The building is their main focus in giving the loan. However, the bank also evaluates you as a credit risk.

Especially when you're starting out as a real estate investor, the bank will have a magnifying glass on you and your credit. This is why we see so many of our students taking the time to get their CRIS (Certified Rental Investment Specialist) certifications. This certification, as well as the CPMS (Certified Property Management Specialist), goes a long way in showing the bank that you have taken the time to learn your craft and are qualified to run this property. All banks understand that the most critical time is the first six months to a year you own a property. This is when most property owners start running into trouble due to poor management, which has a negative impact on the property's cash flow. We will spend more time on property management later in this book.

Since you and your credit will be under a magnifying glass, let's take a moment to learn more about how to improve your credit and dispel some myths about credit scores. If you are going to invest in an investment property, it's wise to first invest in yourself. You're already investing in yourself by reading this book and learning more about real estate. Make another investment by checking your credit rating and seeing what you can do to improve and/or safeguard it. If you have read books about what the rich know that the rest of us don't, you will know that a good credit score is as powerful as money in the bank. It can buy you a lot.

CREDIT SCORES 101

Your credit score (also called your FICO number) is used by most mortgage lenders to determine whether to lend you money and at what interest rate. Think of these scores as being like your grades in school. Your credit scores are a numerical expression of the likelihood that you will repay a loan and pay on time. The better (higher) your credit rating, the lower the interest rates you will be charged because you will be viewed as less of a risk.

FICO scores range between 300 and 850. Scores of 700 and above are considered excellent (an A) and get you the best rates on mortgages. Scoring between 600 and 699 (a B) are good. You could end up qualifying for a slightly higher rate, generally less than one percentage point more than someone with an A grade. If your FICO score is between 500 and 599 (a C) you will likely have to pay at least two percentage points or more over the best rates offered. A score below 499 (a D) means you will pay three or more percentage points above those best rates.

This score is based primarily on credit report information, typically from one of the three major credit bureaus: Experian, TransUnion, and Equifax. These bureaus collect data from retailers, credit card companies, and other places where you pay your bills and credit accounts. Your credit report lists your balances, your payment history, balances owed, and available credit.

Americans are entitled to one free credit report within a twelve-month period from each of the three agencies. The three credit bureaus run Annualcreditreport.com, where users can get their free credit report, normally without credit scores. Credit scores are available as an add-on feature of the report—for a fee, of course!

Even a good income-producing property can become a not-so-good deal if you have to pay a high interest rate on your loan because your credit doesn't qualify you for a good rate.

Know Your Credit Score

The first thing you can do to improve your credit is get a free copy of your credit report. Credit bureaus make mistakes. The information they get from retailers, credit card companies, and others can be wrong. If so, take control and contact one of those three agencies and let them know about the errors. Ask them to remove that wrong information from your report. When they do, your credit score will be recalculated and go up.

Whether you have a good credit rating that you'd like to improve or bad credit that needs repairing, there are at least five steps you can take to improve your score:

Pay Your Bills on Time

Thirty-five percent of your credit score is determined by payment history. That is the most important factor used to calculate your score and the hardest to fix. How important are on-time payments? Depending on other factors, missing even one payment can knock 50 to 100 points off a good score. What you've done most recently carries more weight than what you did five years ago. So, if you've had payment problems in the past don't despair, just take action and start making your payments on time and your score will improve.

Know How Much You Charge . . . and Your Credit Limits

What are your credit card debts/balances and your total credit limits? Credit score calculations are also based on the relationship between these two numbers. If you don't carry a balance from month to month that's good, but credit reporting agencies don't distinguish between those who pay off each month and those who don't. They simply look at the total number of dollars charged. So, if you pay cash more frequently and use your credit card less often, you can improve your credit score! You may love the airline miles and other "rewards" you get when you charge everything, but a lower interest rate on the purchase of your four-unit building should really put a smile on your face.

If you're in the first stages of thinking about an investment property purchase, now is the time to start paying down those balances.

Don't Close Old, Paid-off Accounts

Most people close out an account once they pay it off. Why does closing down accounts hurt? Since credit scores are largely determined by comparing your balances due to your available credit, when you close an account you decrease the amount of available credit you have. That makes even small balances seem larger. Also, credit reports are based on your credit history. The longer the period of time showing you're a good credit risk, the better. If you close old accounts, you're shortening your credit history.

If you carry balances or charge a lot, leave all your old accounts open, especially if you're about to apply for new credit.

UNDERSTAND THE LOAN TO VALUE

When a lender evalutes your rental investment they will use what is called loan to value, or LTV. The loan-to-value ratio is a way that lenders determine the risk they will be taking on in providing you with money to purchase your rental investment. Technically, LTV refers to the relationship between the amounts borrowed and the price or value of the investment property purchased. If you are a general whose task is protecting your soldiers (dollars), then the bank's loan officer is also a general, with the task of protecting the bank's dollars, and he or she uses LTV to evaluate the risk.

Example: If I bought a rental property for $100,000 and acquired a mortgage for $80,000 this would produce an 80 percent loan-to-value ratio. An easy way to figure out LTV is to subtract whatever percentage you are putting down from 100, and that's your LTV. A 10 percent down payment gives you a 90 percent LTV; if you put down 25 percent, your LTV is 75 percent.

The loan-to-value ratio is used by the lender to determine perceived risk in making the mortgage loan. The lower the LTV, the lower the risk to the bank. The way the bank sees it, the more the investor comes out of pocket, the more that investor is tied to the deal. If his own hard-earned money is invested in the deal, he's less likely to default on the loan. A greater LTV means there may not be enough cash flow to cover the loan amount if the lender must foreclose and sell the investment property. Keep in mind as well that higher LTVs will increase the interest rate on the deal as well. Typical LTVs are from anywhere between 75 and 80 percent of market value.

HOW INTEREST RATES ARE SET

Sure, you want to know whether or not you got the loan. We are conditioned to wait with our fingers crossed for the bank to evaluate us and approve us. But in real estate investing, you actually need to evaluate and decide if you are willing to accept the bank's loan offer. The loan they offer you might not work with your investment. This ability to control your own investment destiny—to be in the driver's seat—is one thing I love about real estate investing. *You* get to decide if a deal is a go or not! You don't get to do that in the stock market. IBM has never called me up to ask me if they should make a business deal that impacts my stock account!

One important factor in determining whether or not to *accept* a bank's offer is the interest rate they will offer you. Interest rates for investment property are created off a "spread" over a selected index. Indexes are financial indicators that may rise or fall. This rising and falling is usually affected by the ebbs and flows of the economy. The index your lender uses is based on the type of lender as well as their source of funds.

Types of indexes include:

- U.S. Treasury bonds.
- CMT (Constant Maturity Treasury Rate): This is an average yield on the U.S. Treasury securities that is adjusted to a constant maturity of one year.
- Prime rate: This is the interest rate that banks charge to their most creditworthy customers.
- LIBOR (London Interbank Offered Rate): This is the world's most widely used benchmark for short-term interest rates. It is the rate at which the world's most preferred borrowers are able

to borrow money and the rate upon which rates for less preferred borrowers are based. LIBOR is derived from an average of the world's most creditworthy banks' interbank deposit rates.

Before I really understood how this big picture, or macroeconomics, worked, I began following these indexes and watching the CNBC reports. By paying attention I began to learn how each part of the economy impacts another and how it is all linked together. I recommend you do the same. It's like watching a game of football when you don't understand the rules. If you watch it long enough and listen to the reports, you will begin to see how it works. To begin learning you can follow these indexes on my website.

I said before that if you want to become a master negotiator, then learn how the other person gets paid! This holds true with dealing with lenders, who get paid off the spread. What is the spread? The spread is the difference between the index (described on page 89) and the interest rate you were quoted by your lender. It's the "markup" on the loan. The spread will reveal the lender's profit.

Sometimes an investor will accept a higher interest rate in order to achieve other goals:

- A chance to exercise a prepayment clause
- To set a closing date
- To create greater leverage, i.e., receive a higher loan-to-value. This means you may accept a higher interest rate to put less down on a property.

PREQUALIFYING YOURSELF

Before we get to talking about the different types of loans offered, we need to figure out exactly how much money you qualify to borrow. If you can get prequalified for that amount, you can move swiftly when you find a property that fits your SEOTA qualifications. I suggest you meet with your loan officer *before* you start looking so you know your limits and you don't get attached to a property that you can't afford. There's no sense pursuing a deal if you know you won't qualify for a loan of that amount. "Prequalifying" means knowing in advance what amount a bank is likely to loan you. Be prepared to supply the necessary information. Here is what you will need to have on hand:

- Name, Social Security number, date of birth, contact numbers and email, and your home address.
- Employment information: name of company, address, and phone numbers. (Note: you need to show at least two years of employment history and address history. If

you have changed jobs or moved within two years be ready to provide previous employment or home information.)

- Gross monthly income. This is your income before any expenses are deducted. If you are self-employed and do not receive a W-2, the lender will look at your tax returns. You'll also need to have any other income information available. Be prepared to submit copies of your last two years' tax returns.

- Your current monthly housing expenses. This constitutes your first mortgage, second mortgage, principal, and interest payments. You'll also need hazard insurance figures and what you pay in taxes. If you pay mortgage insurance, have that amount also.

- Assets and liabilities. Gather information on your checking, savings, and any other accounts that you have money in, as well as stocks, bonds, and 401(k)s. Assets are very important for two reasons. One, this information shows where your down payment is coming from. Two, it shows what you have in reserve. Be prepared to submit copies of recent account statements for each asset you list.

All the money in your accounts needs to be **seasoned** for at least two months. Seasoned is a term used to describe how long the money has been in an account. The term can also refer to how long you have owned a property or how long the seller has owned the property.

- Value of your business if you own one.
- Information on all real estate owned. You should create a spreadsheet for your properties so you can keep track of them, but also so you have the information ready when acquiring a loan. Here is what you need to put on that spreadsheet for each property:

1. Address of the subject property
2. What type of property (single family, duplex, or commercial)
3. How the property is owned (owner occupied, investment, or second home)
4. Present market value
5. Mortgage balance
6. Mortgage payment
7. Purchase price
8. Date acquired
9. Rental income
10. Who is on the title
11. Flood area?

I have just given you a road map. Now it's up to you to have all that information ready, and I promise you that the loan process will become a lot easier—especially once you have become an investor and are purchasing multiple properties. To streamline things, I keep an up-to-date copy of my personal financial statement containing all the information above. I also keep scanned copies of my tax returns, a copy of my driver's license, and other information noted above all together in one zip file. When I have to submit this information, it's easy and organized.

TYPES OF MORTGAGES AVAILABLE

You will want to secure the best loan for your situation out of the many different types of loans available. Here are the most common with brief explanations of each.

RULE OF THUMB

If you're just starting out in rental property investment, be careful of "exotic" mortgage options to improve a property's return or to qualify if your credit isn't good. Variable-rate loans, no-money-down loans, and other financing options that seem too good to be true probably are. Unless you really understand all the ins and outs of the loan and the possible negative consequences, these loans can be risky (if you can even qualify for them anymore—lenders are increasingly cautious after the mortgage crisis of 2007–08).

Fixed Rate Investor Mortgage Loans

The thirty-year fixed rate mortgage is the tried-and-true offering. For a long time this was the only type of mortgage available for investors. You pay at a fixed rate which doesn't change for the life of the loan. The loan is fully amortizing—that means that at the end of the term the loan will be completely paid off. A fixed rate mortgage is easy to understand and will not surprise you down the line.

Pros of a thirty-year fixed rate:
- The monthly payment stays the same over the term of the loan. You can plan for it and will not be surprised with an increased payment amount.
- Since it is designed to hold property long term, it allows you to spread out the total amount over thirty years, which can reduce the monthly payment amount.

Cons of a thirty-year fixed rate:

- Since this is a more conservative loan, you are usually charged a higher interest rate to pay for the fixed stability than you would be for another loan type.
- If interest rates drop, you do not benefit. You continue to pay the same amount you originally agreed to.

The Adjustable Rate Mortgage (ARM)

ARMs have become nearly as common as fixed rate loans for residential home buyers and for investors. Unlike a standard fixed rate mortgage, an ARM has a variable interest rate. ARMS are usually linked to a published interest rate index like United States Treasury bonds. The lender then adds a spread to that number.

ARMs have an initial fixed rate period that usually lasts three years, five years, seven years, or ten years, during which the payment stays the same. After that the rate adjusts based on the index the lender has it tied to. Let's say you take out a 5/1 ARM. That means you have a fixed rate for the first five years, then it adjusts every year after that. Most ARMs have limits on how much the rate can reset in any given year, as well as a limit on the amount the rate could rise or fall over the life of the loan.

The advantage of an ARM is that you have a lower interest rate initially than you would for a fixed rate loan. The disadvantage is that you can't predict how those indexes will adjust, high or low, which changes your payment amount. While they have come under a lot of fire as a result of the mortgage crisis of 2007–08, don't write off these loans entirely. For investors, they can be a good alternative—if you know how to handle them. Always work with an experienced and trusted mortgage broker to help you navigate the pros and cons.

Pros of an ARM:

- In the first years of the ARM, you typically pay a lower interest rate, which means a lower monthly mortgage payment. This results in greater cash flow.
- If interest rates goes down, your loan adjusts and you benefit from this change.

Cons of an ARM:

- If interest rates go up, not down, your loan adjusts higher and your payments increase.
- It's more unpredictable. For the luxury of having a lower interest rate initially, you run the risk of higher payments down the line.

Interest Only Real Estate Investor Mortgage Loans

As the name says, on these loans you pay only the interest portion of the mortgage for a set period of time. That can generally be as few as three years and as many as ten. You are not paying any principal to reduce the balance of the loan. After the initial period ends, the bank reamortizes, or recalculates, the loan and you have to pay off the principal over the years left on the loan.

When that initial period ends, you have three choices: pay the increased amount, refinance the loan, or sell the property.

You can generate more cash flow immediately on the investment because your monthly payments will be lower during the interest only phase of the loan. However, you are not paying down principal and when the interest only period ends you need to be prepared to either refinance or pay a higher payment amount.

Pros of interest only:
- Interest-only loans typically have significantly lower monthly payments during the initial phase of the loan. This greatly increases your cash flow.

Cons of interest only:
- You are not paying down your principal and reducing your debt.
- When the interest-only phase ends, you will still owe the entire principal and must be ready to refinance or pay a much higher payment amount.

KNOW YOUR EXIT STRATEGY

It is important to understand your exit strategy *before* selecting financing. Those investors who plan to purchase below-value property, rehab it, then quickly place the property back on the market will typically want to secure variable rate mortgages. A short-term investor may find variable rate mortgages more attractive as the interest rates on these loans are often initially lower and the investor plans to sell the property before the loan resets to higher payments. An investor whose strategy is long term may want to look at a fixed rate or an ARM for the first five years to help maximize cash flow. But the investor who anticipates future interest rate hikes will want to stay with the fixed rate.

My suggestion is to work with a mortgage broker who understands income-producing properties. She can help provide valuable insight on how each of these loans will ultimately affect the property's cash flow. At the end of the day, it always boils down to cash flow. For a real estate investor coach, visit **landlordacademy.com**.

Keys to Securing Financing, Even in Cautious Times

1. **Pick wise investments.** Use the SEOTA method to zero in on the right property, and use that same due diligence information to discuss the property with your lender. Your subject property must have positive cash flow. In other words, it must cover the monthly debt.

2. **Have a résumé.** In cautious financial times, you must have more than just a pulse to get a loan. You must come to the table with credibility. When lenders are more cautious in giving loans, the more you can do to assure them you are educated, trained, and prepared to manage a rental property, the more you are reducing their risk.

3. **Be prepared to put more down on the property than you would have to in less cautious times.** You may need to put more cash down to make your loan less risky to the lender.

4. **Safeguard your credit.** Make sure you improve your credit and keep it in good standing.

5. **Develop the right professional relationships.** Work with mortgage brokers who specifically understand investment property.

THE LOAN APPROVAL PROCESS

With today's technology, we are accustomed to instantaneous responses. Our iPhones, Black-Berrys, and instant messaging have spoiled us. In this fast-paced world, it can be surprising and frustrating to realize that getting approved for an investment property loan is not a one-step process. You will have many hoops to jump through and tests to pass before you secure your loan. It can take up to thirty days to complete the process, depending on the size of the deal. Let me outline the steps for you. The better prepared you are to submit the needed information when requested, the faster this process, called underwriting, will go.

The Appraisal Step

Your lender will assign an appraiser to perform a thorough evaluation of the subject property. Appraisers are trained to evaluate market conditions. They will inspect the property and measure the square footage of its interior and exterior. They will review all leases and rent rolls. Basically they will be performing their own SEOTA process. This is why I like to work with the appraiser and share my own SEOTA research with him. Because this is a very important part of the underwriting process, I want to be sure the lender gets the most accurate picture of the property possible.

You should be prepared to pay for this appraisal. Appraisals can often hold up the underwriting process while the lender is waiting for you to make payment and to schedule the appraiser.

Property Inspectors

Your lender may contract out an environmental and structural inspector to take a look at the subject property.

Credit Agencies

Your lender will surely want to take a look at your creditworthiness. This is a major part of how they will determine your interest rate. The better your credit, the more favorable rates you can obtain.

Underwriters

The bank's underwriter will conduct an overall evaluation of all the reports previously mentioned. The underwriter will also conduct her own evaluation on the subject property's income and expenses to determine your property's debt to income ratio. She will also evaluate market conditions. Then after completing her evaluation, she will make recommendations to the loan committee at the bank. The committee can sometimes change the rate as well as the LTV required on the property.

Triple Checking the Details

If the purchase is a residential investment, the processors for your loans must pre-underwrite files before sending them into underwriting, by documenting and verifying all of the information you provided. This process also includes DU, aka desktop underwriting, which analyzes accuracy of income, assets, Real Estate Owned (REO), taxes, insurance, and debt to income ratio factors. Once loans have passed the DU process and a preapproval has been given, the file goes to the underwriter. He will verify all the information that the processor has done for continued accuracy and may request additional information if he feels it's needed to strengthen the file. The underwriters are responsible to make sure that all files have the adequate information. Once the file passes the criteria and conditions it is cleared to close. But wait one more minute. The lender can pull your credit once again to make sure that you have not incurred any *new* debt that could affect your loan qualification. If you have, the lender can cancel the loan even as you are sitting down to sign the loan documents.

Approval Committee

This is the final step before the investor receives the loan for the subject property. After this committee agrees on the subject property, you move to closing. When dealing with lenders, you will again use your skills as a master negotiator. After submitting your rental investment's financials, the lender should send over to you what is known as a letter of intent. The letter of intent should reflect:

- Proper agreed-upon LTVs (loan to value)
- Correct interest rate
- Nonrecourse or recourse loan (Typically these terms are for commercial deals over two million dollars. Nonrecourse means that the borrower does not have any personal liability for the deal.)
- Correct balloon terms
- Correct lender fees, i.e., points, and what they are charging for appraisal or any other fees
- Maximum Debt Coverage Ratio (DCR)
- Prepayment terms
- Agreed estimated closing date

Your job is to make sure this deal gets to the closing table. Having a strong SEOTA package to deliver to the lender will help to make sure this happens.

Possible Lender Land Mines

Keep in mind that while you are going through the underwriting process, the clock is counting down on your purchase contract. At some point your money will go hard and become nonrefundable. Don't forget this, because your lender won't. I have dealt with some lenders who used this ticking clock to back my team into a corner by using some of the following lender land mines.

- Lenders have been known to drag things out. Be mindful of this, especially when you have deposit money that can go hard. Some lenders are unscrupulous and will know this date and then change the terms of the LOI they submitted after it passes and your money is nonrefundable. You can find yourself with a higher interest rate or larger down payment requirement if you're not careful!
- The lender may not have a strong grasp of the current rental market cycles that pertain to your investment. This is why submitting a well-executed SEOTA package to the lender is key.

- Lenders may not be as concerned about your deal's time line as you are. Be careful when dealing with a lender's secretary or assistant who is slow to get you important documents in the required time. Don't assume that the lender will do everything within the time frame that they agreed to. Make it your responsibility to follow up. After all, it's your money on the line.

- Your appraisal value may come in lower than expected due to quickly changing market conditions. This is why I like to provide the lender as well as the appraiser with my SEOTA package. The SEOTA helps the appraiser to see the value you see.

- The report of rent rolls should reflect the property's current rents, tenants' lease terms, as well as the amount of deposits each tenant has paid in. Before closing, request a current rent roll to see if anything has changed.

- Fraudulent documents may be provided by the seller. As you become a more experienced investor you learn to discount almost everything the seller provides you pertaining to the investment property. Items like current vacancy rate, rents, and deposit money can all be fudged. This is why you must check and recheck during the due diligence process. It was Ronald Reagan who said it best, "Trust but verify."

A CASE IN POINT

Recently a seller tried to pull the rent-roll trick on me. At the closing table, the seller signed what she said was the most recent rent roll, showing the current rents as well as the current vacancy rate on the property. The document showed five units vacant at closing. This was more than there had been when we did our due diligence on the property weeks prior. When we finally did set foot on the property, we realized there were five more vacant units than reported. Usually we like to walk the rental property prior to closing, but the seller refused. She told us that the tenants were getting upset about the sale of the property and she did not want them to react negatively to the selling. As you can imagine, these vacant units create a negative effect on the bottom line. Luckily, we were prepared for such tricks and in the contract we had a clause that said that the title company should hold in escrow one month's rents until the accuracy of the rent roll was verified. In hindsight this was a very smart move on our part.

MY FINAL THOUGHTS ON CREATING LEVERAGE

The main focus for me as an investor when procuring a loan is how that loan affects my cash flow. Can I borrow money and still produce a competitive cash return? I hope that the questions you've answered so far throughout this process will allow you to answer "yes" to that question. If not, it's probably best to keep looking.

Though it is crucial to know various types of loans out there, the key for me as an investor is to focus on five key steps. In keeping with the way I approach real estate—like a game of chess—I like to call these steps The Five Key Moves to Checkmate.

- First move: Understand my credit standing as an investor so I can determine my borrowing power. This borrowing power lets me use maximum leverage.
- Second move: Understand the current market conditions that affect supply and demand in my target area, as well as the entire economy.
- Third move: Understand the DNA of the property to help determine what the projected returns will be.
- Fourth move: Prepare myself for the lending process, i.e., the lender's evaluation of the property and myself. Then determine if the loan allows me to achieve the projected returns calculated in move three.
- Fifth and final move: Put my property under contract and close my deal! Checkmate. The Due Diligence Action List (page 79) will help you keep your details organized as you move forward.

Understanding the Responsibility of Leverage

It is important to note that there are some drawbacks to using leverage—the main one being that you are adding an additional investor to your team. Understand that this investor/partner may not have the same vision as you, and he likely has only one true goal: to recoup his investment. So you need to make sure that you know, without a doubt, who is responsible for paying off the loan if all fails and the property does not perform to expectations. Are you personally guaranteeing the loan? If so, that means the bank or lender will expect you to personally cover any balance owed.

When the market crashed in 2008, a lot of people were overleveraged on their properties, and they couldn't refinance, so they had major problems on their hands. Those "experts" I mentioned in the beginning of the book were preaching "zero-money-down" techniques, and that left a lot of people on the hook for their investments. The economy had softened, and without the rent money coming in as income—which many investors were using to make the mortgage payments on their properties—they couldn't make the payments. But had they put 30 percent or some other amount down, their mortgage would have been a little lower.

But that doesn't mean that leveraging is *always* wrong. If you have to learn anything from 2008, it should be this: Sometimes it's wise to use leverage, and sometimes it's wiser to put money down. It really depends on the financial circumstances of you and your family. You have to figure out what risks you're willing to take, and what risks you're not willing to take—but you need to remember that every successful business venture involves some form of risk. The people who got really hurt in the downturn were those who took no risk at all. They didn't get hurt because they were leveraged, they got hurt because they weren't leveraged *properly*.

The more time you spend in real estate, the more quickly you will realize that there are no sure things when it comes to owning rental property. *But*, you can safely hedge your bets if you pay careful attention to the information detailed in chapter 4. The type of rental property, as well as its demographics (which are typically determined by its location), will play a major role in the ability of the investor to stabilize the property and begin to turn a profit.

SINGLE-FAMILY PROPERTIES—TIPS TO LIVE BY

Single-family homes are "break-even ratios." This means they offer you only one major source of income to pay expenses. Make a wrong calculation when investing in a single-family home and it can prove devastating, because you won't have the benefit of multiple tenants to absorb extra expenses.

Do not make a purchase based on speculation. If you need convincing, just remember the overwhelming number of foreclosures that happened after the market crashed—and those that are still on the market. Many of these foreclosures are a direct result of investors speculating. Make sure you understand the rental market in your target area. Here are a couple of tips:

- Once a base rent has been established for the target area, look for undervalued deals through foreclosures, bank short sales, or owner-distressed properties.
- Only select a rental investment and loan that will allow you to cover the base rent in your target area. If at the current sales price and financing terms you find yourself with very slim margins or the inability for the property's income to cover all expenses, then renegotiate the asking price or simply walk away.

In this chapter we've learned the first basic aspects of real estate financing—including how to make yourself attractive to lenders and how to get financing at the most favorable terms possible. Real estate is such a powerful investment opportunity, in part due to your ability to leverage the money you invest. Your financing of a deal is the key to this powerful ability to leverage and grow wealth. Numbers and financing may not be your strong suit, but the first step to being successful in real estate is learning the principles of how these number games work. Then, if you are not a numbers person, the second step should be selecting a person to be on your "dream team" who is great at financing!

ARE FORECLOSURES TOO RISKY?

The Fundamentals of Foreclosures

After the housing market crashed, foreclosures dominated the real estate headlines in the United States. As a result of unscrupulous lenders and unwary buyers, foreclosures reached record numbers, and while it was a sad state of affairs for many people, it also created opportunities to acquire a foreclosure property. And that property can be an opportunity for all parties involved, not just the purchaser. The acquisition of such a property can free up a person who has gotten himself behind the eight ball with his home payments. It can also be an opportunity for the bank to get the debt off its books. And the good news is that these opportunities still exist, despite the improvements in the economy. I only need to look out my back window to know this is true. According to RealtyTrac.com, 449,900 homes were repossessed by lenders in 2015, with Florida, New Jersey, and Maryland leading all states. This number is 57 percent lower than the peak number of foreclosures in 2010 (a staggering 1.1 million), but it is a 38 percent increase over 2014 totals. To put it simply, there will always be opportunity to take advantage of foreclosed properties. But it is important to proceed with caution. This chapter will show you how to investigate whether a foreclosed property is right for you.

Basketball coach John Wooden used to say, "Be quick but don't hurry." I interpret this to mean: learn to make decisions, don't procrastinate, but don't be in such a hurry that you overlook the details. By now we all know where the devil hides: in the details. As you master the SEOTA process outlined in chapter 4, you will no doubt learn to make quicker decisions as your experience and confidence increase. The most important thing an investor needs to know about foreclosures is how a property will perform as a resale or as a rental.

WHAT TO LOOK FOR IN A FORECLOSURE PROPERTY

1. **Realistic sales comps.** Overly optimistic sales prices are what got a lot of people into foreclosure in the first place. Be realistic in your sales comparisons of similar properties in the same area.
2. **Favorable financing.** Do not inherit someone else's mistake by financing a property under terms that are not favorable and do not provide positive leverage.
3. **Accurate operating expenses.** Or, if your intent is to quickly resell, accurate holding costs.
4. **Accurate rental market surveys.**

Be prepared to be an "accidental landlord." Many "flippers" who cannot resell their property in the current market are now what I call "accidental landlords." Since most of these investors, or speculators, did not intend on being landlords, they did not do market rent surveys or inspect their expense load. Many are finding they cannot rent the property for enough to cover their mortgage payments and expenses. Remember, evaluating a rental property is all about cash flow. Be prepared that in a slow real estate market, you may have to rent out a property for a while before you can sell it.

WHAT CAN GO WRONG?

First, an investor must factor financing into a foreclosure deal. What I mean is this: As an investor, you must hope for the best plan but plan for the worst. As a backup, the financing you obtain must factor in either holding expenses and/or the current rental market, that is, going rents in the target area. Most investors will meet the same fate as the speculative investors who snapped up all the preconstruction homes and condos only to be left holding the bag when economic conditions changed. Instead of "house flippers" they became "accidental landlords." The problem for these speculative investors is that the mortgage payments on these homes are extremely high compared to what the rental market will bear for rent. This causes the property to bleed cash flow, and the investor has to put his or her own money into the property to stay afloat. Most of these investors will find themselves in the same position they found the original seller in—foreclosure.

If you are going to capitalize on the foreclosures in the market, you must understand what got the seller into foreclosure in the first place, and then don't repeat their mistake. I am turning down deals left and right in this market because a seller refuses to lower the asking price to one that will allow the property to produce positive cash flow. Sellers tell me if they lower it to what my DNA strand says is an appropriate price, they will either lose money or just break even and make no profit. My answer remains the same. I am not going to overpay for a property just because the seller overpaid. I don't care how great the area is or what renovations the seller made, if the going market rent in the area won't allow some cash flow at the asking price, I walk away. I won't inherit someone else's mistake.

FORECLOSURE BASICS

A foreclosure takes place when a homeowner or investor is unable to make her monthly mortgage payment and is forced by the lender to give up her property. You can find statistics on foreclosures by reviewing the report put out annually by the Mortgage Bankers Association of America.

- **Buying a foreclosure sale:** Foreclosure sales are acquired through a court auction process. The highest bidder will be awarded title of the property. The property is acquired "as is."
- **Buying a pre-foreclosure property:** The process happens after a homeowner or investor has defaulted on his mortgage but before the home or investment property has made it up the courthouse steps. You, as the buyer, will negotiate with the owner to take over the existing mortgage and any other debt that the property may have.
- **Purchasing from a lender after a foreclosure sale:** Here you are dealing directly with the lender. Keep in mind that lenders are in the business of lending money. They are not property managers. Lenders may be more willing to sell a property at a price more favorable to the investor because they do not have the staff or systems to manage a property.

By law, foreclosure auctions must publish a notice locally. In the past, going down to your local county clerk's office to find foreclosures was the norm. Now with the use of the Internet, foreclosure listing companies are a dime a dozen. As an investor, you should work with a company that provides not only up-to-date listings but also provides a high level of education about the process. For recommended companies, visit **landlordacademy.com**.

PULLING THE TRIGGER

Auction Sale

If you are going to pull the trigger with a foreclosure auction sale, then make absolutely sure you have a title company perform a title search on the property. This will help you determine the true market value. From there you will be able to plug in your operating expenses and acquisition costs to determine the property's true value. You want to see if the property will be a cash-flowing asset or a money pit liability.

Pre-Foreclosure

With a pre-foreclosure, you will want first to make contact with the owner. Most investors start by mailing a letter to the homeowner letting him know that they are willing to purchase the home, thereby freeing the homeowner from his financial problem. Usually the letter will highlight how this process is designed to help the homeowner by providing a way out.

Usually, telling an owner that they can avoid having the foreclosure appear on their credit report by allowing you to purchase it is an important inducement. You will want to set up a meeting with the homeowner, so your letter should end by suggesting that one be scheduled. As you can see, there are a lot of steps to buying a foreclosure. Thankfully there are kits you can buy that lay out this process for you. They even provide you with the proven techniques and letters you will need to ensure a smooth transaction. For a complete list, visit **landlordacademy.com**.

PART III

LANDLORDING ESSENTIALS

So far you've learned about a systematic approach to targeting potential rental areas, evaluating properties, and then negotiating and executing a contract. Now the investor becomes a landlord. This process can be the difference between winning or losing, failing or succeeding. It's that simple. Your success as a landlord will largely depend on your ability to follow the systems provided for you in the following chapters. Remember, these systems will run your rental business and you will maintain the systems. This will create a formula for overall success!

Let's get started.

There are scores of books on buying an investment property, but most of these books don't tell you what to do with it once you buy it. The foundation of any wealth-building real estate strategy is the day-to-day management of the property. This is where income is collected and expenses are controlled. The biggest mistake I see most investors make is failing to approach the management of their property as a business. They treat it as an afterthought. But rental management *is* a business, and you are in charge of running it. You need systems and training to run it correctly. Property management is where most real estate deals fall apart.

We talked a bit in the beginning of this book about how franchises are run on operations systems. Imagine that you bought a fast-food franchise and when you opened the doors for business, you had no systems and no training. You just fired up the grill and started taking orders. You had no instructions—you were just winging it. Do you think you would make a profit? Do you think your customers would be happy and come again? Do you think your life would be organized and stress-free? Of course not. So why would anyone approach managing a rental property worth thousands or even hundreds of thousands of dollars with any less business sense? Now, since you are reading this book, I know you are wiser than most. I know you have already realized that you have to treat your investment property like the business it is.

In the chapters that follow, I will provide you with the training and systems to help you manage your property profitably. In property management, the key is always to maximize your income and minimize your expenses.

There are no victories at bargain basement prices.
—Dwight D. Eisenhower

WHO WILL LIVE THERE?

Attracting the Right Tenants

Remember we said earlier that bricks and mortar don't pay rent, people do. Your tenants do. Since rent is your key source of income, choosing the right tenant to pay the rent is a key element in profitable management. One of the most expensive and unexpected costs you can have as a rental property manager is high tenant turnover. Not only do you lose money while the unit is vacant, but you have to constantly ready the unit between tenants by painting, cleaning carpets, and changing locks. You have advertising costs, and if you have a lot of turnover you will inevitably be evicting some tenants, so you have eviction costs. Therefore, picking the right tenants and managing them well while they're in your building are key skills you need to develop as a landlord.

I am constantly asked by landlords how to reduce evictions, how to get tenants to pay on time, and how to get tenants to follow the rules. I've heard some pretty creative strategies on getting tenants to pay rent from so-called "experts" on landlording. I've heard about offering your tenants a ceiling fan if they pay on time, giving them a discount in rent for paying on time, and other dubious schemes. These strategies may work, they may not—but personally I am an advocate of steering clear of tricks and gimmicks to get a tenant to pay rent on time. Instead, I focus more on getting the right tenant in the first place. A person who you don't *have* to trick into doing what she is supposed to do—pay her rent on time. The number one way to reduce evictions and get paid your rent on time is to get the right tenant to begin with.

READYING YOURSELF TO RENT

Along with readying your unit to be rented, you will need to ready yourself as well. There are a few key decisions to make before you are ready to start talking to prospective tenants:

- What will you charge for rent?
- What is your application fee?
- What is your security deposit?
- Are you requiring first and last month's rent?
- What credit score are you requiring?
- What type of criminal records will you accept, if any?
- Are you allowing pets? If so, what kind, and will you charge a pet fee?
- Are you paying utilities or is the tenant?

In the market surveys you conducted during your SEOTA and due diligence process, you have already determined what the average market rents are. You learned what the typical security deposit amounts and application fees in your target area are. You also have an accurate, complete list of your expenses so you can make sure that minimally your rental amount will cover these expenses. Use this information to determine what you can command in rent in your target area and what you can ask for regarding security deposits and fees.

Another decision you will have is how you will equip your rental unit. What type of floor, bathroom and kitchen faucets, sinks, and so on will you provide? To decide this, you have to remind yourself to keep your prospective tenant in mind. It's easy to select things *you* like and think are useful. However, you have to consider the demographic and psychographics of your prospect. What does he like? What does he need?

Imagine that you and I both own duplexes next door to each other in a part of town where demographics show that most residents are young to middle age with an average of two or three children. Our duplexes have identical floor plans and are in identical condition. We are charging the same in rent. The only difference in our properties is that I have tile floors and you upgraded to high-quality Berber carpet. Who will most likely rent our unit first? Well, psychographics tell us that statistically the larger family demographics prefer tile to carpet. So chances are I will rent mine first.

Understanding psychographics helps you know what will induce a tenant to rent from you. I learned this firsthand on a project several years ago in which we were completely renovating all the units. Since we were replacing everything, we were allowing tenants to choose if they wanted carpet or tile. After the third time we ran out of tile, I decided to check into the matter. I was suspicious . . . was someone stealing supplies? After I checked all the records, though, I realized what was happening. Our tenants, most of whom had larger families, were choosing tile five to one over carpet. Anticipating your prospect's needs and wants, likes and dislikes in advance will allow you to be in touch with your prospective tenant. This will dramatically reduce any vacancies and help increase lease renewals. Remember our Wal-Mart discussion? It's just like choosing plastic pools or lawn furniture. Know your target tenant.

You want to decide these things in advance so that when you begin taking inquiries about the rental you have answers, and consistent ones. We'll talk more about Fair Housing in a moment and the importance of consistent answers.

RENTING SINGLE-FAMILY HOMES

I recommend that landlords renting out single-family homes ask for a security deposit equal to at least one month's rent. Single family means just that, one household. You have more risk because you can rent to only one tenant at a time, and little mistakes can be more costly. If your unit is not rentable while you are repairing things, you don't have any other units bringing in income to help pay expenses.

Next, we want to make sure that you are ready for contact. I am going to remind you again and again about the importance of professionalism. Your first chance to show your professionalism is in how you handle incoming phone calls about your property.

Always have your property's information readily available so you are never caught off guard when a prospect calls. Information you will need handy includes:

- Address of property
- General area of town the property is located in and nearby attractions
- Type of dwelling (single family, duplex, multiunit)
- Square footage
- Number of bedrooms and bathrooms
- Amenities (washer/dryer, pool, garage, etc.)
- Pets allowed? If so, what kind and what is the pet fee?
- Rental rate
- Security deposit required
- Application fee

Create a Phone Card so that when you receive phone calls about your rental property, you can put all the relevant information about the prospective tenant onto a standardized form. Essentially, a Phone Card is just an organized list of all the information you need to gather from prospective tenants. And it can be as low- or high-tech as you want. When *Buy It, Rent It, Profit!* was published in 2009, I had physical cards printed with a line for every piece of data I needed to collect. That approach certainly still works, or you can create a virtual card in an Excel spreadsheet on your computer, or in an app on your phone. Whatever works. Your goal will be to get as much information about the prospect as possible from that first phone call. You can use this information to help prequalify them by explaining the rental rate, application fees, and security deposits. Phone Cards not only allow you to be organized, but they also give you contact information so you can follow up with prospects who called you to encourage them to come view the property.

A sample blank Phone Card is included in the Appendix.

PHONE CARD (FORM 11)

Date: _____ 4/1/09

Name: _____ Joseph Conroy

Address: _____ 129 W. Clearview Ave., Columbus OH 43907

Telephone: (H) (614) 555-1212 _____ (W) (614) 555-3541 _____ (C) (614) 555-0746

Type of rental home desired: _____ 2 BR

How many will live in home: _____ 1 person

Price range: _____ $500-650

Date needed: _____ 5/1/09

Pets: _____ 1 cat

Why moving: _____ Wants more space

Comments: _____

How did you hear about us?

❏ Referral

❏ Newspaper   ❏ Flyer/brochure

❏ For Rent sign   ❏ Locator service

☒ Yellow pages

Other: _____

Appointment scheduled: _4/5/09 at 11am_

7 KEYS FOR SUCCESSFUL PHONE SKILLS

1. **The most important key: Get the caller's name!** The more personal you are, the better the chance to close the deal with your prospect. You can't get personal if you don't know someone's name! One study showed that 34 percent of callers did not hear their name during the conversation. Establish rapport. The first step in doing this is to get the caller's name and use it.

2. **Be present to the conversation.** Stop what you are doing and pay attention!

3. **Slow down!** Ask the caller why they are moving.

4. **Ask the prospect what their needs are.** Forty percent of callers' needs are unknown.

5. **Determine two or three preferences of your caller.** Don't overwhelm them. Save some for later.

6. **Talk about benefits, not features.** A feature is an item—an alarm system, for example. Talk about how they will benefit from this feature. For example, their family will be safer.

7. **Tell them what is in it for them to make an appointment**—they won't have to wait to see you, they won't be interrupted by other viewers, etc.

If your caller is interested after you give the rental details, the next step is to prequalify your prospective tenant. Remember, waste of time is your most costly expense. And if wasted time is your most costly expense, then gas is probably your second highest cost! You don't want to waste your time or your gas going to show prospects your rental if they don't qualify.

To prequalify your prospect, prepare a statement of qualifying criteria (see Form 13 on page 238 of the Appendix). This is your list of minimum standards. Common criteria include the minimum credit score you will accept, minimum monthly income, if you will accept criminal records, if you require any rental history, and so on. You will need to adjust your criteria from target area to target area. You may need to lower your minimum credit score or income in certain demographic areas or you will not find any renters that meet your criteria. But the sample will serve as a guide for you.

When you prequalify your prospective tenant over the phone, be polite about it. Don't interrogate them. I like to start by explaining, "I know your time is important to you. Before you take time to come out to view the property, let me share with you our qualifying criteria to make sure you are comfortable with them. We require . . ." Most people will not waste their time or their money on an application fee if they know they won't pass your standards.

Here are some great prequalifying questions to use with your caller:

"Great, how did you hear about us?" (This helps you find out which of your marketing sources are working.)

"When are you looking to move in?" (This helps determine the urgency and availability of your rental units.)

"We have a great corporate discount package, may I ask where you are employed?" (This helps determine income qualification.)

"Great, may I ask how long you have been working for the company and what is your position?" (This helps determine income qualification and the stability of the prospective tenant.)

If you have a model unit or are on-site, use a Guest Card, similar in form to your Phone Card, for face-to-face meetings.

If a prospect does not schedule a meeting or return your call, use the information you collected on the Phone Card or Guest Card to call them. Some people may be on the fence about renting your unit. Your call may be enough of a demonstration of interest to them that they decide to make a decision and rent from you.

GUEST CARD (FORM 12)

Date: _____ 6/1/09

Name: _____ Madolin Burns

Address: _____ 5529 Edgewater Dr., Denver, CO

Telephone: (H) __(303) 555-1212__   (W) __(303) 555-1111__   (C) __(303) 555-2222__

Type of rental home desired: _____ Studio

How many will live in home: _____ 1 person

Price range: _____ $800-850

Date needed: _____ 7/20/09

Pets: _____ None

Why moving: _____ new to area

Comments: _____

How did you hear about us?

❏ Referral

❏ Newspaper   ❏ Flyer/brochure

❏ For Rent sign   ❏ Locator service

☒ Yellow pages

Other: _____

Appointment scheduled: _____

SHOWING YOUR UNIT AND CLOSING THE DEAL

In addition to readying yourself, you need to ready your unit for show. Studies indicate that most people make up their mind about renting somewhere within the first few moments of seeing a property. If this is the case, then you can see how important your prospective tenant's first impression is.

To make a good first impression, you should pay close attention to your curb appeal. This is how your property looks from the street; it's what prospective tenants see when they first arrive. To have good curb appeal:

- Clear away any trash from your yard or curb
- Make sure the grass is cut
- Make sure there is no junk or old items visible in the yard
- Have a good paint job
- Make sure the window dressings (curtains, drapes, blinds) look nice and consistent from the outside view
- Keep any landscaping trimmed and in good condition

It's a good idea to arrive a little early. One time I pulled up at the same time my prospect did only to find that a dog had gotten into someone's trash can and the contents were strewn across my front yard. Not a great first impression.

Appeal to the Senses

The interior of the property should appeal to your prospect's senses. Studies show that impressions are triggered by not just visual, but other sensory responses.

  · Light candles or have a pleasant air freshener
  · Vacuum away any footsteps so nice, clean vacuum lines show in the carpet
  · Have light refreshments, bottled water, cookies, etc.
  · Play soothing music like jazz, classical, or nature sounds
  · Have lighting bright enough so the prospective tenant can see in all rooms

If you are thinking to yourself that this is common sense, go view a few rental units. You will see that many landlords do not even have electricity turned on in their units! You can barely see the walls, much less notice if there were any pleasant smells or music.

A Tip for Staging Your Rental Unit

Take a day and visit luxury apartment communities in your area. Act like you are looking to lease and let them take you through the whole experience. Pay attention to how their units are decorated. The multifamily industry spends a lot of money to stay up to date on the demographics in their area and what they like. You may not be able to afford, nor can your tenants afford, some of the items they display, but you can get a general idea of the "look" of the place and emulate it more cost effectively. Also pay close attention to how the management company shows the unit. In the industry we call this "shopping your competition." Most luxury leasing agents are well trained in showing units and closing a deal.

LEASING TOOL KIT

If you will be traveling to and from your property and don't have a model set up, pack a leasing tool kit to keep in your car so you are always ready to show your property.

Leasing Tool Kit Checklist
  · Silk plants
  · iPod or other portable music player with external speakers
  · Air freshener or candle and lighter
  · Shower curtain
  · Vacuum
  · Fair Housing poster

- Yarn
- Cardboard cutouts
- Cookies, muffins, or other individually portioned baked goods
- Coffeemaker and supplies or bottled water

Now, some of these items might sound a bit odd. Let me explain. Things like silk plants or a shower curtain are good "fillers" that help make a place seem homier. You want to help your prospective tenants envision your unit as their home. These things also can help disguise some of your unit's features that may not be the most attractive or that you haven't had a chance to repair yet, like recaulking a bathtub or covering a carpet stain. Of course you will need to repair these things before the tenant moves in, but since we are dealing with first impressions here, fillers can be a good tool.

Yarn and cardboard cutouts also help you overcome a very common hesitation prospective tenants have. Many times, prospects hesitate because they are not "sure if their furniture will fit." Yarn can be used to measure and lay out furniture, and cardboard can be cut out in the shape and size of typical furniture like sofas and beds.

LEASING NOTEBOOK

I also recommend that you have with you all the items you need to lease your unit if the prospect is ready to close the deal. You never want to have to get back to someone and risk losing the deal. Be able to close on the spot. Your notebook should include:

- Floor plans of your unit(s)
- Community information
- Photographs
- Maps of city for tenants new to the area
- Applications
- Guest cards
- Qualifying criteria forms
- Move-in cost sheet
- Lease forms
- Pen and paper

You may not be familiar with some of these tools yet, but we will cover them later in this chapter.

SHOWING YOUR UNIT

The most powerful thing you can do to lease your property is to realize that your rental unit is not the product. The experience your prospect has with you is your "product." Anyone can provide a rental unit. You can't control the other rental properties in your area. What you can control is the experience your prospect has with you.

Keys to a Great Open House Experience

- **Luxury Service.** People of all income levels like luxury service. It makes them feel appreciated. I like to offer my prospective tenants beverages and snacks. Aside from making them feel respected and appreciated, it also helps make sure that they aren't distracted by being thirsty or hungry. I know my demographic works, sometimes at physically demanding jobs. If they rush from work to view my rental unit, I don't want the visit cut short or them to be distracted because they are thirsty or hungry.
- **A "Tour" of the Model Unit.** Anyone can "show" a unit. Instead give a "tour." And call it that, a tour. Tour the area, the outside and the inside. Even if you don't have a model unit, use your leasing tool kit to set up your vacant unit like a model.
- **Professional Management.** All tenants want to be treated with respect. If you seem unorganized and unprofessional in the beginning, the type of tenants you truly want renting your unit will be turned off by your lack of professionalism. They want to rent from someone they can trust to be responsible, who will provide a quality place to live and respond quickly to their needs.

A great example of this is on an apartment complex I own called The Palms Apartments. It's a midsize complex with thirty-two units. There is a similar complex across the street. Recently a young couple came to view our apartments. We greeted them and offered them a tour of the property. They told me that they had just left the complex across the street. They went there first because it looked a little nicer from the outside. (It had nicer landscaping than we had at the time.) The landlord took them to an empty unit, unlocked the door, told them to have a look around, and come get her when they were done. They said we were much more professional, that they felt more appreciated and respected. They chose to rent from us.

BE A LEASING MEGASTAR

Pay attention to your personal appearance. Be neatly dressed, well groomed, and aware of your personal hygiene. Have a good attitude. Don't let having a bad day come across in your demeanor and cost you a deal. Have good listening skills. The questions your prospective tenant will ask will clue you in to their needs. Develop closing skills. Ask for the lease, close the deal. And follow up. You work hard to generate leads. Work hard on following up and closing them.

As Dale Carnegie said, "You can make more friends in two months by becoming interested in other people than you can in two years of trying to get other people interested in you." The same applies for leasing. You can lease more rentals by becoming interested in your prospect's needs than you ever can by trying to get the prospective tenant interested in your rental.

The most important key to closing the deal is to be proactive. When you are done showing the unit, ask them if they would like to rent the unit. If they say yes, the next step is to process their application and screen them.

SAFETY IN SHOWING

1. **Make a copy of photo ID.** You can ask prospective tenants to bring copies of their photo IDs with them, for safety purposes, or you can simply use your smartphone to take a photo and store it with others in an app like Box, which gives you access to all of your files from any device. (More on how Box and other technology can transform the way you do business later.)
2. **Always let the prospects enter the unit in front of you.** If you go in first, they can push you inside and slam the door, trapping you.
3. **Do not close the door.** Leave it open.
4. **Turn the dead bolt.** When you flip the dead bolt, if the prospect tries to slam the door and trap you inside, it will not catch and will bounce open, giving you the few seconds you might need to escape.
5. **Always keep a clear line to the door.** Don't let a prospect box you in a closet or behind a wall.
6. **Let someone know where you are.** In fact, make a phone call to someone or call out to a neighbor so your prospect can hear you. This lets them know someone is aware of your whereabouts and will miss you if you are gone for long. This may deter someone who was considering attacking you.

THE APPLICATION APPROVAL PROCESS

The first tool you will use is your Statement of Qualifying Criteria, which we discussed earlier. Even if you went over this information on the telephone with your prospect before the meeting, you should now officially provide a written copy. Let them review it, then sign it, and return it to you. Many people will stop here, before wasting their application fee, if they know they will not qualify. This is good; you don't want to waste your time either. This checklist also serves you well to comply with Fair Housing, which we will discuss in depth at the end of this chapter. It shows you apply the same criteria and standards to everyone.

After the Statement of Qualifying Criteria (see Form 13 on page 238 of the Appendix) is signed, have your prospect complete an application (see Form 14 on page 240). This form is a must and cannot be overlooked. Information shouldn't be taken down casually or in any other format. Why is this so important? The application is the cornerstone of your tenant's file. It authorizes you to run their credit and perform a background check, and it gives you all their contact information. Down the road, if you have to evict or report money owed to a collection agency, you will need the information on the application. So make sure it's complete and legible.

Next, make sure you collect your application fee. This amount should minimally be enough to cover what it costs you to process the application. You can charge more than that, as long as it's a competitive rate in your area. I see a lot of people get overly greedy with their application fees. Don't price it so high it deters people from applying. After all, the point is to rent the unit and collect rent, not an application fee.

A technique for closing the deal is to go ahead and collect a security deposit or have your prospect sign a lease or both, if you can. You want the prospect to mentally decide they want to rent from you. Most people do not like to be in transition. They want to know where they are moving so they can get utilities transferred, plan the move, register their kids for school, and so on. Though their lease is dependent on their application coming back approved, you want to go ahead and close the deal by collecting their security deposit and having them sign a lease, if you can.

TENANT SCREENING

Why is this *so* important? Tenant screening is critical to reduce the number of problem tenants and the cost of high turnover. Key things you will review in the screening process are:

- Credit score
- Eviction check
- Criminal background check
- Rental collection search, which shows if they owe any other landlord money
- Employment verification

Again, you should already have established the minimum standards you will accept and what you will deny when you created your qualifying criteria. Now you are just gathering the information to see if your prospect meets those standards.

MOBILE TENANT SCREENING

In today's world of technology, you are able to screen tenants from anywhere, at any time, and get an almost instant response. You can go to **landlordacademy.com** and process an application from anywhere via the Internet. You can also fax in applications. This makes it much easier to approve a prospect quickly. When I first started in the business, it took about three days to get an approval, and in the meantime I would lose some prospects when they found something cheaper or closer to their work. Today, technology makes tenant screening accessible from anywhere.

TIP: TENANT SCREENING IN TOUGH TIMES

In the affordable housing market where you are renting to low- or middle-income tenants, you can be hit hard by slow economic times. You may find it hard to find a tenant who will meet your qualifying criteria, particularly one who meets your credit score requirement. You may, during tough rental times, need to take a more detailed look at your prospective tenant's credit report than just looking at the overall score. In tough times, I may overlook student loans and hospital bills. I pay more attention to former evictions, monies owed previous landlords, and late payments made on utility bills. If a tenant can't make electric or phone payments on time or owes a previous landlord money, I am more apt not to approve them than if they have some hospital bills they can't afford to pay.

If your prospect's application comes back meeting all your criteria except for the credit score, you can still approve them if you want to. My suggestion is to require them to prepay the last month's rent. Be sure to have them sign something indicating why they had to prepay last month's rent. Remember, you always want to consistently document every transaction.

If you don't approve the application, you are required by the Fair Credit Reporting Act, which is a national regulation, to provide the prospect with a letter informing them they were not approved and telling them what agency you used to process their credit, and providing contact information so they can obtain a copy of their credit report. This is the law. Here is a sample letter:

TENANT REJECTION LETTER (FORM 17)

To: _Joseph Conroy_   Date: _4-10-09_

Address: _129 W. Clearview Ave., Columbus, OH 43907_

We regret to inform you that your application for residency has the following adverse action:

_X_ Your application for rental has been declined.

___ We are requesting a larger security deposit for approval.

     Total deposit required $_____

___ You must provide us qualified lease guarantor for approval.

The reason for this is based on one or more of the following reasons:

___ Residence History	_X_ Credit History
___ Employment Information	___ Public Criminal Records
_X_ Insufficient Income	___ Public Eviction Records
___ Other _____	

___ Information that resulted in adverse action was received from a person or company other than a consumer reporting agency. You have the right to make a written request to us within 60 days for a disclosure of the nature of this information.

_X_ Information that resulted in adverse action was obtained from the following consumer reporting agency: _XYZ Consumer Credit_

The consumer reporting agency did not make the decision and is not able to explain why it was made. According to the Fair Credit Reporting Act, Public Law 91-508, you have the right to review all consumer reporting information used in the evaluation of your application, and you also have the right to dispute any information on file. If you would like to receive a free copy of the information used in the decision, contact the agency within 60 days. Include your full name, date of birth, Social Security number, current and former address, daytime and evening phone numbers. You have the right to dispute directly with the consumer reporting agency the accuracy or completeness of the information in your file. The agency must then, within a reasonable period of time, reinvestigate and modify or remove any inaccurate information. There is no charge for this service. If reinvestigation does not resolve the dispute to your satisfaction, you have the right to prepare a consumer statement of up to 100 words explaining your position, which will be kept in your credit file.

Sincerely yours,

Patricia Allen

Printed Name of Owner/Agent

Hand delivered on date: _____ by (name): _____

or

Mailed on date: _4-10-09 by Patricia Allen_ by (name): _____

WHY NOT TO SKIP TENANT SCREENING

Skipping the tenant screening process can be one of the biggest mistakes you can make. And I never understand why some landlords skip it. After all, you collect an application fee from your prospective tenant. This will cover what you are charged for the screening process, so why would you skip something that not only protects you but doesn't cost you anything?

DON'T JUDGE A BOOK BY ITS COVER

Some of the worst mistakes I've made in tenant selection were made when I first started out. I would judge people based on how they looked. One time I watched two young guys arrive at a rental. They pulled up in an older, rusty car that had shiny rims on it. When they got out I saw they were in their early twenties. They wore their baggy jeans hanging down low, and white tank tops, showing lots of tattoos up and down their arms. "Oh, Lord," I said, "these are horrible prospects, what a waste of my time." Not knowing how to decline without being out-and-out rude, I showed them the unit. They liked it and filled out an application. As I processed their application, they passed all the criteria and were approved. So I moved them in, with many reservations.

Later I learned that if I had declined to show them the unit based on their looks, I could have also left myself open to a Fair Housing complaint. But it turns out that I also would have missed moving in two of the most dependable, respectful tenants I've ever had. They worked minimum-wage jobs at Home Depot, and they liked to wear their pants baggy and show their tattoos. But they paid rent, on time, every month. They never caused a disturbance. They didn't have a lot of furniture, but they kept their unit clean. One day I pulled up and even saw them helping an elderly neighbor carry groceries into her home.

Contrast that with a luxury property I once worked on. When I took that job, I thought, "I'm going to have it made. I'll be renting to rich people. This will be a piece of cake." Boy, was I mistaken. Some of the clean-cut men in fancy suits driving BMWs were among the worst tenants I've had. They had good-paying jobs, but they paid their rent consistently late. And they had loud parties, left trash in all the common areas, and did more damage to their units than their security deposits would cover. So don't judge a book by its cover. In fact, don't judge your prospects at all. Just follow your approval process and let it do its job. It will weed out the undesirable tenants far better than you can with your uninformed judgment.

FOLLOW YOUR SYSTEMS

I'm often asked how to handle the following situation. Say you receive an application from someone who looks like a marginal approval. She has an okay job, and some rental history. Then you receive a second prospective tenant who looks far better. What can you do?

It's simple: You process the application that was turned in first with an application fee. You can't pick and choose who you think looks better to process first. And again, don't assume that someone who looks more qualified will turn out to be. Always follow your systems, they will always work better than your opinions will.

FAIR HOUSING

I want to stop for a moment and discuss the Fair Housing laws. This is something that landlords often pay little attention to. They tell me that they know they can't discriminate so they just use their common sense. Many go on to say, "I've been a landlord for thirty years and I haven't gotten in trouble yet." Well, common sense doesn't get you very far with Fair Housing. There are some quirks in this law that don't seem to make sense, and your common sense and trying to be helpful can get you sued. Today, technology is having a huge impact on Fair Housing claims. Before, to file a claim a tenant would have to take off work, find the government office that handled Fair Housing claims, go down there, find parking, file the claim, and later take more time off work to attend depositions, and so on. This is assuming they even knew what their rights were. Nowadays, I see advertisements informing people of their Fair Housing rights on TV and in prime time. There are billboards all over town, in English and Spanish, telling you who to call if you have been discriminated against. And you can file a claim, online, from anywhere, twenty-four hours a day, seven days a week. Things are changing, and people who slipped through the cracks before will get caught.

You must follow Fair Housing guidelines in *every* phase of the landlording process. That means from showing and leasing your property to prospective tenants and throughout your entire relationship with the ones you lease to, and ones you turn down. Violations can bring fines in the tens of thousands of dollars. I don't want you to be afraid of Fair Housing, but respect it. If you establish a consistent system that follows the law, you can avoid having a legal judgment against you that could lead to financial disaster.

Here are the basics of the Fair Housing laws. This information should not replace you consulting with an attorney or officials at the department of Housing and Urban Development.

The Fair Housing Act prohibits discrimination in the sale or rental of housing on the basis of:

- Race—treating someone differently due to their origin, characteristics, physical traits, or appearances
- Color—treating someone differently due to their skin pigmentation being lighter or darker than yours
- Religion—treating someone differently due to their belief, observance, devotion, or practice of a religious faith. This protected class includes the lack of a religious belief.
- National origin—treating someone differently due to their place of birth or their ancestors' place of birth
- Sex—treating someone differently because they are a man or a woman
- Familial status—treating someone differently due to the presence or expected presence of children under eighteen, pregnant women, or individuals securing the custody of children under eighteen
- Disability—treating someone differently due to a mental, physical, or sensory disability, AIDS/HIV, or persons recovering from addiction

Here are some examples of Fair Housing violations:

- Refusing to rent housing based on any of the above
- Falsely denying that a property is available for inspection or rental
- Making housing unavailable
- Refusing to allow a disabled resident to make a reasonable modification

DISABILITY AND FAIR HOUSING GUIDELINES

Disability compliance is an area of Fair Housing where mistakes are common. The law says you have to allow a disabled person to modify the rental dwelling. However, the cost of the modification is the tenant's responsibility, not yours. Tenants are also responsible for applying and paying for any permits and are responsible for the cost of returning the unit to its original condition when they move out.

This last condition is sometimes a gray issue, though. If the change won't impair your ability to re-lease the unit or impair the new tenant's living condition, it doesn't have to be changed back. So for example, if a doorway is widened an inch to allow wheelchair access, it will not have to be changed back. The new tenant may not even notice it was done. However, if the kitchen cabinets are lowered so they are wheelchair accessible, you can require that they be put back in their original condition, as they may make it hard to re-lease the unit.

- Asking questions during the application process about an applicant's disabilities that were not necessary or appropriate
- Setting different terms, conditions, or privileges for the rental of a dwelling
- Directing a renter to a specific neighborhood, area, or community based on one of the protected classes
- Advertising or making a statement that indicates a discriminatory presence
- Refusing to allow a therapy animal, most commonly a Seeing Eye dog

THERAPY ANIMALS AND FAIR HOUSING GUIDELINES

Legally you cannot deny a disabled person a therapy animal, even if you have a no pet policy. A therapy animal is most commonly a Seeing Eye dog, but I've seen some other unusual therapy animals in my day. You cannot charge a pet fee for a therapy animal.

Everyone must adhere to the seven protected classes. Individual counties and cities often have additional protected classes. Common ones may be age and sexual preference. Check your local statutes for any additional protected classes you need to be aware of.

The only reasons you should be rejecting a potential tenant are the reasons on your qualifying criteria, which are not based on any of these protected classes. They are based on credit, income, criminal background, and so on. This is why following your approval process is so important. You want to have clearly defined reasons to deny someone, not just your "intuition." You don't want to leave the door open for someone to say you denied them because of their race, color, or another protected class. Again, let your qualifying criteria do its work.

OCCUPANCY STANDARDS

Can you turn away prospective tenants if there are too many people to reasonably live in the unit? This makes landlords nervous, because they don't want to be held responsible for familial status discrimination by turning away a prospective tenant who has children.

However, you are allowed by law to follow occupancy standards for your unit. There is no specific law outlining occupancy standards. The closest thing we have is a national guideline called the Keating Memorandum. This allows two heartbeats per bedroom. A baby isn't counted until he or she is one year of age. So if a family with six people wants to rent your two bedroom they can be denied, not because they have children, but because they exceed your occupancy standards. Always check your local law to see if there are different occupancy standards in place.

PREPARING FOR MOVE IN

If the applicant is approved, do the following:

First, complete a Move-In Cost Sheet (see Form 15 on page 243 of the Appendix) to explain all of the up-front costs of moving in. This form is essential to avoid any confusion on move-in day about any monies due. Never allow a tenant to move in without collecting all the money due to you. I don't care what kind of sob story they have, do not let a tenant move in owing you any money. This may sound harsh, but I have learned the hard way that you don't want to move a tenant in, only to have to evict them because they never bring you that first month's rent they promised.

The Move-In Cost Sheet helps you outline exactly what monies are due. The form should indicate what fees you have already collected and which are still due. This also ensures there is nothing missed if another team member handles the move in for you.

DO NOT ACCEPT CHECKS FOR FIRST MONTH'S RENT

Do not accept a personal check for first month's rent. You want to have a cashier's check or money order so you know the funds are available. Again, you don't want to have to evict a tenant whose first-month rent check bounced.

Next, schedule a move-in meeting. One of the most important parts of move in, other than collecting monies due, is to conduct a Move-In Inspection. We'll talk more about this in the next chapter.

In this chapter we learned about preparing both your unit and yourself for showing. We learned keys to staging a unit and keys to being a leasing megastar. We discussed the importance of treating your tenant, no matter what the demographic or income level, with respect and appreciation. We learned how to close a leasing deal and process an application for approval. We discussed the importance of your qualifying criteria and why you should never skip the tenant screening process. We have learned what the seven protected Fair Housing classes are and how to avoid violating them. And we have a tool to outline what monies our tenant needs to bring to our move-in meeting. In the next chapter, we will learn how to conduct a professional move-in meeting that also protects us from many costly mistakes down the line.

> Unless a man undertakes more than he can possibly do,
> he will never do all he can.
> —Henry Drummond

NINE

WHEN CAN THEY MOVE IN?

Understanding the Basic Components of a Lease

In this chapter we will cover the best way to move a tenant in to set the groundwork for a good, long-term relationship—and to protect yourself in case it doesn't turn out so well. I always follow the saying, "Hope for the best, but prepare for the worst." Three key tools for both a good tenant relationship and for protection are the Move-In/Move-Out Inspection Report, the lease, and the application (the latter was discussed in the last chapter).

TENANT RELATIONSHIP

Let's talk for a moment about your relationship with your tenants. Ideally you want it to be a friendly one—but be very clear, it's not appropriate for a tenant to be your friend. What do I mean by that? You should absolutely, always treat your tenants with respect and professionalism. You should interact with them, get to know them. Ask how they are, how their family is, and always be polite and professional. But do not cross the line into being overly familiar. Be cautious about inviting tenants into your home or babysitting their children, and never, ever lend them money.

Now with that said, your tenants are people. If you don't like people, landlording might not be the best business for you. I hear so many investors say, "I like owning rental property, I just can't stand the tenants." I understand this relationship can be a frustrating one at times. You will get taken advantage of and probably lied to. Even with the best of preparations, you may get burned occasionally. But again, bricks and mortar don't pay the rent, people do. So if you aren't good interacting with people, you might want to try some other type of investment! As the professional in this relationship, you are the one that will need to be respectful, but firm in your implementation of your rules.

THE MOVE-IN MEETING

I always recommend that you schedule a move-in meeting. Aside from being the appropriate time to sign all documents and collect any remaining monies, this is another way you can give a new tenant a quality experience—and it doesn't cost you a thing. This is something you can provide that other landlords won't, and that will differentiate you from the rest. Remember, you don't just want to sign tenants; you also want to keep the good ones happy.

Don't just hand over the keys and call it a day. Walk your tenant through all the amenities you have on the property. Show her the laundry room, point out where the Dumpster is located, and show her her mailbox. In a single-family home, give them a lesson on the alarm system, or how the pool equipment functions. Make them feel appreciated, and smooth their transition to their new home.

It's always a good idea to prepare your paperwork in advance for a move-in meeting. Fill in blanks and dates on any document that will be signed. Review your copy of the Move-In Cost Sheet so you know what monies are still due. And please, check the key to make sure it works! Once I had a new tenant who worked long hours and had to move in in the evening after work. When he finally got his U-Haul packed up and drove to the unit to unload it, he found out that the keys didn't work. He was stuck, locked out, at midnight with a U-Haul full of furniture. This was *not* a good start to our relationship.

Here is a checklist of everything you should complete at the move-in meeting to ensure a smooth, successful move in of your new tenant.

MOVE-IN MEETING CHECKLIST (FORM 19)

Use the checklist below to complete all the actions necessary to ensure a smooth, successful move in of your new tenant!

Prior to your move-in meeting:
_____ Complete Lease filling in all blanks (Form 20 or 21)
_____ Complete any Addendums filling in all blanks (*example: Lease Addendum—Pet*, Form 18)

At move-in meeting:
_____ Review Lease and have tenant sign if it is not already signed
_____ Review any Addendums and have tenant sign
_____ Review Rules and Regulations Form (Form 22 or 23)
_____ Collect security deposit if you haven't already
_____ Collect first month's rent (*certified check or money order*)
If you are requiring last month's rent, collect that also
_____ Collect any other fees due, such as a pet deposit or pet fee

_____ Conduct inspection of unit using the Move-In/Move-Out Inspection Report (Form 24)
_____ Give tenant keys

After the move-in meeting:
_____ File documents in tenant's file
_____ Calendar a "check in" with your tenant for one week away
_____ Contact all utility companies to confirm accounts are transferred from your name to tenant's name

---

BRYAN'S TIP ON UTILITY BILLS

Make sure you contact the utility company(s) when a tenant moves in to make sure the accounts have been transferred to your tenant. If you rely on the tenant to transfer the accounts, it won't always happen and you will be left with their bills to pay!

LEASE REVIEW

The first step is to allow your new tenant to review and sign the lease, if she didn't already sign the lease when she applied. When you review the lease with your tenant, go over it carefully and in-depth. Don't try to skip over or be vague about penalties, breaking the lease, or other negative things. Be clear and address these issues directly. You want your tenant to be aware of the consequences of violating the lease and also to be clear what she is agreeing to. You don't want confusion after she takes residence on what she is or is not allowed to do.

The lease is where I see a lot of landlords take shortcuts. It bewilders me why investors will spend money on asset protection plans and insurance coverage, and yet cut corners on their first line of defense, which is their lease. Of course I recommend asset protection planning and insurance coverage on *all* properties; you always want to be protected. But the truth is, you may or may not get sued—you could go for your entire landlording career without a lawsuit or a serious claim. You will, however, almost certainly have to evict a tenant at some time during your career as a landlord. This doesn't mean you are a bad landlord or even that you had a bad tenant. Even good people lose their jobs or fall on bad times and have to be evicted. But the truth is, eventually you will have to evict someone—and the lease is what the judge will look at every single time to see if you are justified in your eviction.

In fact, any dispute or disagreement you have with your tenant will always come back to the lease. The lease contains the rules you and your tenant have agreed on. And keep in mind, you sign the lease at the beginning, when your tenant moves in. Everyone is happy then. The tenant is happy to have found a place to live, and you are happy to have leased your unit. Months down the line, when the tenant is breaking the rules or not paying rent, you have to play by the rules you set in place at the beginning, when everyone was happy and you signed the lease. You cannot change a lease midway through a tenant's lease term. You are stuck with the one you signed until the lease term is up, which is usually twelve to twenty-four months or even longer. Therefore, you want a lease that is prepared to deal with a variety of things that might happen during that time. So be careful about downloading free leases, or using ones that are not prepared by someone familiar with landlord tenant law. Free doesn't always equal valuable.

A well-written lease should address the following issues:

1. Recognize all parties involved
- Use the correct legal names.
- State complete address, rental unit number, street address, city, state, and zip code.
- Give a very detailed description of the premises that will be under lease contract.
- Give the name of the managing agent or owner or rental community name (if any).
- Recognize all occupants that are of legal age and require them to sign the lease. (Check with your local landlord tenant attorney. This is not a requirement in all states.)

2. Identify the duration and payment terms
- State the duration of the lease term, beginning date, lease date, and expiration date.
- State rental amount.
- Outline utility payment policy.
- State security deposit amount and where it is being held. In some states, like Florida, this is required and you also must indicate if it is held in an interest- or noninterest-bearing account.
- Outline parking provisions.
- State required methods of payments, i.e., check, certified check, or money order.
- Underline when the rent is due and amount of any late fees that are assessed.
- State where the payments are to be made.
- Spell out clearly the returned check policy.

3. Address legal issues
- State acceptable uses of the premises.
- Specify landlord or landlord agent's right of access.
- State causes for any legal action.
- Contain radon gas language (if required in your state).

(A common item now included in many leases or in an addendum is "mold language." This is a quickly growing cause for litigation against landlords.)

4. Contain provisions for occupancy and end of occupancy issues
- State termination procedure and tenant's requirement for submitting notice to vacate.
- Give holdover tenant language.
- State terms and conditions of rental increase.
- Contain abandonment language.

5. Identify other key issues
- Who is responsible for certain maintenance issues.
- Condition of premises.
- Subletting policy.
- Any pet policies or procedures.

Those are the basic items to be covered in the lease. Always check with a local landlord tenant attorney to see what other language your state's statutes indicate should be in your lease. You want to add any language your state's laws allow to protect yourself. Remember, it is important to have a complete team on your side, and a landlord tenant attorney on your roster is a must-have.

That said, let's take a look at a few of the items on the list above and define a few key terms.

TERMS OF THE LEASE

Identifying Who Is Who

In order for a contract to be valid, the two parties have to be who they claim to be. During the tenant screening process, you asked for various forms of identification. This is the reason why. If you want to enforce any parts of this agreement/lease, or if you want to initiate any action to end this contract, or if you need to defend yourself against any legal action, you need to have accurate information about who is on the lease. If the tenant's name is on the lease, then he or she is legally bound by its provisions. I know of several landlords who ran into problems because they did not accurately account for who was occupying the rental property and whose name was on the lease.

Length of the Lease

In almost every case, you will want to have your tenants sign for a one-year lease. Anything longer than that and you won't have the opportunity to raise the rent in a timely manner. You cannot typically raise rent in the middle of a lease term. So if you have a tenant sign a lease for three years, you are stuck with the same rent for three years. Any length of time shorter than a year means a lot of turnover/vacancies, and you want to limit the amount of time your property is not producing income for you. If you are doing seven-month leases, every seven months you have a possible turnover in tenancy, which means you have to paint, clean, and ready the unit for a new tenant. In addition, you have to market the unit, which costs money, and that unit will probably be vacant for a period of time in between leases. In certain circumstances, you may allow a month-to-month tenancy, but those circumstances are not ideal. We will discuss month-to-month tenancies later.

Tip: Check your state law regarding lease term lengths. Some states require that leases be longer than seven months.

FINANCES

Security Deposits Returned

We've already covered security deposits, but in addition to what you've already learned, a good lease will lay out all the terms related to the landlord's responsibilities (and the limits of those responsibilities) when it comes time to return that deposit. It also will specify that you can make claims of damages that will result in the loss of a portion of the deposit. In addition, it spells out the terms of any legal dispute regarding the security deposit and that the prevailing (winning) party will be entitled to have the losing party pay the court costs and attorney's fees.

As with all elements of leases, be sure that your security deposit policy complies with all applicable state and local laws. Your lease should clearly state what time frame you will have to return a security deposit or provide a notice of what charges you are deducting, as well as the time frame the tenant has to dispute those charges. Your state law should tell you what these time frames are in your state. So, for example, in Florida I have fifteen days to return a security deposit in full. I have thirty days to notify a tenant of charges we are deducting, if any. And the tenant has fifteen days to dispute those charges.

Security deposits are a hot item for landlords to get sued over these days, so we will spend more time talking about them later. But for now, remember to make sure your lease complies with your state's rules about security deposits.

SECURITY DEPOSIT PLEDGE

You should have two separate bank accounts: one for depositing your security deposits and one for your rent. A security deposit is not your money. You may not spend it. The IRS likes to see that the funds are *not* commingled. This is a must for security deposits. I recommend you use a bank that returns canceled checks to help you with maintaining your documentation.

Rent

You need to be as specific as possible about when and where the rent is to be paid. That can either be in a locked communal rent box, mailed, or dropped off in person at a management office, your residence, or wherever else you specify. You can even specify that you require a one-party check or money order. Cash is a legal and acceptable form of payment. Not accepting a cash payment could negate the resident's rent responsibility for that month. I don't recommend that you do cash transactions routinely—you should do everything you can to discourage tenants from paying with cash. Clearly, you need to be careful when handling cash payments—knowing how to identify counterfeit bills is important—and you should deposit the cash as soon as possible. Carrying large amounts of cash is a real safety issue and if there is a dispute between you and your tenant on payment of rent, cash is hard to track and prove receipt of.

Late Fees

As a part of the rent portion of the lease, you should also be sure to include a late fee. Generally, I have imposed a onetime per month late fee of $50 any time a tenant has not paid the rent by the fifth day of the month. Having your tenants initial this part of the lease when you review it with them prior to signing is a good policy. I know of several landlords who have a $50 late fee and add on $2 a day for every day after the rent deadline has come and gone without payment. This method is good for encouraging tenants to make rental payments in a timely manner. Just be careful with daily charges. Many judges have deemed this excessive.

Utilities

Along with specifying whether you or the tenant is responsible for each utility (water, gas and electric, phone, cable) you should also include a statement to this effect: "*We are not liable for any interruptions or malfunctions of service. You may not occupy your apartment without electric service except during brief interruptions beyond your control.*" Hard to believe, but landlords have had tenants who either never had their utilities turned on or who had them shut off for nonpayment and continued to try to live that way. Requiring electric is one way to protect the condition of the property.

Whether you pay for utilities or the tenant does is a matter of knowing your market. You will figure in the cost of utilities when you set your rent, so go with whatever seems to be customary in your market area.

Parking

Your lease should clearly state where a tenant can park. If you have assigned parking, it should state that as well. If you have multiple units, one of the most common complaints you will receive will be about parking. You do not want to get in the middle of resolving a parking argument. No matter how you decide, it will end up being "not fair" to someone. You want your lease to have good, clear rules about parking. This includes where parking is allowed, how many parking spots each tenant gets, and where visitors should park. For a single-family house, you still want to address parking in your lease. Indicate where parking is allowed (e.g., not on the grass) and how many vehicles are allowed. Pay particular attention to any rules your community has about parking. Also address where recreational vehicles or trailers should be parked. This includes boats, trailers, and Jet Skis.

With regard to parking, your lease should also state that all vehicles must be currently licensed, with the license displayed as required by law, be in good operating condition, and not be unsightly. This keeps tenants from storing cars with no tags, or junk cars, on your property.

Bounced Checks

Your lease should state your returned check fee. I usually charge $50, so my lease specifies that $50 charge plus late fees. Remember, if your tenant's check bounced, his rent is late, so late fees and nonpayment procedures apply. The lease should also state that if a check is returned for insufficient funds, you have the right to require all future rent payments to be made via money order. This avoids having to accept checks from a tenant who routinely writes NSF checks. Remember, you have a mortgage and expenses to pay, and having checks returned constantly can cause problems with your own funds.

LEGAL ISSUES

Acceptable Uses of the Premises

Your lease should state what constitutes acceptable use of the premises. For example, you may state that a business cannot be run out of your unit.

Access

Your lease should state your right to enter. As the owner, you have the right to enter your unit. It's good practice to issue a Notice of Resident Manager's/Owner's Intent to Enter (see Form 36 on page 284) at least twenty-four hours in advance so your tenant knows you are coming. You don't want the tenant to feel his privacy has been violated. You do have the right to enter your unit at any time if there is an emergency. For example, if a lower floor unit has a leak coming from the ceiling you can have your maintenance team enter the top-floor unit to see where the water is coming from. There might be a burst pipe or defective water heater that will cause extensive damage if you do not enter the premises and deal with it. Always notify your tenant that you entered the unit and why. Even though you have the right to enter, remember you always want to be professional and respectful.

Mold

In Florida, where I live and work, mold has become a real issue. We have a warm, moist climate and mold grows easily. Because it creates a potential threat to health and to the structure, the issue must be addressed. Here is what I include: "You must take steps to limit the growth of mold in your apartment. This includes operating your heating and air-conditioning system as appropriate to reduce humidity, using appropriate ventilation, limiting evaporation of water, promptly removing any visible mold, and immediately reporting to us any leaks or other water intrusion into your apartment or any visible mold that you cannot remove." Again, knowing the particulars of your area and its needs is important. The language here is that specific because the problem in Florida is that common. In other areas, it may be radon gas that you have to address.

Policies

In your lease, clearly state any other policies about the use and care of your unit. Common policies are:

- Whether or not you allow water beds.
- Locks may not be altered, added, or changed by tenant.
- No spikes, nails, screws, or hooks may be drilled into walls other than small nails for decorative purposes.
- Window coverings must have a white exterior so that window coverings are uniform from the outside.
- No loud noise or music that may disturb other tenants or neighbors.
- Patio areas and balconies must be kept tidy and not used as a storage area.

Along with the notice about policies be sure to include a provision that tenants may not make alterations or additions to their unit without written consent. Common alterations or additions are painting, changing doors, adding lighting fixtures, or adding a garbage disposal.

Repair and Maintenance

We will spend a lot of time on maintenance in the next chapter, but basically you need to let your tenant know what he is responsible for and what you will take care of in terms of maintenance and repairs. This includes not only who will *do* what, but who will *pay* for what.

OCCUPANCY

Permissible Occupants

Only those persons whose names appear on the lease may occupy the rental property on a full-time basis. If tenants want guests to be able to reside there temporarily, they must get your permission in writing. I generally limit these guest stays to seven consecutive days and a total of fourteen days in a year. I also require tenants to notify me if they will be away from the unit for more than fourteen consecutive days.

Subletting

When someone to whom you are leasing a unit enters into an agreement with a third party to lease the property the practice is called subletting. I do not allow this. Anyone residing in the unit should be on my lease and in an agreement with me. As well, the lease cannot be assigned to someone else. Exceptions to this rule do exist. I know that in some major markets with low rental occupancy rates overall, it is sometimes easier and more desirable for a tenant to find someone to occupy her unit during a long-term absence than it may be for a landlord. For the most part, I suggest you avoid this potential web of complications. If you do allow subletting, talk with an eviction attorney first to make sure you understand the ramifications if this sublet tenant breaks rules or doesn't pay rent.

END OF OCCUPANCY

Renewal

The renewal language in your lease addresses several matters. First, it clarifies that the lease continues in force unless the tenant gives you thirty days' notice before the end of the lease term, or you give them notice that you will not renew the lease thirty days before the end of the lease term. So, if your lease is scheduled to end June 30th, written notice of nonrenewal to the other party should be given no later than the last day of May. Your lease not only clarifies that written notice must be given, but it also means that if the tenant remains in the unit after the end of the lease term, all the rules of the lease are still in force so he has to abide by them. A good lease will also state that the lease will automatically go "month to month" after it terminates. This means that each month he can give thirty days' notice that he is leaving, or you can give him thirty days' notice that he must leave, but all the rules of the lease are still in force. It is not ideal to go month to month for long. For stability you want to know a tenant is locked in for a year and you are not having vacancies pop up unexpectedly each month. But in some cases, a tenant may need an extra thirty to sixty days before he can arrange to move. He may be waiting for a job transfer or to find another place to go. If you do not have a new tenant waiting for the unit, no sense in letting it sit empty. You can let the tenant go month to month. At the end of the lease term, you should go ahead and increase his rent to be comparable with market rents in the area, and in addition charge a month-to-month fee. This is like a convenience fee for the tenant's ability to cancel the lease in thirty days. Again, month to month isn't a good long-term approach, but cases will occur where it makes sense as a temporary solution. Check your state statutes for any particular time lines required to give notices of renewal or nonrenewal.

CONDO AND HOMEOWNERS ASSOCIATION RULES

These days, with many rental properties being located in a condo association or in an area with a homeowners association, it is very important for your lease to state that if the rules of the association change, the tenant is obliged to follow the new rules. You can't change your lease in the middle of the term, but association rules can change at will, and you want your lease to be able to hold the tenant in compliance with any change in rules. For example, a student of mine rented a condo out. When he came to my class, he was not on what I would call a well-written lease. His tenant owned a small computer company and drove a car with his company's advertisement on the side. The condo association put rules in place that no commercial vehicle could be parked on the property. The owner (my student) received a citation from the association for his tenant's car. He asked the tenant not to park it there, but the tenant refused. It was his only vehicle and his lease said nothing about not being able to park it where he lived. So he continued to do so. And the owner continued to receive citations from the association and eventually paid several fines. He was stuck in the middle between the rules he agreed to with his tenant and the changing rules of the association. A good lease will foresee this situation and plan for it. Here is condo/home-owner association language from the lease form included in this book:

> If the leased premises are included in a condominium association or homeowners association, you agree to abide by its bylaws, rules, and regulations including as they may be amended and that failure to do so is a violation of this lease.

THE LAST WORD ON LEASES

I've provided two sample leases for you. One is for single-family rentals and the other for multiple unit rentals. But remember, each state has its own laws pertaining to leases, so you should have an attorney review your lease and make any needed adjustments. The cost of some good legal advice now will be much less than the cost of a messy eviction later.

ADDENDUMS

In addition to your lease, you may have addendums for your tenant to sign. These are additions to the lease, but contained on a separate document. This allows you to have one "master" lease that addresses issues common to all your rental units. Then addendums can address something related either to a specific property or to a specific tenant. A common addendum is a Pet Addendum. Not all tenants have pets, so this is something signed only if needed. (See Form 18 on page 247 of the Appendix.)

Rules and Regulations Form

Your rules and regulations form is a comprehensive and detailed list of rules on your property. It is technically an addendum to the lease, so it is considered legally binding. Here is a sample rules and regulations form.

RULES AND REGULATIONS ADDENDUM FOR MULTIFAMILY RENTAL (FORM 23)

This form should be signed in addition to your lease. Use this Rules and Regulations for a multiunit rental. Use Rules and Regulations Form 22 for a single-family rental.

**THIS ADDENDUM IS HEREBY MADE A PART OF THAT CERTAIN LEASE AGREEMENT DATED
_____, 20_____, EXECUTED BY _____ ("Resident").**

The following Rules and Regulations have been established by the Owner/Management and are considered an addendum to your Lease Agreement. Failure to comply with said Rules and Regulations may, at the discretion of Owner/Management, be grounds for termination of the Lease Agreement.

1. RENTAL PAYMENT: Rent is due on the first day of each month. Rent received after 5:00 p.m. on the fifth (5th) must include the late fee specified in the Lease Agreement. Checks which do not include the late fee as required will not be accepted. All late payment checks and charges must be paid by cashier's check, certified check, or money order. After you tender two (2) NSF checks during the term of the lease agreement, personal checks will no

longer be accepted and all monies due must be paid by cashier's check, certified check, or money order. Please mail or deliver your rental payment to the business office.

2. MAINTENANCE REQUESTS: Maintenance requests should be made by phone or in writing to the business office. Maintenance hours are weekdays from _____ a.m. to _____ p.m. In case of an emergency, call the office and you will be given an emergency number to call. Emergencies include fire, flood, electrical shortage, and sewer backups. Your maintenance request cannot be fulfilled if pets are left unattended. It is not our policy to make appointments for maintenance work.

3. LOCKS: You are prohibited from adding, changing, or in any way altering locks installed on the doors of the residence.

4. ENTRANCES, HALLWAYS, WALKS, AND LAWNS: Entrances, hallways, walks, lawns, and other public areas should not be obstructed or used for any purpose other than entering and exiting.

5. PERSONAL PROPERTY: Due to legal limitations, it is not possible for us to insure your personal property. It will be necessary for you to obtain rental dweller's coverage at your expense from a local insurance agent to cover any possible loss of personal property.

6. DELIVERY OF PACKAGES OR FURNITURE: Our employees are prohibited from receiving packages for anyone. Please make your own arrangements for such items. If you are expecting delivery of furniture, appliances or repairs to these items, you may leave a key at the office for the serviceman, but you must sign a release of responsibility for theft or damages. We will not be able to accompany any serviceman to your residence.

7. SPEED LIMIT: The maximum speed limit throughout the Community is 10 m.p.h. Please drive carefully and watch out for children.

8. PARKING FACILITIES: Our parking lots are not to be used for abandoned or inoperable vehicles. The determination of whether a vehicle is abandoned or inoperable shall be within the discretion of Management, but a vehicle will be deemed to be inoperable if not "street legal." All vehicles must be periodically moved to prevent buildup of dirt and debris. Automobiles should not be parked on the grass. Recreational vehicles and trailers may only be parked in certain areas, which are clearly marked for recreational purposes. Vehicles not conforming to these rules may be towed away at the owner's expense.

9. PEST CONTROL: Residence units are sprayed on a regular basis. If you have a special problem with pests, notify the office and the exterminator will pay special attention on his next visit. You are asked to assist our pest control by maintaining a high standard of good housekeeping. It you have a pet and it becomes necessary to spray for fleas, you must pay an additional charge.

10. GROUNDS UPKEEP: The Owner maintains a high degree of grounds maintenance. Owner/Management requests that you help in maintaining our high standards.

11. DUMPSTERS: There are Dumpsters conveniently located throughout the Rental Community. Please ensure that your trash is placed in plastic bags and securely tied before placing it in the Dumpster, not beside it. You must break down boxes before placing them in Dumpsters.

12. GUESTS: You are responsible and liable for the conduct of your family, invitees, licensees, and guests. Acts of these persons in violation of the Lease Agreement, or one of these or future rules and regulations, may be deemed by Management to be a breach by you which may result in termination of the Lease Agreement.

13. POOL: Pool Regulations are posted at pool area. Children under age _____ must be accompanied by an adult. Older children may use the pool without supervision as long as they have parental permission and behave in a responsible manner.

14. MOTORCYCLES, MINIBIKES, ETC.: All state regulations that apply on the street will apply in the Rental Community. All vehicles, including motorcycles and minibikes, must be properly licensed, and all operators must be licensed as well. No one underage is allowed to operate a motor vehicle of any type on the grounds of the

Rental Community at any time. All motorcycles and minibikes must be parked in the parking lot, and may not be placed in the rental unit.

15. PLUMBING: A charge will be made for unclogging plumbing equipment, in cases where malfunctions are caused by the introduction of improper objects therein, such as toys, cloth objects, grease, and other foreign matter. The cost of repair or replacement of other equipment or furnishings of the Owner will be borne by you.

16. LOCKOUTS: It you find it necessary to have authorized personnel unlock the rental unit after hours you will be charged a fee of $_____ payable at time of entry. If this service is not available at the Rental Community it will be necessary to call a locksmith and you will be responsible for locksmith fees.

17. DRAPERIES: Window treatments must have white linings or a white shade. Bed linens, towels, tinfoil, flags, reflector film, etc., are not acceptable. You are requested to comply within ten (10) days of move in.

18. TELEPHONE HOOKUPS: Telephones may only be placed at previously wired locations provided by the telephone company. Additional drilling, cutting, or boring for wires is not permitted without written permission from Owner/Management.

19. WATER BEDS: Water beds are allowed subject to Owner/Management's prior written approval.

20. STORAGE: No goods or materials of any kind or description which are combustible or would increase fire risk shall be placed in storage areas. Storage in such areas shall be at your risk and Owner/Management shall not be responsible for any loss or damages. Heating/air-conditioning or water heater closets are not to be used for storage purposes.

21. RECREATION: You agree to abide by rules and regulations established for use of recreational and service facilities provided by Owner/Management.

22. ANTENNAS: Radio, television, CB, or other types of aerials or antennas should not be placed or erected by you on the roof or exterior of any building.

23. DISTURBING NOISES: Your family, invitees, licensees, and guests shall have due regard for the comfort and enjoyment of all other residents in the Rental Community. Your Residence is your home, free from interruption by Owner/Management, unless you or your guests disturb other residents of the Community. Televisions, stereo units, radios, and musical instruments are not to be played at such a volume or time that will annoy persons in other residences.

24. SIGNS: You should not display any signs, exterior lights, or markings on the rental unit. No awnings or other projections should be attached by you to the outside of the building of which the rental unit is a part.

25. PATIOS: All balconies or patios must be kept clean and clear of storage items. Hanging of clothes, garments, or rugs over railing of balconies or patios will not be permitted. Patios or balconies should not be used for anything except patio furniture, flower boxes, and plants. They are not to be used for storage under any circumstances. For safety, please do not place plants on balcony railings.

26 PETS: No pets allowed except with the permission of Owner/Management and the execution of a Pet Addendum. An additional fee will be required, a portion of which is nonrefundable. The entire fee may be applied against damages to the residence in the event of default by you under the Lease Agreement.

27. LAUNDRY ROOM: If the Rental Community provides laundry facilities, please remove clothing from machines promptly. Do not use tints or dyes. Report any malfunction of machines to the office.

28. ALTERATIONS: No apartment alterations allowed without Owner/Management's prior written approval.

To avoid misunderstandings regarding the **SECURITY DEPOSITS** that are made at the time you sign your Lease Agreement, the following information is provided:

RELEASE OF THE SECURITY DEPOSIT IS SUBJECT TO THE FOLLOWING PROVISIONS:

1. Full term of lease has expired and all persons have vacated the Residence.

2. **A written notice** of Intent to Vacate effective the end of the calendar month must be given by the 1st of the calendar month prior to said vacating.

3. No damage to property beyond normal wear and tear.

4. Entire Rental Unit including range, refrigerator, bathroom, closets, and cupboards are clean. Refrigerator to be defrosted.

5. No unpaid legal charges, delinquent rents, or late fees.

6. **All** keys must be returned.

7. **All** debris, rubbish, and discards placed in proper rubbish containers.

8. Forwarding address left with Owner/Management.

9. Move-In/Move-Out Inspection Report must be completed when you move in and signed by the Owner/Property Manager and you. This form must also be completed and signed by both parties when you move out.

QUESTIONS AND ANSWERS ON SECURITY DEPOSIT POLICY:

Q. What charges are made if the prerequisite conditions are not complied with?

A. The costs of labor and materials for cleaning and repairs will be deducted. Also, any delinquent payments including late charges will be deducted.

Q. How is the Security Deposit returned?

A. By a check mailed to your forwarding address. The check is jointly payable and addressed to all persons who sign the Lease Agreement. No pick ups from the office.

Q. Can the Security Deposit be applied to any rent still outstanding during the lease term?

A. No. All rents must be paid separate and apart from the Security Deposit.

ADDITIONAL RULES AND REGULATIONS (if any):

_____

INITIALS (if any additional rules and regulations)

I/we hereby acknowledge that I/we have read the foregoing Rules and Regulations and hereby agree to abide by each and every one.

Date	Resident
Date	Resident

I've provided another Rules and Regulations form on page 261 of the Appendix that is more appropriate for a single-family rental home.

COLLECT ANY MONIES DUE

If you did not collect a security deposit as part of your closing technique when you were showing the unit, be sure to collect it now. Also collect the first month's rent. If it is not the first of the month, prorate the rent. Divide the total monthly rental by the number of days in the month to get the daily rate. Then multiply the daily rate by the number of days the tenant will occupy the unit that month. So if the monthly rent is $900 and the tenant is moving in on June 18, divide 900 by 30, since June has 30 days. The daily rate thus becomes $30. Since the tenant is occupying the unit for 13 days, multiplying 13 by $30 gives you your prorated rent of $390. Remember not to accept cash for first month's rent.

Also collect any other fees due, like a pet fee, or last month's rent if required.

A NOTE ABOUT PET FEES

Be careful not to refer to a pet fee as a pet deposit. I hear a lot of landlords call them nonrefundable pet deposits. Deposit implies it will be held, and therefore can be refunded. So it's an oxymoron to call something a nonrefundable pet deposit. Call it a pet fee, that's what it is. It's a fee that will not be returned, to compensate you for the additional cleaning a pet will require. And pets do require additional cleaning, particularly of carpets. Usually an additional cleaning treatment will be necessary to rid the unit of pet-related odors.

MOVE-IN INSPECTION

Now to my favorite technique, the move-in inspection. This is my favorite technique because it has kept me out of arguments, disagreements, and lawsuits so many times and with such ease. Unfortunately, it's the most overlooked tool by landlords. If I can say one thing with certainty, it's that when your tenants move out, you and they will not see eye to eye on what the condition of the unit was when they moved in. You will have very different memories of what damages were preexisting and different opinions about which were caused by the tenant. I'll share one of my mistakes with you, so you can learn from it. I once allowed a tenant to move in early. The move had been scheduled for a week later, but he called me in a panic and needed to move that day—which should have been my first clue. He had a great sob story and he had all his move-in money, so I agreed. Now there is nothing wrong with accommodating a tenant who has all his move-in money and has been properly screened. The problem was, I hadn't had anyone available to conduct a proper move-in meeting the day he moved. So a few details were missed. One of these was the move-in inspection. Not two weeks later, when the next month's rent was due, this tenant failed to pay. I ended up having to file on him for eviction. In response he wrote a long letter to my eviction attorney stating that the unit was a wreck and we hadn't made necessary repairs. Now this was all false, but because I hadn't scheduled a proper move-in inspection, I couldn't prove it. What should have been an easy, quick eviction ended up going to a hearing. I ultimately won, but it took much longer, and time is money when a nonpaying tenant is in your rental unit. Let's review what a move-in inspection is and how to conduct one properly so you can see how important it is.

The Move-In Inspection is a form you complete with your tenant. You should walk through the rental unit together, at your move-in meeting, before the tenant obtains keys. After checking off and identifying any existing conditions of the unit, like a scratch on the stove or a stain on the carpet, you both sign the form. If you explain to your tenants that this protects them from being charged for any damage they didn't cause, they are usually very agreeable about participating. Shown here is an example of a completed Move-In Inspection Report.

MOVE-IN/MOVE-OUT INSPECTION REPORT (FORM 24)

Resident(s) Name: _Sarah Koenig_   Date: _3-1-09_

Address: _22 Caraway Ln., Tempe, AZ 85280_   Unit #: _3-B_

PRE/AT OCCUPANCY	ND=No Damage		POST OCCUPANCY			
ITEM	Condition (unless noted otherwise in exception column)	Note Exception to Condition	Move-Out Condition	Cost per item to clean or replace	#	Total Cost
Kitchen:						
Floors	Clean, ND					
Walls/Ceiling	Paint Good					
Counters	Paint Good					
Cabinets/Drawers	Clean, ND					
Stove/Oven	Clean, ND					
Drip Pans	Clean, ND					
Hood, Filter Fan	Clean, ND					
Refrigerator	Clean, ND	_scratch on door_				
Dishwasher	Clean, Working, ND					
Sink & Stopper	Clean, Working, ND					
Lights	Clean, Working					

		1	2	3	1	2	3		
Windows/Track, Screens	Clean, No Breaks								
Other									
Living & Dining Area:									
Floor/Carpet	Clean, ND or spots								
Carpet Rips/Tears/Burns	Clean, ND								
Vacuuming Only	Clean, ND								
Walls/Ceiling	Paint Good								
Lights, Dimmer Switch	Clean, Working								
Heating, AC	Clean, Working								
Blinds	Clean, Working								
Windows/Tracks, Screens	Clean, ND								
Fireplace	Clean, ND								
Ceiling Fans	Clean, ND								
Bedroom:		1	2	3	1	2	3		
Floor/Carpet	Clean, ND								
Carpet Rips/Tears/Burns	Clean, ND								
Vacuuming Only	Clean, ND								
Walls/Ceiling	Paint Good, ND								
Lights, Dimmer Switch	Clean, Working, ND								
Blinds	Clean, ND								
Windows/Tracks, Screens	Clean, No Breaks								
Closets	Clean, ND								
Other									
Bathroom:		1		2	1		2		
Floor	Clean, ND								
Walls/Ceiling	Paint Good, ND								
Sink	Clean, ND								
Vanity/Counter	Clean, ND			*chipped*					

Vent Fan	Clean, Working							
Lights	Clean, Working							
Tile/Grout	Clean, ND							
Bath/Shower Enclosure	Clean, ND							
Toilet	Clean, ND							
Towel Bar/Soap Dish/ Mirror	Clean, ND							
Windows/Tracks, Screens	Clean, No Breaks							
Halls:								
Walls/Ceiling	Paint Good, ND							
Cabinets/Closet	Clean, ND							
Floors/Carpet	Clean, ND							
Patio/Balcony:								
Floor/Door Cleaning	Clean, ND							
Patio Door Replacement	Clean, ND							
Storage Area	Clean, ND							
Misc. Other:								
Fire Ext./Smoke Detector	Clean, Working, ND							
Drywall Repair	Clean, ND							
Trash Removed								
Doors—Interior Replace	Clean, ND							
Doors—Exterior Replace	Clean, ND							
Other								
Pet Deodorization								
			TOTAL					

Comments: _____   Comments: _____

_____   _____

_____   _____

Resident has inspected the Rental Unit prior to occupancy and accepts same as noted above. Resident understands that upon vacating the rental unit cleaning will be charged as set forth above and he or she will be responsible for damage as provided in the Rental Agreement.

Resident has inspected the Rental Unit subsequent to vacation and concurs in the above except as noted.

Dated: _March 1_____, 20 _09___

Dated: _March 3_____, 20 _10___

_____Sarah Koenig_____
Resident

_____Sarah Koenig_____
Resident

_____
Resident

_____
Resident

_____
Owner/Management

_____
Owner/Management

File a copy of the Move-In Inspection Report in your tenant file. When the tenant moves out, which, remember, can be a year later and possibly not on friendly terms, you will use this form to compare the condition of the unit. It allows you to avoid any disputes about whether or not a tenant damaged something.

Once this form is completed, you can turn over the keys to your tenant.

TENANT FILE ORGANIZATION

A best practices habit to develop is to immediately place documents in your tenant's file. Don't let them stack up. Things can get lost or damaged. These forms provide you with valuable protection if there is a problem with your tenant. They also provide protection if you ever receive a Fair Housing complaint and are audited. Below is a suggested organization for your files.

Prospective Tenant File
What to Keep:
- Application
- Guest Card
- Copy of Driver's License
- Credit Report
- Qualifying Criteria
- Move-In Cost Sheet
- Copy of Any Checks Received
- Adverse Action Letter

Tenant File

Right Side/Back to Front:

- Applicant Screening Report
- Move-In/Move-Out Inspection Report
- Rules and Regulations Form
- Lease Addendums, if any
- Guest Card/Phone Card
- Application
- Lease

Left Side/Back to Front:

- Qualifying Criteria
- Copy of Any Checks Received
- Copy of Any Notices Given During Occupancy
- Copy of All Work Orders During Occupancy
- Copy of All Receipts for Repairs
- Receipts for Any Monies Received
- Copies of Any Correspondence w/Tenant
- Tenant Contact Notes Page

Move-Out Tenant File

What to Keep:

- All of previous, and . . .
- Written 30-day notice (from tenant)

Or:

- Notice of Nonrenewal
- Completed Move-In/Move-Out Inspection Report
- Copy of Notice to Impose Claim on Security Deposit
- Certified Mail Receipt
- Documentation and Photos of Damages

FOLLOW UP

The final thing you should do to complete your move-in process is another way to distinguish yourself as the best, not the rest. Place a follow-up call to your tenant a week after move in. Ask how things are going, if they have any questions or problems. Aside from providing great service, this is a great time for a tenant to ask you again how the pool pump works or the alarm works before they damage anything.

Follow these steps and you will be moving in a happy tenant and setting yourself up with the most possible protection if needed in the future. In the next chapter, we will discuss some common scenarios where you will need to put these rules into play and you will see how important it is to have a well-written lease and all your ducks in a row—for your cash flow, your legal protection, and your sanity!

> Never throughout history has a man who lived a
> life of ease left a name worth remembering.
> —TEDDY ROOSEVELT

WHAT DO I DO WHEN MY TENANTS BREAK THE RULES?

The Most Common Tenant Issues and How to Solve Them

By now you've screened your tenant and approved him, and moved him in with a proper move-in meeting. So far you've done a professional and efficient job of working with your tenant. But I want to spend some time in this chapter talking about some common problems that can happen during your tenant's lease term and how to handle them.

I was fortunate, when I first started my business, to read a book called *The E-Myth* by Michael Gerber. This book emphasized the importance of systems. As you know from reading earlier chapters of this book, I'm a big fan of establishing good systems for every step of the landlording process. Systems keep you out of trouble, make you more efficient (which means more profitable), and they allow you, or anyone on your team, to produce a consistent result. My goal is to prepare you, not just with knowledge, but with systems to help you manage your property.

HOW DO I COLLECT RENT?

First, let's talk about the most important process you need to master as a landlord: rent collections. Think of it this way: The main source of your income from your property is from rent, and without proper rent collection you can't do anything else you need to do in order to keep the building running. The terms of your lease will specify the date the rent is due, which is typically the first of the month. Most landlords also include a grace period in their lease. This is a period of time after the due date during which rent will be accepted without a late fee. A typical grace period is until the third day of the month, or perhaps the fifth day of the month. If rent is not received by the end of the last day of the grace period, late fees go into effect and the rent is considered officially late. See the calendar that follows.

MAY

Sunday	Monday	Tuesday	Wednesday	Thursday	Friday	Saturday
				1 *Rent is due*	2	3
4	5 *Grace period ends at end of business day*	6 *Late fees go into effect*	7	8	9	10
11	12	13	14	15	16	17
18	19	20	21	22	23	24
25	26	27	28	29	30	31

All tenants should be on the same schedule. It is too difficult and time-consuming to track different due dates and grace periods.

When you've collected the rent, do the following:

Step 1: Make copies (or take photos) of all rent checks or money orders.

Step 2: Post your checks in the ledger you are keeping to track which tenants have paid and which have not. If you don't have property management software, you should post your checks or money orders in a program that will keep track of the entries and balance your books.

Step 3: Immediately endorse all checks "For Deposit Only" as a safety measure against theft or loss.

Step 4: As soon as possible, deposit all the checks. Staple your deposit slip to the copies of the checks for that particular deposit. Match those deposit slips to your ledger entries. Staple the checks, deposit slips, and ledger report and file.

Continue this process each month when you receive and deposit checks. Separate your records by month to create an easy to use system. Keep your records in a secure but easily accessible place.

Late Rent

Property management is a very interpersonal job. You have to be able to work with all kinds of people and wear many different hats during the course of a single day. One of the most potentially uncomfortable tenant conversations is the late rent discussion. Many books on landlording and rental property investment just flat-out refuse to deal with the subject. Obviously, this is a very unrealistic approach, considering that rent is the major source of income for your property. We're going to tackle this subject head-on.

The first step is to spell out very clearly the terms and conditions of the rental payments (including late fees, etc.) within the lease contract. We discussed this in chapter 9.

Be very persistent. Always remind a tenant in person, via phone, and/or via email when he or she has not paid rent.

Follow your procedure consistently in all cases. Do not procrastinate on handling late rent.

Pay or Quit Notice

If rent has not been paid by the end of the grace period, promptly address the late rent on the next business day. If you are managing multiple units, the best way to address late rent is to run a delinquency report. A property management software program can run such a report to show you who is late on rent. It gives you a complete and accurate list to work off of so nothing is missed.

For each tenant who has not paid rent, prepare a notice to pay or quit. This tells the tenant to pay the rent within a specified period of time or to vacate the unit and return possession of it to you. Check your state law to see how many days your state specifies for its pay or quit notice. Most states give three or five. In most states, the pay or quit notice must be delivered and the specified time period must expire before you can begin an eviction proceeding.

So, for example, if you have a five-day grace period and your state requires three days for this notice, the time line would be as shown on the calendar that follows.

Typically some days cannot be counted toward the days until your notice expires:

1. You cannot count the day of delivery. If you deliver the notice on Monday, you start counting the days until expiration beginning Tuesday.
2. You cannot count weekends.
3. You cannot count holidays. Usually if the clerk of court in the county your property is located in is closed, that's considered a holiday.

MAY

Sunday	Monday	Tuesday	Wednesday	Thursday	Friday	Saturday
				1 Rent is due	2	3
4	5 Grace period ends at end of business day	6 Deliver pay or quit notice	7 Day 1	8 Day 2	9 Notice expires at end of day	10
11	12 File for eviction	13	14	15	16	17
18	19	20	21	22	23	24
25	26	27	28	29	30	31

The next business day after your notice expires you can file for eviction.

An example of a Notice to Pay Rent is shown here.

NOTICE TO PAY RENT OR DELIVER POSSESSION (FORM 25)

Sample completed form—to be issued when tenant is late on rent.

TO: *Mr. Elijah Wade*   DATE: *06/05/05*

   1023 Bulls Drive

   Tampa, Florida 33615

YOU ARE HEREBY NOTIFIED THAT YOU ARE INDEBTED TO US IN THE SUM OF: $ *$500.00 and a late*
fee of $50.00 for a TOTAL of $550.00

FOR THE RENT AND USE OF THE ABOVE REFERENCED PREMISE IN *Hillsborough* COUNTY,
STATE OF *FLORIDA*, NOW OCCUPIED BY YOU AND THAT WE DEMAND PAYMENT OF SAID

RENT OR THAT YOU SURRENDER POSSESSION OF THE SAID PREMISES WITHIN THREE (3) DAYS (EX-CLUDING SATURDAYS, SUNDAYS, AND LEGAL HOLIDAYS) FROM THE DATE OF DELIVERY OF THIS NOTICE:

ON OR BEFORE THE _8th_ DAY OF _June_ 20_05_.

YOUR FAILURE TO COMPLY WITH THIS NOTICE MAY RESULT IN EVICTION PROCEEDINGS BEING INSTITUTED AGAINST YOU. WE WILL RETAKE POSSESSION FOR YOUR ACCOUNT IN THE EVENT YOU VACATE OR ARE EVICTED. YOU WILL BE HELD LIABLE FOR PAST DUE RENT, AND FUTURE RENT DUE UNDER THE FULL TERM OF YOUR RENTAL AGREEMENT MINUS ANY RENT RECEIVED FROM RE-RENTING THE PREMISES, ANY CHARGES DUE UNDER THE TERMS OF YOUR RENTAL AGREEMENT, DAMAGES TO THE PREMISES, ATTORNEYS' FEES AND COURT COSTS.

Jim Landlord
Owner/Agent Signature and Printed Name
Happy Apartment Management
Property/Company Name
1044 Wisdom Lane, Tampa, FL 33615
Property/Company Address
_813-100-1514_
Telephone Number

CERTIFICATE OF SERVICE

I hereby certify that a copy of the above notice was:

_____ delivered to _____ by hand

__X__ posted on the premises described above in the tenant's absence

on _June 5_____, 20_05_.

By:

___Jim Landlord_____

Owner/Agent

Note: Check your state law for any additional requirements for notices to pay rent.

TIMING OF NOTICES

Be careful when mailing notices with time lines, particularly pay or quit notices for rent. Some judges have ruled that since you mailed the notice you have to allow five extra days on the expiration date to allow for mail time.

It is good practice to run another delinquency report on the next business day after your pay or quit notices expire. So, using the calendar example above, you would run a new delinquency report on the twelfth. This will show you who still has not paid rent so that you can start the eviction process.

The amount you include on the three-day notice should be the amount of rent owed only, unless your state allows you to specify that any late fees are considered *additional rent*. If it does, you can add those fees.

DELIVERING A NOTICE

There is certain protocol required to deliver a notice.

1. Most states require notices to have a certificate of service, or similar language, at the bottom of the notice. This indicates how the notice was delivered—whether you handed it to the tenant, to someone else who was in the unit, or left it taped on the door for them. See the bottom of the Notice to Pay Rent or Deliver Possession form on page 270 for an example of a certificate of service. Don't leave the notice with a child unless you know the child meets the age requirement set by your state.

2. Take two copies of the notice to deliver it. You need one to give to the tenant or leave on the door and the other to bring back for your file after you've made sure to fill out the certificate of service on your copy.

3. Knock and see if the tenant is there before you leave the notice on the door. It's good business practice to give the tenant the courtesy of personally handing them the notice. If no one is home, you can leave the notice on the door, but leave it folded or in an envelope. Do not tape the notice open for others to read. Aside from being unprofessional, it can get you sued in some states.

4. I do not recommend you open the door and leave the notice inside. It is legal in some states but I have seen cases where landlords entered a unit to leave a notice and were accused of stealing. You are not required to leave it inside, so I don't open that door, no pun intended.

Partial Rent

Sometimes landlords or property managers will accept partial payment of rent. If you choose to do that, you should still follow the steps above. Do not skip issuing the notice to pay or quit. Issue the notice for the amount still owed. Let's say a tenant says that he can give you only $500 of the $850 owed for the month. When you fill out the notice to pay or quit, the amount due should reflect the balance owed to you: $350. Issue this notice on the spot when accepting a partial payment. Even if you agree to give the tenant more than the number of days listed on the notice, you should still issue the notice immediately. Also, accepting any amount of rent usually negates any notice you issued the tenant regarding rent. This lets the required number of days tick by while you are waiting on your tenant to pay rent. You do not have to file immediately for eviction on the day after the notice expires. You can wait until the agreed upon payment extension date before you file. The point of issuing the notice is that if the tenant doesn't show up on the day promised, you can immediately file for eviction. If you had not issued the notice, you would have to issue it at that point and lose more time waiting for the days to expire.

For example, say Mr. Smith's rent of $850 is due on the first, but he has a grace period through the fifth. On the fourth day of the month, he tells you he has been sick and missed some work and has only $500 of the rent but can pay you the rest in ten days when he gets paid again. It is up to you if you accept this arrangement, but Mr. Smith has always paid rent on time before so you agree. You should accept the $500 payment and have Mr. Smith put in writing that he agrees to pay the remainder within ten days. This is called a promise to pay. Then you immediately issue him a notice to pay or quit showing the $350 remaining and your late fee, if your lease supports this. While you are waiting those ten days, your notice to pay or quit will have already expired. If Mr. Smith does not show up by the end of the tenth day with his remaining rent, you can file for eviction on day eleven. If you had not issued the notice when you accepted the partial payment, you would have to issue the notice on day eleven and wait for it to expire before filing for eviction. I usually accept partial rent unless it's a really troublesome tenant and I prefer to move toward eviction as fast as possible. A bird in the hand is worth two in the bush. But I follow my late rent procedures to reduce any time delays if I do have to evict.

With that said, be careful of accepting partial rent. If a tenant has a good track record of paying, you may want to accept this offer. However, keep in mind that a tenant may be asking for more time *not* to raise the balance due but to move out and abandon the property or to file for bankruptcy. Bankruptcy will stop your eviction process cold. Once a tenant files for bankruptcy, you must stop all your attempts to collect overdue rent.

If your tenant does file for bankruptcy, contact your attorney immediately. Your lawyer will check to see if a bankruptcy has actually been filed. Your attorney will then file a motion to obtain relief from the automatic stay of bankruptcy. You must petition the bankruptcy court to allow the stay to be lifted so that you can collect the debt or continue the eviction process. You don't want a unit sitting there occupied by someone who has no intention or ability to pay. This process of securing permission to go after your tenant can take anywhere from thirty to sixty days. All this quickly adds up to lost money and an unhappy owner. You can't afford either of those two so use your discretion when accepting partial rent, especially with a single-family rental because you have only one source of payment.

Returned Checks

Your returned check policy will be spelled out in your lease. If a resident's check is returned for insufficient funds, be sure to note that in your file and rent roll ledger and consider that tenant unpaid and delinquent.

DISHONORED CHECK NOTICE (FORM 29)

June 6, _____, 200 _8_
(date)
Samantha Green _____
(name of check writer)
99 Cranberry Lane #2 _____
(rental unit street address & number)
Portland, ME 09326 _____
(city, county, state, zip)

You are hereby notified that a check, numbered _763_ , in the face amount of $ _700_ , issued by you on _June 1, 2008_ , drawn upon _Cranberry Bog Bank_ , and payable to _Kimberly Hildebrand_ , has been dishonored. You have 7 days from receipt of this notice to tender payment of the full amount of such check plus a service charge of $25, if the face value does not exceed $50; $30, if the face value exceeds $50 but does not exceed $300; $40, if the face value exceeds $300; or an amount of up to 5 percent of the face amount of the check, whichever is greater, the total amount due being $ _735_ and _00_ cents. Unless the amount is paid in full within the time specified above, the holder of such check may turn over the dishonored check and all other available information relating to this incident to the state attorney for criminal prosecution. You may be additionally liable in a civil action for triple the amount of the check, but in no case less than $50, together with the amount of the check, a service charge, court costs, reasonable attorney fees, and incurred bank fees, if payment is not made within 30 days.

Kimberly Hildebrand _____
(signature)
Kimberly Hildebrand _____
(name and title)
Hildebrand Rentals _____
(community name, if any)
55 Oak Street _____
(street address)
Portland, ME _____
(city, state)
_555-2396_ _____
(telephone number)

Sent certified mail # _009823568_ _____ on _June 6, 2008_ .

Mailed by:
Kimberly Hildebrand _____
(signature of person who mailed it)

- Put the name(s) of *all* persons named on the lease on the dishonored check notice.
- Send this form out by certified mail immediately when you've received an NSF notice regarding the payment.
- Include late fees and NSF charges as indicated in your lease.
- Include a Notice to Pay or Quit for the amount that was not paid and is now late.

Follow these steps for an NSF check:

1. Send a Dishonored Check Notice (see sample on previous page) to the tenant and include a notice to pay or quit as soon as possible. This informs the tenant of his or her delinquency. Most states require you to send the Dishonored Check Notice by certified mail and be sure that it is signed for by the tenant.
2. Make a copy of the Dishonored Check Notice form and a copy of the bank's notification of insufficient funds. Make a copy of the check, too, and place all of these in your tenant's file.
3. Update the tenant's account ledger to reflect this nonpayment. Add the charge for a returned check. (You will have specified this amount in your lease.) It is very important to update your ledger as soon as you receive the notice from the bank about the NSF.
4. Add your tenant's name, address, check amount, and check number to your monthly NSF log. Use this log to keep track of and to follow up on all NSF checks and to make sure that all rents are collected.

RULES VIOLATIONS

When you conducted your move-in meeting, you reviewed with your tenant and had them sign your rules and regulations form. Enforce your rules consistently in all situations.

Despite your preparations, you will still have some tenants who violate those rules. Here are some common types of violations and how to deal with them.

Disturbances

Disturbances are usually loud parties, loud music, or loud arguments. If a disturbance is reported to you, you should deal with it promptly.

1. Issue a Disturbance Notice (see Form 28 on pages 159 and 275 of the Appendix). Be very specific and detailed in your description of the violation.
2. Deliver the notice using the same delivery guidelines above.

3. Be sure to note any subsequent conversations and/or correspondence you exchange with the tenant in regard to the rules violation. Place these notes in the tenant's file.

For these typical types of disturbances a disturbance notice will usually suffice. Don't be too aggressive for these general disturbances. Address the matter, but don't overreact. Some tenants just require occasional reminders of the rules. Again, this is a people business and these people pay the rent. Think to yourself, is one loud party every six months worth eviction costs, paying to ready the unit for a new tenant, vacancy costs while you find a new tenant, and marketing costs? Probably not.

I had one tenant named Ritchie on a property I managed who, every eight months like clockwork, had a party that got a little too loud and disturbed his neighbors. So every eight months like clockwork I issued a Disturbance Notice to Ritchie. He would apologize and behave for eight months until it happened again. We did this for five years because other than the occasional reminder to keep the noise down, Ritchie was a good tenant. He paid rent on time and kept his unit in good condition.

Now, had Ritchie broken the rules too often, where he was really bothering the neighbors, I would have taken the following steps:

- If a tenant continues to violate the rules, issue a Lease Violation Notice with Option to Cure (see Form 26 on page 271 in the Appendix) to them. Again, be very specific when describing the reason for the notice. An option to cure means you are not evicting them, but you are giving them a certain number of days to comply with your notice—that is, to stop whatever they are doing that is breaking the lease. This notice should state that if the problem happens again during their lease term, you will evict them. It's a much sterner notice than a Disturbance Notice.
- Deliver the notice using our delivery guidelines.
- Be sure to note any subsequent conversations and/or correspondence you exchange with the tenant in regard to the rules violation. Place these notes in the tenant's file.
- If a tenant continues to break the rules after the notice expires, you have the legal right to evict the tenant.

FIRST-TIME OFFENDERS

In most states judges will not evict a tenant for a first-time typical disturbance, like having one loud party. This is why documenting each disturbance with a Disturbance Notice is important. Then, if the unsatisfactory behavior gets out of hand, you have a documented history of the problem and are more likely to persuade a judge to evict the tenant.

LEASE VIOLATION NOTICE, WITH OPTION TO CURE

There are typically two types of lease violation notices: option to cure, and notice to vacate or terminate. The difference is an Option to Cure means you are giving the tenant a chance to rectify the problem. These notices usually have a specified time line, like seven days, in which they must fix the problem or you can evict them. So, for example, if you find out your tenant has a pet and she is not supposed to have one, you issue a Lease Violation Notice with Option to Cure. This gives her a certain time period to either get rid of the pet, come sign a Pet Addendum and pay the pet fee (if you accept pets), or vacate the premises and return possession to you. Other common scenarios are:

- Continued, documented disturbances
- Illegal occupation (someone who has moved in but who is not on the lease)
- Gross uncleanliness
- Damages to property

Illegal Occupants

Illegal occupants are people residing in the unit who are not on the lease, therefore not authorized to be there. This is a problem you should immediately address. Your lease should state that any person not on the lease cannot be in the unit for more than seven consecutive days or a total of fourteen days over a year. This is to control who is living in your units.

You always want anyone living in one of your apartments to be on the lease. First and foremost, you want them to complete an application so you can screen them. Now, if the original tenant has already met your credit, income, and/or employment criteria, the additional, new tenant may not need to meet those guidelines. However, at the very least you must run a criminal background check to make sure this person meets your criminal background criteria. You want to know who is living in your unit and who you are exposing your neighbors to. Second, you want each person living in a unit to be on the lease, therefore legally bound by the rules and responsible for payment.

LEASE VIOLATION NOTICE TO TERMINATE/VACATE

The second type of lease violation notice is to terminate or vacate (see Form 27 on page 273 of the Appendix). This means you are not giving the tenant an option to fix the problem. You are notifying him he has violated the lease and must vacate the premises by a specified date. If he has not moved out by the time the notice expires, you can file on him for eviction. This notice is usually issued for very serious circumstances where a tenant must go, even if you know you will have financial consequences. Common examples are:

- Severe, continued, and documented disturbances
- Illegal activity
- Extensive damage to property

USING THE RIGHT NOTICE AND PROPER NAMES

Be sure that the name that you place on the notice is exactly the same as the one that appears on the lease. Also, if more than one name appears on the lease, be sure to put all the names on the notice.

IMPORTANT FORMS FOR DEALING WITH TENANT PROBLEMS

These notices will be the most common ones you issue as they address 95 percent of the situations you will face as a landlord: late rent, loud disturbances, unauthorized occupants or pets, uncleanliness, and damages.

Let's take a look at several of these forms as well as go over a checklist of dos and don'ts for each.

DISTURBANCE NOTICE (FORM 28)

TO: _Kevin Stein and Erica Jackson_   DATE: _December 15, 2008_
    42 Ridgeway Street #4, Los Angeles, CA

YOU UNREASONABLY DISTURBED YOUR NEIGHBORS BY: _Throwing a loud party, playing music at a disruptive level after 10pm, and smoking in the common area of the apartment building._

IF YOU UNREASONABLY DISTURB YOUR NEIGHBORS AGAIN DURING THE NEXT 12 MONTHS, YOUR LEASE MAY BE TERMINATED AND YOU MAY BE REQUIRED TO VACATE YOUR UNIT WITHIN 7 DAYS OF TERMINATION. IF YOUR LEASE IS TERMINATED, WE WILL RETAKE POSSESSION OF YOUR UNIT. YOU WILL STILL BE LIABLE FOR RENT AND LATE CHARGES UNTIL THE LEASE EXPIRES, LESS ANY

RENT WE RECEIVE FROM RERENTING THE PREMISES. IF SUIT IS FILED YOU ALSO WILL BE LIABLE FOR OUR SUIT COSTS INCLUDING ATTORNEY'S FEES.

Laney Kohl
Owner/Agent Signature and Printed Name
Vista Property Management
Property/Company Name
9984 Hollywood Boulevard
Property/Company Address
_310-555-1212_
Telephone Number

CERTIFICATE OF SERVICE

I hereby certify that a copy of the above notice was:

_____ delivered to _____ by hand

__X__ posted on the premises described above in the tenants' absence

on _December 15,_____, 200_8_ .

By:

_Laney Kohl_____

Owner/Agent

Issue this notice when . . .

Your tenant has caused a disturbance for the first time and it does not warrant threatening them with terminating their lease. The Disturbance Notice is used when a resident has broken the rules of your lease or addendums. Be sure to include the names of all the persons named on the lease on the Disturbance Notice and be very specific in describing how the rules were broken.

Delivery options: Legally, the notice can be posted on the resident's door, sent via mail, or hand delivered.

Check with your attorney to see if state or local laws require this form to be filed in order to terminate a lease.

- Don't accept rent if you are aware of a tenant's noncompliance and intend to issue a Lease Violation Notice to Vacate.
- Don't accept rent when a notice is pending, and don't issue a notice to pay or quit for nonpayment.
- Don't be vague in your description of the noncompliance.
- Don't issue a lease violation notice for a first-time disturbance. Use a Disturbance Notice.

LEASE VIOLATION NOTICE WITH OPTION TO CURE (FORM 26)

Sample completed form—to be issued when tenant breaks a rule of the lease and you wish to give them 7 days to correct the problem and remain in your rental unit.

TO: _Arianna McDowall_____   DATE: _06/05/05_____
_3333 Celtic Drive_____
_Tampa, Florida 33615_____

YOU ARE NOTIFIED THAT YOU HAVE VIOLATED YOUR RENTAL AGREEMENT AND/OR THE LAW AS FOLLOWS:
_Presence of a pet without approval by management or execution of a Pet Addendum_____

DEMAND IS HEREBY MADE THAT YOU REMEDY THE NONCOMPLIANCE(S) WITHIN SEVEN (7) DAYS OF RECEIPT OF THIS NOTICE OR YOUR RENTAL AGREEMENT SHALL BE DEEMED TERMINATED AND YOU SHALL VACATE THE PREMISES UPON SUCH TERMINATION. IF THIS SAME CONDUCT OR CONDUCT OF A SIMILAR NATURE IS REPEATED WITHIN TWELVE (12) MONTHS, YOUR TENANCY IS SUBJECT TO TERMINATION WITHOUT YOUR BEING GIVEN AN OPPORTUNITY TO CURE THE NONCOMPLIANCE(S).
WE WILL RETAKE POSSESSION FOR YOUR ACCOUNT IN THE EVENT YOU VACATE OR ARE EVICTED. YOU WILL BE HELD LIABLE FOR PAST DUE RENT, AND FUTURE RENT DUE UNDER THE FULL TERM OF YOUR RENTAL AGREEMENT MINUS ANY RENT RECEIVED FROM RERENTING THE PREMISES, ANY CHARGES DUE UNDER THE TERMS OF YOUR RENTAL AGREEMENT, DAMAGES TO THE PREMISES, ATTORNEYS' FEES, AND COURT COSTS.

_Jim Landlord_____
Owner/Agent Signature and Printed Name
_Happy Apartment Management_____
Property/Company Name
_1044 Wisdom Lane, Tampa, FL 33615_____
Property/Company Address
_(813) 100-1514_____
Telephone Number

CERTIFICATE OF SERVICE

I hereby certify that a copy of the above notice was:
_____ delivered to _____ by hand
__X__ posted on the premises described above in the tenant's absence
on _____June 5_____, 200 _5_ .
By:
____Jim Landlord_____
Owner/Agent

You may be wondering why you shouldn't collect any rent if you have issued a Lease Violation Notice to *Vacate*. If you do collect the rent, that will cancel out what you are intending to do in the lease violation notice: that is, to initiate immediate eviction proceedings. Taking the tenant's rent invalidates that notice, so don't do it. Don't send a mixed signal by collecting rent and telling a tenant she has seven days to clear up a problem. Legally, she will have the right to remain in the unit until the end of the month covered by the rent you've just collected from her.

GAINING ENTRY TO A TENANT'S UNIT

The last of the most common tenant problems is getting into a tenant's unit or single-family home legally. Many states have laws requiring that the landlord or property manager send a notice alerting the party of the landlord or property manager's intent to enter the rental property for a nonemergency reason. You will always have the right to enter a rental property in the case of an emergency. Cases where there is not sufficient time to alert the tenant of an emergency include:

- Fire or smoke coming from windows or doors
- Excessive water leaking out of doors, windows, floors, walls, or ceilings
- Loud screaming
- The smell of natural gas
- No answer at the door or not hearing from a tenant for an unusually long period of time

Tips on Notifying a Tenant of Intent to Enter
- Always provide the tenant with written notification (see Notice of Resident Manager's/Owner's Intent to Enter on page 284 in the Appendix).
- Give the tenants as much prior lead time as possible. (Check with your local landlord tenant attorney regarding any required compliance to this lead time.)
- Try to enter the unit at a time when the tenant is home to avoid any false claims of theft or other improprieties.
- Do not force your way into a tenant's home if there is no emergency.

Do
- Put the name(s) of *all* persons named on the lease on the Notice of Resident Manager's/Owner's Intent to Enter.
- Post this notice at least twelve hours prior to entering the residence.
- Post this notice between normal business hours as specified in your lease.
- Check with your attorney to see if state or local laws require this form to be filed and the above provisions adhered to.

Don't

- Do not enter the residence alone.

Delivery options: Legally, the notice can be posted on the resident's door, sent via mail, or hand delivered, but it must be at least twelve hours prior to entering.

NOTICE OF RESIDENT MANAGER'S/OWNER'S INTENT TO ENTER (FORM 36)

Send this form to any tenant to notify them you need to enter their unit.

Date _____

To _____

_____

_____

Please be advised that the manager/owner of _____ will be entering your residence on the _____ day of _____, 20___, in order to _____

_____

_____
Owner/Agent

CERTIFICATE OF SERVICE

I hereby certify that a copy of the above notice was:

_____ delivered to _____ by hand

_____ posted on the premises described above in the tenant's absence

on _____, 20___.

By:

_____
Owner/Agent

MAINTENANCE/HANDYMAN: A WEALTH OF INFORMATION

Maintenance men are a great way to get information on your tenant's compliance with the lease and rules they agreed to. When a maintenance technician enters a unit to handle a work order or does a routine maintenance checkup he can report back to you if the unit is unclean, if there are pets living there, or if people are living there who are not on the lease. A good maintenance man is a wealth of information and an important key to you knowing what is going on inside your unit. I've had maintenance techs report back that my tenants had moved boyfriends or girlfriends in, that they had pets—and once, even, that the tenant had marijuana growing in the linen closet! Pest control or other routine vendors can also serve in this role if you develop a good rapport with them.

With these forms and checklists, a well-thought-out lease, and your consistent and prompt application of your rules and consequences, you will be able to take care of any tenant-related problems you encounter very quickly. When other tenants who comply with the rules and pay on time see how effectively you address these issues, you will take the most important step in creating a culture for your tenants of professional, quality management and in letting your blue-chip tenants know that you really care about the building and the quality of life of all those who reside in it. You will greatly reduce turnover in the units this way and keep that income stream flowing regularly. A well-run building is an income-producing building.

REALITY REAL ESTATE

Now, let's end this chapter with some Reality Real Estate examples. These are true stories of tenant situations I have dealt with. I always believe it's great training to share not just the legal formalities required of you as a landlord, but how to make it work in real life, with real tenants.

Read the real-life situations below and write down what notice should be used. The correct answers are listed at the end of this chapter.

1. On a new property I acquired, an immediate problem I saw was the clutter and mess most tenants kept on their patios. It was unsightly and hurting my "curb appeal," as discussed in chapter 8. And it was also a safety problem, as the clutter was blocking the exits. What form did I send to the offending tenants?

2. While conducting a work order to repair a leaky bathroom sink, William, my former maintenance director, reported back to me that he saw women's toiletries in the bathroom. A significant number of items indicated a woman was living there. He also noticed women's clothes hanging in the bathroom. This unit was leased to a single man. What notice did I deliver to handle this situation?

3. I received a notice on May 10th that Mr. Jackson's rent check had bounced. What notice did I deliver to handle this matter?

4. I had a tenant, Kathy, who moved in on a Wednesday. On Thursday morning at ten o'clock it was reported to me that she was on her patio, drunk as a skunk. She was announcing loudly to all her neighbors that she was "celebrating her new apartment" with a few drinks (at 10 a.m.!). As she continued to "celebrate," becoming more and more inebriated, she was getting louder and louder, disturbing everyone.

What notice did I deliver to handle this problem? And what would I do if this happened again, which it did?

5. A tenant of mine got into a fight with his wife. In anger, he threw a chair through the sliding glass door. I was notified by the police, who were called out by some neighbors to handle the domestic disturbance. How did I handle this situation?

REAL-LIFE ANSWERS

1. I issued a Lease Violation Notice with Option to Cure to handle the messy patios. The rules in my lease stated that patios should be kept clear of clutter. However, I did want to give these tenants the option to clean up the mess and continue to live there. And they did.

2. I issued a Lease Violation Notice with Option to Cure stating that the woman who moved in had seven days to come fill out an application, pay an application fee and, if her criminal background check was approved, be added to and sign the lease.

3. I updated my rent roll to reflect that Mr. Jackson had indeed not paid rent, as the funds were insufficient. I added him to my NSF list. I completed and mailed an NSF notice to Mr. Jackson along with a notice to pay or quit for nonpayment of rent.

4. I issued a Disturbance Notice the first time Kathy caused a problem. After the second incident, I issued a Notice of Lease Violation with Option to Cure. When it happened a third time within six months, I issued a Lease Violation Notice to Vacate, giving her seven days to move out or I would evict her. After three times of drunken disturbances, I was at risk of her neighbors, who were good tenants, moving out.

5. I immediately issued a Lease Violation Notice to Vacate. I have a no-tolerance rule for illegal activity on my property. In addition, intentional damage this serious in nature would be enough of a reason for me to require someone to vacate my premises.

Success, the real success, does not depend upon the position
you hold but upon how you carry yourself in that position.
—TEDDY ROOSEVELT

ELEVEN

HOW DO I MOVE MY TENANT OUT?

Ending the Lease Term

At the end of a tenant's lease term, your tenant will either be staying or going. Either way, there are important steps to follow to avoid financial loss and lawsuits. If your tenant will be staying, you have lease renewal procedures that include rent increases. If your tenant will be moving out, you have required notifications, move-out procedures, and security deposit issues to handle. In this chapter, I will share with you the proper procedures for renewing a lease or moving a tenant out. We will also discuss the less desirable and more complex scenarios of evicting a tenant and handling an abandoned unit to make sure you are prepared for the best and worst possible circumstances.

RENEWING A LEASE

Typically, the landlord will have the option to either renew or not renew a lease. In most cases, you do not have to give a reason for not renewing a lease; it's simply at your discretion. The tenant also has the right to choose not to renew the lease. As the landlord, you always want to know as early as possible your tenant's intention to stay or leave so you can begin looking for a new tenant if needed. This will minimize the amount of time your unit is vacant and you are incurring the cost of vacancy loss.

To aid in determining a tenant's intentions, I recommend that you send out a Renewal Notice forty-five to sixty days prior to the end of the lease term. The Renewal Notice informs the tenant that you wish to renew the lease and explains the new rental rate. (See the sample on page 167.)

When you renew a lease, you should always have a tenant sign a new lease stating the new lease term and new rental amount. It also gives you the chance to have your tenant sign a new updated lease with any new legal changes or provisions in it. You should have your lease updated periodically as laws change and attorneys learn better ways to protect you. You can either include the new lease with your Renewal Notice for the tenant to sign and return to you, or ask the tenant to meet you and sign a new lease.

RENEWAL NOTICE (FORM 32)

Date: _7/1/09_

To: _Lee Gallagher_

94 Rumble Dr.

Cherry Hill, NJ 08063

This letter is to advise you that in accordance with paragraph _____ of your lease agreement, I am giving you official notice that your lease is due to expire on _September 1, 2009_ . **Please be advised your new monthly rent amount shall be $** _$785_ **a month.** Please be informed it is imperative you come to _14 Main St._ _____ during the hours of _9–5_ on the days of _Monday–Friday_ _____ as soon as possible to have a new lease signed. In the event you choose not to renew your lease, this is your official notice that I will not allow you to remain as a month-to-month resident. You will be required to vacate the premises on the _31st_ day of _August_ _____, 20_09_. If you fail to turn in your keys, you will be considered a holdover resident and charged accordingly.

Larry Kohl

Owner/Agent

CERTIFICATE OF SERVICE

I hereby certify that a copy of the above notice was:

_X_ delivered to _Lee Gallagher_ _____ by hand

_____ posted on the premises described above in the tenant's absence

on _7/2_ _____, 200_9_ .

By:

Larry Kohl

Owner/Agent

The Art of the Rental Increase

The rental increase is one of the most important processes a landlord/property manager will have to master. Without periodic rental increases a rental property could stand to lose a considerable amount of cash flow. Conversely, a well-thought-out rental increase plan can benefit you in many ways:

- Offset the rising cost of doing business
- Recover any losses suffered by the investment
- Provide additional amenities
- Upgrade and make needed repairs on the rental property

Being able to raise the rent is one of the things that make rental property a solid investment. It's a good hedge against inflation.

A lot has been written on how and when to tell a tenant that the rent she is currently paying will be increased. Landlords/property managers have been known to offer new microwaves, TVs, ceiling fans, and other items at the end of a lease term as an incentive for lease renewal. The end of the lease term is also when the rent is usually increased, so these incentives are thought to help sugarcoat the rent raise.

It has been my personal experience that tenants respond more positively to an increase in rent when they have been treated with respect and the landlord/property manager has maintained their rental property. I once conducted a poll of tenants whose leases were coming up for renewal and their current rents were to be raised. My staff and I were pretty shocked to discover that most tenants decided to renew their leases not because of a free microwave or a free TV, but because of, as most tenants put it, our professional management and the feeling that they actually mattered to our staff. Moreover, the study showed that our attention to detail and timing with respect to maintenance requests was a huge deciding factor in persuading tenants to renew their leases. In a highly competitive rental market, maintaining high levels of tenant satisfaction is one way to increase retention. If you're a numbers person, reducing the number of units that have to be "made ready" for another tenant will have a direct positive effect on your net operating income (NOI). For the owner, this translates to return on investment.

Simple techniques can help in the rental increase process:

- Let your tenants have plenty of notice of their rental increase. The number of days' notice will depend on your type of lease.
- Be ready to deal with tenants who will want to negotiate the rental increases. Be firm and stick to your procedures.
- I have found it useful to raise the rent after a lease term, even if it is only a few dollars. This gets the tenant accustomed to a rent increase at the end of each lease term. Otherwise, a sudden increase after a long positive relationship may cause problems.
- Always be prepared to explain and justify a rent increase. Increases are used to maintain the property, keep up with the local rental market, and provide new amenities. I like to point out that the new rental amount is average for the area so tenants are not likely to find anything less expensive, plus they would have the cost of moving, which is expensive.

Month-to-Month Leases

Previously, I mentioned that on occasion you may allow a tenant to go month to month on their lease. You may be allowing them to stay for a brief period while they finalize moving arrangements. Usually you do not want to turn a long-term lease into a month to month, but occasionally it might make sense for you and the tenant. Preferably the month-to-month term should be no more than ninety days. Remember, you don't want the unpredictability of a month-to-month tenant up and leaving you with a vacant unit for long.

On the first month after the lease term is over, the rent due is the new rental rate that you put on the renewal form (the market value rent). Your lease should also state that you charge a month-to-month fee.

If the tenant chooses to pay rent without the new rental rate and additional month-to-month fee, you should immediately either send the rent back with a notice to pay or quit, or else accept the rent, but immediately issue a notice to pay or quit for the balance due. If you have not collected all the rent by the time the pay or quit notice expires, you can prepare the file for eviction. Communicate with your tenant during this process. Eviction should be the last resort.

You or the tenant can terminate the month-to-month arrangement with a thirty-day written notice.

MOVE OUT

Step 1

Upon receiving notice from a tenant of their intention to vacate, or if you notify a tenant you are not renewing their lease, you should immediately schedule a move-out meeting. During this meeting the tenant should return the keys to you, provide a forwarding address if he hasn't already, pay any balance due, and accompany you on a move-out inspection.

Step 2

At the move-out meeting, use your Move-In/Move-Out Inspection Report (remember the one you used in your move-in meeting way back when you moved your tenant in?) and walk through the unit, noting any damages or areas in need of repair. Indicate any damages that were not marked present at move in.

For example: If an appliance had chipped paint prior to move in, that damage should have been noted on the form from the move-in inspection. Be detailed and accurate in differentiating the old damage from any new damage. Clearly explain to the tenant that he will not be charged when he moves out for any damage noted on this form at move in.

Your tenant's recollection of the condition of the rental property as it was when he moved in may differ from yours, so always utilize your Move-In/Move-Out Inspection Report along with photographs of the unit before and after.

MOVE-OUT INSPECTION

If possible, schedule your move-out inspection after *the tenant has removed his or her furniture. It is easy to hide stained carpet or holes in the wall behind a sofa!*

If a tenant is very hostile upon move out and you feel he or she would cause a problem during the move-out inspection, then perform the inspection accompanied by a friend or staff member. Never perform a walk-through or a move-out inspection alone if you question your safety.

If a tenant does not show up for the move-out meeting, or "skips out" on you without notice, you can perform the inspection without him. Your tenant's signature on the Move-In/Move-Out Inspection Report upon move in, agreeing to the condition of your rental unit when he took possession, along with photos of the current condition, is all the evidence you need.

We recommend, if possible, to go ahead and conduct the move-out inspection with your tenant and to discuss any disputes then and there, rather than prolong them.

Step 3

After your meeting with your tenant, back at your office calculate the cost of repairing the damages reflected on the Move-In/Move-Out Inspection Report.

Step 4

Prepare a **Notice of Intention to Impose Claim on Security Deposit.** This form itemizes what you are deducting from the security deposit and formally notifies the tenant of these charges. Most states will have specific legal requirements and time lines for notifying a tenant about their security deposit.

Be sure to show a calculation of all damage charges found in the unit. Show the deduction of these charges from the security deposit. (See the example of a completed form on page 171.)

Step 5

Mail the notice of intention to impose claim. You must send the notice to either the last known address or any new address the vacating tenant has provided. If a new address was not provided, mail it to your rental unit's address. Typically, a tenant will have put in a forwarding request for mail and will receive the notice. If you plan to deduct charges from the vacating tenant's security deposit, you usually are required to send the notice *by certified mail*. Include a copy of the

NOTICE OF INTENTION TO IMPOSE CLAIM ON SECURITY DEPOSIT
(FORM 34)

Send this form to your tenant after they vacate your unit to notify them you are deducting charges from their security deposit.

TO: _June Ella_   DATE: _06/28/09_

_____1010 Heat Drive_

_____Tampa, Florida 33815_

THIS IS A NOTICE OF THE LANDLORD'S INTENTION TO IMPOSE A CLAIM FOR DAMAGES UPON YOUR SECURITY DEPOSIT AS INDICATED BELOW. YOU ARE HEREBY NOTIFIED THAT YOU MUST OBJECT IN WRITING TO THIS DEDUCTION FROM YOUR SECURITY DEPOSIT WITHIN FIFTEEN (15) DAYS FROM THE TIME YOU RECEIVE THIS NOTICE OR THE LANDLORD WILL BE AUTHORIZED TO DEDUCT ITS CLAIM FROM YOUR SECURITY DEPOSIT. YOUR OBJECTION MUST BE SENT TO THE LANDLORD AT THE ADDRESS SHOWN BELOW.

Happy Apartment Management

1044 Wisdom Lane

Tampa, Florida 33615

Amount of Security Deposit $ _250.00_

Interest if due $ _0_

Total security deposit and interest (if due) $ _250.00_

Less damages and rent:

Carpet $ _$ 100.00_

DAMAGES

_____ $ _0_

RENT

Total damages and rent due $ _100.00_

Total due to: ( ) landlord

             (x) tenant $ _150.00_

Sent certified mail # _0554893314_ _____ on _June 28_ _____, 20_09_.

Mailed by: _Jim Landlord_ _____

Note: This notice does not waive or limit any of landlord's rights to damages or amounts due which may exceed security deposit or amounts listed on this form.

Move-In/Move-Out Inspection Report in your mailing. Complete and mail this notice promptly to make sure you comply with deadlines for sending this notice.

If a refund of the security deposit or a portion of the deposit is due to the tenant, enclose a check. Check your state statutes with regard to time requirements for return of a security deposit. You can visit our website, **landlordacademy.com**, for more information on state-specific requirements.

The Security Deposit—What to Take and What Not to Take

Security deposit dispute is one of the most common areas of litigation in landlord tenant law. In some states, a tenant has up to four years to sue the landlord over security deposit claims. However, after the first year the chances greatly decline. If you do find yourself in court the best defense, in my opinion, is to be well organized by having the move-out procedure well documented. This book helps provide you with consistency and professionalism.

Tips for Security Deposit Deductions
- A fair price should be charged for repairs and replacements. Judges may rule against you if your fees cannot be substantiated or are exorbitant.
- The security deposit should not be considered a landlord or property manager's source of income. It is not *your* money.
- Do not charge a tenant for replacing an item when it can be easily repaired.
- Always take into consideration the length of the tenant's occupancy. You may find it difficult to collect money for cleaning carpet and repainting walls if the tenant lived in the unit for a period longer than one year. This may be considered normal wear and tear and not something you can charge for.
- Do not charge for conditions that were seen and noted on the Move-In/Move-Out Inspection Report upon the tenant moving in.

Ordinarily you *can* charge for:

- Replacing ruined, stained, or torn carpet
- Replacing chipped tile
- Replacing broken blinds or drapes
- Fixing damaged furniture
- Pest control for flea infestation
- Patching holes in walls
- Replacing broken doorknobs
- Replacing torn or missing window screens

- Replacing broken window glass
- Cleaning for an excessively dirty kitchen or bathroom

You typically should *not* charge for:

- Any condition present at move in
- Replacement of an item that could be repaired

Areas of Common Disagreement

- *Painting of interior walls.* The rule of thumb is if someone has lived in a residence for *more* than one year, the need for new paint is normal wear and tear and should *not* be charged for. If they have lived there for less than one year, and the walls were newly painted upon their moving in, you can charge them for painting. Either way, you *can* charge for repairing walls.
- *Cleaning of carpets.* Again the rule of thumb is one year's occupancy. If the carpet was new upon move in, and is stained and torn within months, you can charge the tenant. This is more than normal wear and tear. If the carpet was already worn upon move in, you should not charge to clean it, even if it looks worse upon move out. This is considered normal wear and tear.
- *Fixtures.* Any furniture, fixtures, or equipment that a tenant attaches to the apartment become the property of the landlord. They cannot be removed by the tenant.

In addition, do not charge a tenant for cleaning if she has already paid a nonrefundable cleaning fee. You can't charge her twice. Also, be sure to charge fair prices for repairs and replacements. This will help you avoid disputes and bad publicity. Security deposits should not be counted on as an income source. Their purpose is to cover the cost of repairs.

EVICTION

The eviction process is one that must be followed precisely to ensure the rules work in your favor. All the attention you have paid to detail, by completing all forms such as the lease and notices properly and maintaining copies, will now pay off for you. I strongly recommend you build a relationship with a good eviction attorney. For a list of eviction attorneys in your area, visit our website.

The most common reason for eviction is nonpayment of rent. Other common reasons include:

- Continued, documented disturbances
- Illegal activity
- Illegal occupant (someone not on the lease living there)
- Illegal pet
- Severe damages
- Holdover tenant. A good lease will include language stating that any tenant who remains in your unit past the lease term, and to whom you have not offered a new lease, is a "holdover tenant" and can be evicted.

Most states require you to issue the proper notice to your tenant to address a problem situation before you evict them. This could be your notice to pay or quit, or your lease violation notice. Sometimes a tenant will move out within the time line outlined in your notice. Sometimes they will not. That is when you have to evict them. The only recourse for removing a tenant from your unit who will not voluntarily leave is eviction.

When you are ready to file an eviction follow these steps:

Step 1: Check the Names

Make a copy of the lease agreement, the application, and the notice to pay or quit three-day notice or other notice you issued. Double-check that the names on the notice match the names on the lease. This is very important.

Step 2: Send the Copies to Your Eviction Attorney

The attorney will prepare a complaint, which is a legal document outlining why the tenant is being evicted. The complaint will be filed with the clerk of court in the county your property is in. Once the complaint is filed with the clerk, the tenant will be served a copy of the notice by a process server. The tenant has two options at this point. She can either file a formal response to the complaint with the court or not. The complaint will give her a certain number of days, like twenty or thirty, to reply. If she does not respond, you win the eviction by default. A sheriff will notify the tenant she must move out and if she does not, the sheriff will physically remove her. You would think the tenant would go ahead and move out when notified by the sheriff to leave. But I promise you, the sheriff and I opened the door to a unit once to see if a tenant had moved out and he was on the sofa playing Playstation.

If a tenant responds to the complaint, the judge will review that response and either schedule a hearing or strike the response as not valid and approve the eviction. If you go to a hearing, your attorney will represent you, and the judge will hear both sides of the story and make a ruling.

DO-IT-YOURSELF EVICTIONS

At this point in the book, you probably know the motto I base my business on: "Maximize income, minimize expenses." Finding ways to minimize expenses is always key to me. However, I see a lot of landlords make what I believe is a crucial mistake when it comes to evicting. That mistake is to try to handle the eviction themselves rather than hiring an attorney. They go for the short-term cost cutter instead of the long-term minimizing of expenses. In doing so they also overlook the cost in time, our most extravagant expense.

When I have a tenant in my unit who isn't paying rent or is violating his lease severely enough to warrant eviction, I do not want to waste time trying to navigate the legal process myself. I am not an attorney, so I hire the expert to handle it for me. I have developed a great relationship with an eviction attorney I respect and trust. He can handle this process much faster than most landlords or other attorneys could on their own. I've evicted hundreds of tenants and I still use an attorney, each and every time. Remember, if you are the smartest person on your team, your team is in trouble!

When you hire an attorney, make sure you are hiring a landlord-tenant law attorney. I am a big believer in using attorneys. I don't like investing millions of dollars on anything with less than the best contracts and legal advice. But, remember, attorneys are like doctors. Each has an area of specialty and no one attorney can master all areas of law and keep up with the changes in all of them. You wouldn't go to a foot doctor for brain surgery. So make sure your eviction attorney is an eviction specialist!

Some tips to remember during the eviction process:

1. Remember *not* to accept any rent or monies from the tenant under eviction.
2. If the tenant calls you to ask about the eviction, respond by telling the tenant to please refer any questions to your attorney. This will protect you.
3. If you are evicting a tenant for breaking the rules, remember to document everything! This includes any conversations or actions taken by this tenant.

ABANDONMENT

Occasionally a tenant will just move out without telling you. We call this abandonment or a "skip out." This can be a delicate situation because sometimes it's not clear that the tenant has actually moved out, and they usually leave a lot of personal property behind. How do you determine if they really have moved out? What do you do with their property?

I had a tenant once who I thought had moved out. We didn't see him for over a week and his electricity was turned off, so we assumed he had left without telling us. I instructed my maintenance team to go in and throw out all the stuff he left behind so we could begin to clean the unit and market it for a new tenant. Well, the tenant announced that he was still living there and threatened to sue me. He claimed he was sleeping in a sleeping bag and came back only late at night because his electricity had been turned off and it was cooler after dark. He further claimed that an antique ring of his had been thrown out when his stuff was disposed of. Whether you believe that story or not, I had not followed proper procedure to protect myself from this kind of claim. And tenants will come up with some very creative ones!

Here is how I learned from this mistake to handle abandoned units properly. First, my lease has abandonment language to protect me from having to be responsible for a tenant's property:

BY SIGNING THIS RENTAL AGREEMENT YOU AGREE THAT UPON SURRENDER OR ABANDONMENT, AS DEFINED BY FLORIDA STATUTES, WE SHALL NOT BE LIABLE OR RESPONSIBLE FOR THE STORAGE OR DISPOSITION OF YOUR PERSONAL PROPERTY.

When I do think a unit is abandoned, I always call my eviction attorney now and run the situation by him for his advice. If he agrees it can be deemed abandoned, this language protects me from any claim from a tenant for their personal property left behind. In Florida, all I have to do is remove the property and place it at the nearest property line. What happens to it after that is not my responsibility. I've found that most states have similar provisions.

Timing is so critical in property management, especially at the end of a lease term. We want to know as soon as possible if a tenant decides not to renew their lease so we are prepared to market and release the unit. We need to have time to schedule vendors, like maintenance or carpet cleaners or painters. It's very frustrating to lose a prospective tenant who wants to rent from you because you can't get a vendor in to ready the unit. Timing is also critical in nonrenewals and evictions. Losing time when dealing with lease renewals, nonrenewals, and evictions literally means losing money. In the next chapter you will learn about a major key to timely releasing, and that is the timing of your maintenance and repairs.

With integrity you have nothing to fear, since you have nothing to hide.
With integrity you will do the right thing, so you will have no guilt.
With fear and guilt removed you are free to be and do your best.
—Zig Ziglar

MAINTENANCE— INSPECT WHAT YOU EXPECT

Tenant and Building Maintenance in the Long Term

The number one reason tenants renew leases is because of good maintenance. The number one reason they leave is poor maintenance responsiveness. Maintenance is also the number one area where you can lose control of your expenses on a property over the years. Considering these factors and their impact on your property's bottom line, you can see why I am devoting an entire chapter to maintenance.

A good maintenance technician or handyman is invaluable for good property management. In particular, a handyman with an understanding of property management is worth his weight in gold. The good ones don't just know how to fix things, they understand the delicate timing of getting things repaired so a tenant can move in, they know how to interact with tenants to make them feel their needs are being met even if there are maintenance delays, and they can provide you with key information on when things need to be replaced or when a repair will suffice. They can forecast for you when to expect large expenditures, like new roofing or A/C work. They also find good vendors, like plumbers and roofers, and interface with them to make sure they do quality work, don't overcharge, and stay on schedule. I don't have the expertise to interview a roofer and know if he is knowledgeable in his craft, but a good handyman will be able to make that assessment.

My business partner, William Cortese, was in the rental maintenance industry for decades. I met William on my very first property management job. I'd just decided on property management as a career and landed my first job. I was young, broke, and thrilled to have a free apartment to live in at the apartment complex I was working at. A few days after I moved in, William entered my unit to fix a leaky faucet I had reported. He noticed my lack of furniture and food, other than the fruit punch and wafer cookies I was living off of until I got my first paycheck and could buy some groceries. When I arrived home that evening, William had stocked my refrigerator with Tupperware containers of food and left an invitation to dinner at his house on the counter.

We worked together for over a decade in the multifamily business. William and I have worked on many rehabs, renovations, lease-ups, and property acquisitions. I am proud to have worked alongside William as partners in our business. Twenty years after we met, he was a trainer for The Landlord Academy. This isn't just how important I feel an excellent maintenance technician is—and William is the best I've worked with—but it's also a perfect example of putting a team together of like-minded individuals. People with the same values, goals, and dedication as myself. People who meet my criteria of the Seven Disciplines of Success I shared with you in chapter 1.

Since William is the master of his craft, he helped me write this chapter, offering his Keys for Excellent Maintenance, his method for conducting a walk-through on a property during due diligence, and some tips on preventive maintenance.

Keys for Excellent Maintenance
1. Organization
2. Attention to detail
3. Follow through
4. Communication with staff and residents

HANDLING REPAIRS

In your lease you will specify how a tenant should report a repair or emergency. Be prepared to receive these requests and check for them frequently. When a repair request is called in, always take down the information on a work order. This is an organized way to obtain the needed information to respond, as well as to file for future reference if needed. (See the sample work order on page 179.)

Work orders should be responded to within twenty-four hours. At the least, the resident should be contacted and given an estimated time when the repair will be made. Even if it is not an urgent repair, make your best effort to get it fixed promptly. Remember our statistic on maintenance being the number one influence on lease renewals.

Notice that on the bottom of the work order form there's a notification of entry. Always leave this for the tenant so they know an authorized person was in their unit and so they know the problem has been taken care of.

Make two copies of the work order. The first should be filed in the tenant's file. The second should be placed in a file that contains all work orders. This is for your maintenance technician to review periodically. It helps forecast preventive maintenance needs or larger repairs coming down the pipeline. A property often tells you through its work order file what it needs and what to expect to replace soon.

WORK ORDER (FORM 30)

Use this form to take down information when a tenant calls and needs a repair made.

Date & Time	11/17/15
Resident Name	Daniel Franklin
Address	99 Bonner Lane, Bend, Oregon

Type of Work to Be Performed
Leaky faucet in the master bathroom

Tools Needed to Complete Work
Wrench, washer

Maintenance Tech or Contractor's Name or Company Name
Top-Flight Plumbing, Reggie Barden

Price of labor/parts	# of hours or parts	Total Cost
1 washer	1 hour	$100
	TOTAL COSTS	$100

Work Performed By:	Date
Reggie Barden	11-17-15

Notes:

Complete Section Below, Tear Off, and Leave in Unit

- -

NOTICE OF ENTRY TO RESIDENCE

Date: 11/17/15	Time Entered: 1:30 pm
Reason for Entering: Maintenance	Time Left: 2:30 pm
Work Completed By: Reggie Barden Top-Flight Plumbing	
Work Performed: Fixed a leaky faucet	
Notes:	

EMERGENCIES

Always have a phone number tenants can use for emergency maintenance needs. Trust me, you want to be contacted as soon as possible about something like a burst pipe. The sooner you can respond, and at least have the water turned off, the less damage you will have to clean up.

I also recommend you establish accounts with vendors you may need in an emergency, like a plumber or electrician, and at a Home Depot–type store. When something goes in the middle of the night and you have to call out for emergency repairs, you don't want to have to try to access large amounts of cash before work can begin. You want to be billed and have thirty days to arrange payment.

WHO PAYS FOR WHAT

I see many landlords pay for repairs that are not their responsibility. If a tenant breaks something intentionally or through carelessness or negligence, many times you can charge the tenant for the repair. If a tenant breaks a window or a toddler clogs the toilet by flushing his GI Joe down, it's not your responsibility to pay for it. Typically, the best course of action is to fix the problem to avoid tenant problems and further damage by letting something stay broken. Then invoice the tenant for the repair. If you wish, you can break the charge down over a few months.

With single-family rentals, many landlords state in their lease that the tenant is responsible for minor repairs under $50. This is common, but after all my years in the industry it makes me nervous when a landlord allows tenants to work on their own units. Many times they cause more problems than they fix. And sometimes those problems aren't discovered until later when the tenant may be long gone.

PREVENTIVE MAINTENANCE

Taking a proactive approach to preventive maintenance will save you a lot of money and time in the long run. It will also play a big part in keeping your tenants happy and increasing your tenant retention.

Preventive maintenance consists of two parts. The first is setting up a schedule to replace certain items in your rental units to prevent them from wearing out and causing major (expensive) damage.

The second part of preventive maintenance is to schedule routine checks of certain appliances and items to be sure they are not wearing out. Often if you catch something early the repair is much smaller, such as simply replacing a hose. Also, if an appliance or plumbing is leaking, a prompt repair will help to prevent water damage to walls, floors, and carpets.

We have provided a Preventive Maintenance Checklist on page 278 of the Appendix. We recommend you complete this checklist at least twice a year, once in the spring and once in the fall.

As you conduct your maintenance checks, keep track of the life expectancy and warranty dates of each of your appliances and fixtures. This will help you budget for replacements. Create a "Reserve for Replacement Budget," setting aside money for replacing items as they wear out or for emergency repairs.

READYING A UNIT FOR TENANTS

Your focus at this point is to fix up, paint, and clean a vacant unit so you can lease it to a new tenant. You want to dress up the unit and make it attractive so that a good prospect will want to rent it from you and at the price you are requesting.

Keep in mind that time is of the essence. You want to rent your unit as soon as possible!

Start by removing any items left in the unit by the last tenant. No new tenant wants to be reminded someone else lived there. They want to feel as if this is their home. Be sure to check top shelves and closets.

Next, clean and dust everything! Leave no stone unturned. Here's a checklist:

- Clean all appliances
- Clean cabinets, inside and outside
- Remove all nonadhesive shelf paper
- Clean the showers and bathtubs
- Clean all sinks
- Clean toilets
- Clean medicine cabinet, inside and out
- Clean mirrors
- Dust miniblinds
- Change A/C filter
- Change locks

Finally, clean the carpets and touch up paint if necessary. For a comprehensive "Make Ready Checklist," visit the Members Section on our website at **landlordacademy.com**.

KEY CONTROL

It is the property manager's or landlord's responsibility to maintain strict key control, and all office personnel and tenants must strictly adhere to the rules of key control. The use of master keys is usually *not* a good practice.

1. Keys should be stored in a key cabinet that stays locked at all times. Only the property manager or landlord should have the key to the key cabinet, and only the landlord or property manager should release the key to an employee.
2. Code all keys with a random code system. Do not make reference to a building or residence. Store the key code away from the key cabinet.
3. Place two keys in the key cabinet for each apartment unit or residence. At move in, one key per adult should be issued. Tenants may be charged for extra keys.
4. Make sure all keys are returned at move out. The total number of keys should be documented on the Notice to Impose Claim on Security Deposit if you are charging for not returning keys.
5. Any time a key is issued to a tenant, vendor, or staff, it should be noted in a key control log located in the general area of the key cabinet. Do not allow the vendor, tenant, or employee to keep the key overnight. All keys must be brought back by the end of the business day. The log should contain the following information as follows:
   For each entry:

   - Date key was borrowed
   - Name of individual checking out the key
   - Time the key was issued
   - Time the key was returned

WILL'S MAINTENANCE TIPS

Below I have explained some common problems that may occur in your home or rental unit. If you are unsure of how to troubleshoot or repair these items, please call your local home improvement store and see if they have a maintenance service that will come to your property and repair the problem. Or you can visit our website at **landlordacademy.com** and visit "Will's Tips" for more detailed information on how to address these common maintenance issues.

1. To sharpen blades on your garbage disposal use ice cubes or crushed ice. Put about two cups of ice into the disposal and turn it on. This will sharpen the blades.

2. If your garbage disposal starts to smell, pour half a cup of lemon juice directly into the disposal. Cover the opening and turn on the disposal. This will help eliminate odor.

3. Change your air conditioner's air filter monthly to ensure proper operation. Do not pile items in the A/C closet or against the return vent. This will affect the cooling performance of your A/C. If there are shrubs around the outside unit they need to be kept at least two feet away from the condensing unit to ensure proper operation.

4. To keep your house cooler and conserve energy keep all blinds closed while you are away from your unit. Keep your A/C set to 78 degrees. You will arrive home to a manageable temperature and it will be easier to achieve a lower temperature. If you turn off your A/C to save money and keep all blinds open, your home can be as hot as 98 degrees when you arrive home. Trying to cool off your home quickly actually wastes more money than simply keeping your blinds closed and your thermostat set to 78 degrees while you are away.

5. At one time or another everyone has loaded the dishwasher only to discover they're out of dishwasher detergent. If you squirt a little dish soap into the dishwasher and a few minutes later come back into the kitchen to find a bubble factory, what should you do? Simply put two tablespoons of salt directly in the dishwasher and turn it back on. Away your bubbles will go down the drain.

APPLIANCE TROUBLESHOOTING QUESTIONS AND ANSWERS

Dishwasher

Q: Why does the motor hum when I turn on my dishwasher?
A: The motor is either stuck or bad. Here is how to determine the problem:
Remove the lower panel below the door. All you need is a Phillips head screwdriver or a quarter-inch nut driver. *Be sure the breaker is off!* Once the panels are removed you can see the motor. Run your hand up the side of the motor until you feel the impeller blades. Turn the blades with your fingers. When the motor frees itself it will feel like a rubber band snapped. The blades will spin freely. Now you can replace the panels and turn on the breaker. Your dishwasher should work. If the blades are really hard to turn, you can either replace the motor for approximately $80 to $100 or replace the whole dishwasher for $180 to $250, depending on make and model.

Q: There isn't any water going to the dishwasher. Why?
A: Check the shut-off valve under the kitchen sink. Check the water supply line for kinks or damage. If you do not see any obvious kink or damage, call a maintenance professional.

Q: The dishwasher won't drain. What do I do?

A: Check to see if the garbage disposal has been replaced recently. Many dishwasher drain lines hook right up to the disposal. If it was replaced and the plug wasn't knocked out, the dishwasher won't drain. Also, the valve or motor actuator arm or pump may not be working properly.

Water Heater

Q: My hot water lasts only five minutes when I shower. Why?

A: There are many things to check:

1. A forty-gallon tall boy has two panels—upper and lower. Behind these panels are a thermostat and an element. The upper thermostat has a reset button on it. If you push it in, and it clicks, you will have hot water in about thirty minutes.

   This happens for three reasons:
   a. The thermostat may be defective.
   b. If the water temperature setting is too high it will trigger a safety default and stop heating water altogether. Turn down the setting.
   c. The element may be bad.

2. Check your temperature setting. All brand-new water heaters are set on something called a "Vacation Setting," which is anywhere from 100 to 110 degrees and will cause your hot water to run out.

3. There are only four things that go bad on a water heater:
   a. Upper thermostat
   b. Upper element
   c. Lower thermostat
   d. Lower element

Electric Stove

Q: I turn on my surface burner and there is no heat to the element. Why?

A: There are three things to check for:

1. If there are any cracks or breaks on the element it will not heat properly.
2. The switch could be bad.
3. The plug for the element is bad.

Q: When I try to use the oven it doesn't heat. Why?

A: Same possible problems as stated above.

Gas Stoves

Q: I turn on my stove and the burner doesn't ignite. Why?

A: Turn the burner off. Check the pilot light. If it's out, relight. Then turn the stove on again. If it still doesn't work, check to make sure it is plugged into an electrical outlet so your igniter can function. (Note: Modern gas stoves have igniters that require electricity.)

Refrigerator

Q: The freezer is cold but the food compartment isn't. Why?

A: The drain line in the back of the freezer may be clogged, blocking the air vent into the fresh food compartment. This could mean the element for the defrost cycle is not working.

Q: Nothing in the refrigerator is cold. Why?

A:
1. The evaporator fan motor is not running.
2. The breaker is tripped.
3. The Freon level is low.
4. The compressor is bad.
5. The defrost timer is defective.

Central Heat and Air

Q: What does it mean when there is ice on the outside copper lines and the A/C is blowing warm air?

A: The ice on the lines could be there for a few different reasons.
1. The filter is extremely dirty! Whenever the A/C turns on, it pulls air across coils. If the filter is dirty, it gets sucked up and blocks the airflow across the evaporator coil. When there is no airflow across the coils they will freeze up.
2. There could be too much Freon in the unit.
3. There may not be enough Freon in the unit.

Q: I turn on the A/C and it blows out warm air. Why?

A: Again, there are a few things to look for:
1. The outside unit may not be running.
2. It may be very low on Freon—or there may be a leak.
3. There may be too much Freon—possible overcharge.

Q: How do I unclog the condensate line?

A: There are a few ways to do this:
1. Outside behind the condenser unit there is usually a white three-quarter-inch

pipe coming out of the ground or the wall. You can use a wet-vac by putting the hose on that pipe. Turn on the wet-vac and extract the blockage.

2. You can use a nitrogen tank and blow it from the inside, providing you have enough space. Simply insert a hose from the nitrogen tank into the drainage hole and blow out the line using the pressure in the tank. *Do not do this from the outside. It will make a horrible mess inside!*

3. As a preventive maintenance tip, buy some "sludge tabs" for about $18 for a bottle of 50 tablets, and put two of these in your A/C drainpipe. That will pretty much take care of your blockage problems and they will last about one month.

WORKING WITH VENDORS

If you don't feel qualified to handle your own maintenance, or you don't want to, be sure to hire someone who is skilled in the areas you need. Unless you know the person well and trust them, be careful of allowing them access to your supply accounts. Be sure to check receipts and invoices carefully. If you don't want to give people access to your accounts, you can have the handyman prepare a list of all needed materials and price them. (If they can't do this, beware of working with them. Any handyman worth anything should be able to think through all the materials needed for a job and price them out.) Purchase a supply store gift card with the total amount needed and let the handyman use this to purchase the items. This practice makes access to your accounts unnecessary and ensures no unauthorized items are purchased.

A vendor is a person or a company who is a separate business entity. That contractor usually performs a specific service or task and is hired to perform jobs that are outside your comfort zone. It's good practice to make sure the individual or company knows exactly what's expected of them. A carefully prepared job specification list is essential (see the Work Order, Form 30 on page 179). This helps you decide exactly what you want the contractor to do for you, because it requires you to be specific. It then helps you make this clear to the contractor, so there is no miscommunication over the details of what the job entails. It also forces you both to have a specific discussion about fees, and get it in writing. Lastly, it requires you and the contractor to agree on time lines. This lets you know what to realistically expect from them and lets the contractor know what you expect also.

A job specification checklist should include the following:

1. Detailed description of the work to be done, including preparation and application
2. Specific materials and equipment to be used
3. Location of the job
4. Time frame for completion
5. Licenses and permits needed

6. Insurance, warranties, guarantees—i.e., workers comp
7. Payment schedules
8. Cleanup required
9. List of references
10. OSHA requirements (Occupational and Safety Hazard Agency)

The Contract

Contracts are used to minimize risk to the property and its owners. The conditions for negotiating a contract and the people empowered to sign a contract are usually covered by company policy or the owner's policy. The scope of the project and the dollar amount may require that a company supervisor or owner sign a contract.

All contracts are subject to local, state, and federal laws. An attorney should review contracts before they are signed to ensure compliance and reduce risk.

A contract should contain:

1. The scope and nature of the work to be performed, outlining the detailed specifications
2. The starting and completion dates
3. A remedies and cancellation clause
4. A hold harmless clause
5. Proof of workers compensation and proof of comprehensive general liability insurance
6. Total cost of work
7. A payment schedule, outlining retainage fees

DUE DILIGENCE INSPECTION

In chapter 4 we discussed in depth the due diligence of a subject property. Here I will outline the top ten most important things to check when buying a house or apartments. I've included my full Subject Property Inspection Checklist (Form 6) on page 220 of the Appendix.

1. Roof: Check when the roof was last replaced or inspected.
2. Water lines throughout building: CPVC or copper are good. If the lines are gray polybutaline, you will encounter problems due to defects in the pipes. Make sure to replace or replumb the whole area.
3. Electrical lines: These should be copper. If they are aluminum, you could encounter problems. Aluminum expands and contracts with heat and cold, which will cause connections to be faulty.
4. Plumbing fixtures and pipes: Make sure to check these thoroughly by turning on and off all kitchen and bathroom taps. Check for leaks at the faucets. Also look

under the sinks to see if the P-trap is PVC or metal. The P-trap is the curved pipe connecting the sink to the wall. If it is metal it may be OK, but I suggest changing it to PVC. Check to see if shutoff valves work under the sinks and beside the toilet. Be sure to flush the toilet and make sure that sinks and tubs hold water.

5. Electrical switches, outlets, and major appliances: Turn all switches on and off to check for proper operation. Check the fridge, stove, dishwasher, and any other appliances for proper operation. Also be sure to turn heat on to check for proper operation.

6. Security: Make sure the key for each unit operates all locks within that unit, especially on dead-bolt and keyed entries. Check any sliding glass doors for proper operation. For added security you can install a "Charlie Bar." A Charlie Bar is a security bar you can add to a sliding glass door. Check that all windows lock properly.

7. Carpeting: A new carpet, if taken care of, should last seven to ten years. Make sure to check for odor, fleas, and pet stains (particularly urine). The carpet can be fogged for fleas and treated/cleaned for smell and stains. If pets were kept inside, check the corners and near doors for damage.

8. Vinyl flooring: Brand-new vinyl can last two to five years, depending on wear and tear. Check edges for corners rolling up. Check for purple or black discoloration near the tub or toilet. Stains indicate that water has gotten under the vinyl, which will need to be replaced. For tile, check for cracks and for proper grout lines.

9. Physical aspects such as drywall, baseboards, and moldings: Make sure there are no large holes in the drywall or brown spots that would indicate water leakage. Check for missing baseboards or crown molding. Also, make sure there are no black or green spots on drywall near water leaks—this could mean mold is growing in the walls.

10. Windows and doors: Check all miniblinds and vertical blinds for proper operation by opening and closing them. While checking blinds make sure to check windows in all rooms. Also, check doors for a proper seal. You don't want any large gaps around the door sides, top or bottom. Remember to check all cabinet doors and drawers for proper operation as well.

Maintenance will have a positive or negative impact on your bottom line. If you are not qualified to handle your own maintenance needs, or don't have the time or desire to, don't hesitate to find a great maintenance person. Look for someone who can be a key player on your team. No other person will have such an ability to impact your cash flow, positively or negatively, or represent you in interacting with tenants as your maintenance technician. The one person I never did a deal without was William. He was like my American Express card—I never left home without him.

> The guy who puts the ball through the hoop has ten hands.
> —John Wooden, UCLA Bruins Basketball Coach

PART IV

BUILDING WEALTH WITH REAL ESTATE

THE TECH-SAVVY INVESTOR

How Your Smartphone and a Few Apps Can Completely Transform Your Business

How would you like to accomplish all of your landlording administrative work in real time and be less consumed with your mountains of paperwork? How would you like to reduce your workload by 80 percent? And how about minimizing your endless trips back and forth to your office to handle tasks like email, picking up forms, or photocopying documents—all of which test your patience and drain your gas tank. Your smartphone can actually accomplish all of these tasks and more. In fact, if you have a smartphone, you already have the equivalent of your very own administrative team at your fingertips. I refer to my smartphone as the "Pocket Property Manager," and I cannot live without it.

But I get it. Many people are hesitant about or downright resistant to change. I was the same way at first. I sometimes just really want to hold the document in my hands as I'm searching for an answer, and I was always oddly reassured by the multiple file folders stacked high in the front passenger seat of my SUV as I traveled around town from property to property. But as my business grew and the demands on my time multiplied, even I had to get with the times—and now I don't know how I managed without my pocket property management systems.

Some of you (fewer every day, but some of you!) remember a time when cell phones didn't exist, when the only way to get in contact with someone when you weren't near your home phone was to stop at a pay phone and drop a quarter in. But mobile phones completely changed the equation. And the technologies I outline below can have the same revolutionary impact on your real estate investment business, whether it's a fledgling two-family home or a sprawling rental-property empire. Here are some of the apps and services I use most regularly and how they help me.

HelloSign (www.hellosign.com)—If you're a real estate investor, you're going to need to collect a lot of signatures. But getting signatures isn't always convenient, especially if you're moving toward a digital, paper-free business system. So how will you get signatures on everything from background check authorizations, to leases, to contracts with third-party vendors if all of the forms are stored on your smartphone? HelloSign makes it easy to secure legally binding e-signatures. Other benefits include the ability to easily request a signature from up to twenty people at a time and automatically receive a copy of the document in your inbox once it's fully executed. And to keep all information secure, HelloSign promises that documents are fully encrypted when they're being sent from one party to another.

Box (www.box.com)—As my business grew, I struggled with lugging around my file cabinet and the individual files on the properties I own or am managing. But it's a universal problem, no matter what the size of your business. Let's face it, nothing is more frustrating when you realize the document you need is back at your office . . . thirty minutes away. With Box, your entire file cabinet is in your smartphone, or your tablet or laptop, or any other connected device. Easy access to every document, from signed leases to photocopied IDs, is as simple as pressing "save."

CamScanner (www.camscanner.com)—If you don't want to carry a bulky file cabinet with you everywhere you go, I know there's no way you want to carry a scanner or a copy machine either. But that doesn't change the fact that you will often need to capture images of documents in your day-to-day business and sometimes send them to other people. CamScanner allows you to scan or take a picture of any document, turn the file into a PDF, and send it electronically to your contacts—as well as to the file cabinet in your smartphone. This includes important notices like rent checks and lease contracts, eviction notices, and any and all letters between owner and tenant. No photocopying necessary, no postage needed, and the tenant receives the document in real time while it's also being saved in the cloud.

Microsoft Office Suite (www.office.com)—Well-known software like Microsoft Word, Excel, and PowerPoint are all available as apps on your smartphone, giving you the same access to these programs that you rely on when you're at your desktop or laptop computer. With the Microsoft Office app on your smartphone, you can work on your documents, as well as send them to recipients, while you're on the go. These apps give you a virtual office in your pocket.

Ruby Receptionist (www.callruby.com)—If there is one app I absolutely can't live without, it's Ruby Receptionist. It has completely changed the way I do business, because instead of spending my days answering phone calls from current and prospective tenants, I can have all calls transferred to Ruby Receptionist and trust they will be handled in a polite, professional manner when I am busy or out checking on properties. Their mission is to "preserve and perpetuate real, meaningful connections in an increasingly technology-focused, virtual world," and the best part is that you don't have to pay for the health insurance or 401(k) of a traditional receptionist.

Bench (https://bench.co)—When you own a business, accounting services can quickly become one of your biggest expenses, but it's a necessary evil, so unless you're a CPA on the side, you're going to need someone to help you with your books. Bench is an online bookkeeping service offering different packages so you can buy only the services you need, including monthly financial statements, year-end financials, and more.

With all of the new and always-changing technology, I would like to address those concerned about security and the legality of the information you are uploading and emailing, especially financial documents and time-sensitive documents regarding eviction. When it comes to security, you first have to be smart and protective of your smartphone to make sure it is in your safekeeping at all times. Additionally, with the personal, classified information in your documents, you do have the option of encrypting these documents on your device. There's an app called the Vault (thevault-app.com) that is available on both iPhones and Androids, and it allows you to store and encrypt any data, including credit card and Social Security numbers. As of this writing, I believe it is probably the best app on the market for keeping documents secure, but as fast as technology is changing, I would encourage you to research additional security apps when the time comes for you to launch your real estate investment business and begin handling secure documents. As for the legality of the electronic signatures and anyone who questions the validity of them, the federal Electronic Signatures in Global and National Commerce Act (ESIGN) was signed into law in 2000 by the U.S. Congress. The ESIGN Act facilitates the use of electronic records and electronic signatures in interstate and foreign commerce, ensuring the validity and legal effect of contracts entered into electronically.

How much is your time worth?

As an investor, you need to ask yourself, "How much is my time worth?" Then ask yourself if your time is better spent doing a task on your own or paying a specialized service to do it for you. Be very honest with yourself. Are you horrible on the phone? Are you great at managing your books? Did you invest in rental properties to spend all of your time doing all of this work?

If you could free up ten to twenty hours per month by making an investment in your business versus looking at it as an expense, how much more productive could you be as an entrepreneur? What kind of return on investment would you place on yourself to grow your business?

Aside from making life easier, many of these services also have the potential to save you a lot of money. With that in mind, I've put together a library of resources for investors online at www.landlordacademy.com/resources. I encourage you to visit our website and sign up for all of the free services, and keep in mind that we've also partnered with many of the services to offer special discounts for our readers. Make sure to sign up for our newsletter as well at **www.landlordacademy.com** for updates on new technology you can use to grow and manage your real estate portfolio.

It is my sincere hope that you will come to understand (like I did!) how technology will allow you to grow your real estate business, while at the same time reducing your workload and eliminating the need for you to hire additional staff to manage your business and your rental properties. This kind of technology was just being introduced into the mainstream real estate space when I first published this book back in 2009. I cannot imagine where technology and smartphones will be in a few more years, but I will gladly embrace whatever the world of technology brings. And if you have any success stories or recommendations with smartphone apps you use, we would love to know about them.

HOW DO I PROTECT MYSELF?

A Legal Perspective

Note to reader: This chapter is written by my trusted attorney, Steve Riley. Steve has been on both sides of the process—as a lawyer for hundreds of deals (including several of my own) and as a landlord and investor himself.

—Bryan M. Chavis

Yes, I am an attorney. I practice law in Florida, but I became a lawyer as a way to get into business. I love real estate, and I imagine that this love affair will be lifelong. When I scraped together my pennies to do my first real estate deal, I bought a duplex. My wife and I lived on one side as I rehabbed it myself and rented out the other. From there I did seventeen single-family home rehabs. Some were rentals, some were flipped to other investors, and some resold on installment sales where I held the mortgage. From single-family homes, I moved on to a commercial office building, a self-storage center, and a multifamily apartment complex. After working as an investor, I started a development company with a partner. We have developed retail centers, strip centers, office buildings, and a small shopping plaza.

In addition to being a real estate entrepreneur, I represent people from one extreme to the other in the real estate world. One client may just be getting started with her first deal, and another may be a very successful mega-wealthy investor in a complex negotiation across the table from a $2 billion company.

So the question is: From what perspective shall I share my experience? With Bryan's permission, I will try to use both perspectives to share what I can. I hope that you find it of value. First, I'd like to share some key strategies to help improve your chances of success in the real estate business.

STRATEGY #1: THERE IS NO "STANDARD AGREEMENT"

Whenever I'm conducting a real estate transaction and someone says they will send me "a standard agreement," I cringe. I cringe because that term has conditioned me to react painfully. It can mean multiple things.

It could be "sneaky speak" for, "Please do not read this, I have hidden something in here that really may hurt you." Or it could be a form the person has used so many times that it appears standard to them—but not necessarily standard to anyone else. It could also be a red flag, meaning that the lender will not change the loan document or negotiate with you, no matter what. It could possibly be a Realtor telling you to sign a standard agreement to "speed up the process" of getting a deal done.

As I look back, some of my biggest frustrations legally have been over so-called standard agreements that my clients signed without having them reviewed. Thus, your first strategy should be to expand your thinking and realize that there is no such thing as a standard agreement. A "standard agreement" is designed to simplify someone else's life, usually not yours. In many cases the "standard agreement" is a great way of putting a legal fast one over on a naive real estate investor. Just a reminder, the term "standard" does not mean acceptable. It means easy and beneficial for the other guy. When I hear "standard agreement," I make sure to read it carefully and think it through.

STRATEGY #2: UNDERSTAND YOUR CONTRACT PROCESS

Now I am going to completely contradict myself. (It's OK, don't panic; I'm a lawyer and this is part of what I do.) Note that in strategy one, I said to be aware of the other party's "standard agreement." But I am going to encourage you to think through, systematize, and, where possible, "standardize" your processes and agreements. If you are going to be in the business of real estate, you want to think through—or better yet, create—your negotiation and contract process. The more routine it becomes, the less complex and painful the process will be for you. You get to create your own "standard agreement."

Do you need an LOI (letter of intent) on every deal? No. My experience, though, is that it helps to think through the framework of the deal before the parties start to have a battle of contracts. The LOI usually sets the tone, addresses key issues, and controls the contractual process. In fact, in certain complex deals I will use an LOI as a framework to make sure I have thought through every issue to discuss. I may not share the LOI, but I use it to help me think through major deal points before I start drafting a contract. Bryan has already shared the major components of an LOI in chapters 5 and 7.

From the LOI phase, the party usually goes to the formal agreement. As I have said, there is no such thing as a standard agreement. However, in many states there is an agreed upon industry standard agreement between the Realtors Association and the Bar Association. These are great starting points because everyone—the Realtors, lawyers, and lenders—knows the agreement. While these agreements are consistently utilized in the residential marketplace, in the commercial marketplace we do not see them used at all. In twenty years, I have not seen any "standard commercial real estate agreement" used in a routine manner.

So what does this mean to you as a real estate investor? You want to understand or create your own process so you won't be caught up in someone else's process. I suggest that you create your own "form bank." This is something lawyers have done commonly for years. When we find contracts that we like we keep them as a resource to look back and learn from. You can also create a "clause bank." The clause bank is basically key language for certain provisions you would like to put in your contracts. Some of my favorites are inspection provisions, financing contingencies, and the post-closing inspection provisions. These are important provisions to understand and utilize for your benefit in any real estate transaction.

Pay attention as you go through your real estate career and accumulate contractual wisdom. If you see a contract you like, capture it. If there is a provision in a contract that you think is great, capture it. My experience is that the more you read, learn, and accumulate these provisions, the more you understand some of the contractual aspects of deal making. You will learn how to make these provisions work to your advantage and protect you from harm.

STRATEGY #3: KNOW YOUR LEGAL ENTITIES

Every real estate investor should have at least a working knowledge of the different types of legal entities out there available for use. I am a big fan of land trusts, limited liability companies (LLCs), and various forms of trusts. In brief, please allow me to explain some basics. Generally, there are four types of business entities to choose from.

1. **Sole Proprietor:** The first and most simple type is the sole proprietorship. This is *not* a corporation or an LLC. In this case you hold your individual self out as a business. There are very few advantages to doing business this way and several big disadvantages. You are 100 percent personally liable for the debts of the business. Also, some of the tax benefits you are looking for may not be available in this particular way of doing business.

2. **Partnership:** The second type of business is the general partnership agreement. When you have a partnership, two or more people have agreed to work in business together. Although there are certain tax benefits to a partnership, the downside is that each partner is liable for the debt of the other partner. So, for example, if your partner gets sued, you are automatically responsible for your partner's debt in most general partnerships.

3. **Corporation:** The third type, the corporation, is a popular type of legal entity due to its flexibility. It basically provides the ability to protect your personal assets from claims against the business. You can elect two different types of tax structure for the business, subchapter S or C corp.

4. **Limited Liability Corporation (LLC):** The fourth type of legal entity is a limited li-

ability company, commonly referred to as an LLC. This is probably the most popular legal entity used to do business because it offers maximum creditor protection and maximum tax flexibility. The LLC provides protection from claims of creditors of the business. However, the LLC has some additional special protections that when used effectively can make it preferable over a regular corporation. First, if there are investors other than you in the LLC, most state laws provide that they are protected from any claims related to the LLC. This provides greater confidence to the investor. Investors know that the only risk they will have is the actual capital they invested. Second, the LLC provides that if a creditor tries to take ownership of an LLC, that creditor cannot seize the ownership. The creditor can receive only a "charging order." This protection makes the LLC preferable to a regular corporation in any situation where there is more than one owner. Please note that in our opinion, if you have a single-owner LLC or a single-owner corporation, the protection is approximately the same. When a business has more than one owner, we believe an LLC offers superior protection strategy. The LLC is also the most flexible from a tax perspective. You generally have four ways to tax it as opposed to the two ways to tax a regular corporation.

i. As a sub-S you elect to treat your business as a small business under the tax code. All profits and losses are directly passed through to the owner. This is sometimes called "pass through" taxation.

ii. As a C corporation your business will be taxed twice: once on the income it earns, then again when the business makes distributions to its owners. This is often called "double taxation." There are two main benefits to a C corporation. First, the ability to accumulate capital inside of it. This is called retained earnings, and it is capital that the business may use for acquisitions or investment. Second, the C corporation has the ability to take greater tax deductions. Most large businesses are taxed as a C corporation.

iii. As a partnership tax status you are taxed on a "pass through" basis as well. Companies taxed as partnerships have quite a few flexible and advantageous tax benefits in the right situation.

iv. A disregarded entity is ignored for tax purposes. If the owners tell the IRS to ignore the business and just tax the owners as if the business was not there, it's "disregarded."

A corporation can be taxed either as a sub-S or a C corp. The LLC may be taxed as a sub-S, C corp, partnership, or disregarded entity. These enhanced protection benefits and greater tax flexibility make the LLC the entity of choice for most investors.

Tax Strategy

Understanding how your entities will be taxed is critical. One of the more powerful advantages of owning real estate can be tax benefits. Most mistakes I see by investors are the result of not understanding the tax ramifications of their legal entities. To cut costs, many go online and decide for themselves how their corporate entity should be taxed without realizing the potential negative consequence or lost opportunity for tax savings. My recommendation is that you have a clear tax strategy for each investment. Will this property make you money or lose you money? What is the depreciation? Is it accelerated or standard? How will this investment impact your personal income? All these issues are important to discuss with your CPA or lawyer before you pull the trigger on how you want to have your entity taxed.

STRATEGY #4: CREATE AND USE A "MANAGEMENT LLC"

One of the things I recommend that you do as an investor is create a brand name around a management LLC. When I use the term "management LLC," I usually mean an LLC taxed as a sub-S corporation. This will not be an entity you own property in. It's a "storefront" that you can do business through. It may own some office furniture and a laptop computer, and it may or may not be licensed as a real estate sales entity, but ultimately it is the name that you hand out on your business card. You use it to make offers for contracts, and to buy office supplies. But you do not use it to own real estate.

What do I mean by that? One of the big mistakes I see investors make is to pile all of the real estate assets they own into one corporate basket. So if there is one lawsuit against that corporation, all of their investment assets are impacted and at risk. Our recommendation is that although you may have a brand name under a corporation entity, you actually will end up owning separate properties under separate corporation entities. This limits the liability of each property but allows you one "brand" to operate under.

STRATEGY #5: PUT ALL AGREEMENTS IN WRITING

One mistake I see investors make on a very consistent basis is reach a verbal agreement, but put nothing in writing. Now, my thinking is simple. If you take the time to come to an agreement, take the time to capture that agreement in writing. There have been so many problems that could have been resolved on the front end through a written agreement that come back and haunt the parties because nobody wanted to take the time or spend the money to put it together in writing.

I don't care if the agreement is with a family member; I don't care if it is your best friend; I don't care if it is "simple." Put it in writing! There have been so many times that I have had someone come in and say, "Well, we agreed to do this, but they are not doing their end of the bargain." I ask, "Let's see your copy of this agreement." The response is, "We didn't put it in writing, we just shook hands on it." If it is worthy enough to shake hands on, it is worthy enough to put on paper.

As a side note, it is also helpful to remember that agreements can be modified. They can be amended and changed as life goes on. Agreements are designed to adjust, they are typically not going to be set in stone.

STRATEGY #6: FIND A GOOD CPA

A CPA is a critical component of your team. You want to make sure that you find one who is orientated toward helping you think through strategic issues, and not just someone who files your 1040 tax return. There are quite a few CPAs out there who are doing "tax planning by word processing" and really provide no "strategic tax advice" to their customers. The number one request I get from my law clients is for an introduction to a CPA who can think strategically. Find someone who can give some advice, wisdom, and counsel.

PROTECT YOURSELF

Here are some of the legal strategies I've helped Bryan and other investors in his investment company, Apartment Investment Advisors, LLC, with. You may want to consider working with an attorney to utilize these in your own protection plan.

Protection strategies are critical, but generally not for the reason you are probably guessing. Yes, it is important to protect what you own and isolate it from the risk creditors. In my experience, one of the most important benefits of examining protection strategies is the massive leap in confidence that I have seen our clients enjoy. Once you are clear about what is protected and taken off the board, so to speak, your confidence will soar. You won't stay awake at night worrying about what happens if this occurs or that occurs.

When you know what assets are at risk and, more important, what is not at risk, you will be more confident about acting and moving forward against the obstacles in your life. This level of confidence cannot be priced. People who are in crisis, or believe they will be faced with a crisis, will not act. They remain frozen until their confidence level is increased or the threat is removed. They will feel they are being backed into a corner and they will not be on the offense. They will be either frozen, or moving backward, running from the obstacles.

It reminds me of the famous quote by General George Patton: "The best defense is a good offense." Sometimes the best thing to do when you feel you are against the wall is to take massive action. But in my experience, no one will do this until they are clear about what is protected.

Consequently, I have outlined four confidence boosters to help you increase your confidence so you can act in the face of fear. I could probably list one hundred strategies, but I've limited it to four.

Confidence Booster One: Protect Your Home

Your home can be your castle, and depending on your state law you may have a moat around it! In many states, the family home, sometimes called a homestead, can be protected from creditors. Different states have different statutory protection for homesteads. What is protected depends on your state law.

For example, if you are a Florida resident, one of your most powerful protections is the protection of your homestead. Your home is clearly your castle and is treated that way by the legislature, the Florida Constitution, and the courts.

If you are in any way, shape, or form concerned about protecting any asset, whether it is equity or cash, the best source of protection in Florida is your home. You can take cash and pay down your home as a way to protect the cash.

Florida, unlike some other states such as New York and California, does not limit the amount of value you can protect. The state limits only the physical land size of the homestead. If you are inside a municipality, you can protect up to half an acre; if you are outside the municipality, you can protect up to 160 acres. Now, I may be oversimplifying this, but in my experienced understanding, how your home is protected is critical, from both a financial and emotional perspective.

There are three common mistakes I see real estate entrepreneurs make with their homes when they are in financial trouble.

The first is to mortgage their home to the hilt. To my mind, you want to mortgage every other asset with the exception of the home. I have worked with many investors who have a first, second, and even a third mortgage against their home. Consequently, they have no equity in their home; however, they have left equity in nonprotected assets because they apparently had confidence that they would be able to pay all the three mortgages on the home. This is a critical mistake. It will not only increase your own anxiety, but it will also increase your spouse's. And when you are under stress, having your spouse stressed-out about the possibility of losing your home will only compound stress everywhere.

Ideally, I would like to keep my client's home free of any type of mortgage. However, I realize that is just an ideal. In some situations, especially among developers and real estate investors, having some form of ability to collateralize a home for financing is critical. In this case, my recommended strategy is simple: a home equity line of credit (HELOC). The HELOC is a wonderful tool. First, most banks provide them without complication. Generally, the costs are nominal. Second, it is there when you need it. Most banks will allow you to keep your HELOC without any time limit. The third reason—my favorite and I think the most unrecognized—is that the HELOC is better financially. I would rather pay a higher simple interest on my HELOC than a lower compounded interest on my mortgage. If you run the numbers on this issue, you'll find that the HELOC wins 90 percent of the time.

Confidence Booster Two: Protect Your Cash

Now this may sound very obvious, but many people do not know how to protect their cash. It is one thing to have a cash reserve, but it is another thing to protect and isolate it from creditors. In Florida, there is no state exemption or protection for cash accounts. In fact, I don't believe there are any exemptions in the country for protection of cash accounts. A creditor can always attach your cash accounts and seize them. For example, if you have cash sitting in a money market account, a creditor can take it from you. There are multiple ways for businesses, as well as individuals, to isolate and protect cash. I have several suggestions for individuals:

Life Insurance

In most states, if not all, life insurance is exempt from claims of creditors. If this is true in your state, use it. Buy life insurance, or utilize life insurance as a protective strategy. Certain types of life insurance have an investment component that allows you to put cash in where it is protected, then pull cash out if you need it. While not all policies are conducive to this strategy, some policies work very, very well. Unfortunately, due to the length constraints of this chapter, we cannot spend a tremendous amount of time on this topic. But keep in mind that life insurance is valuable not only for its death benefits and liquidity for your family, but it can be a great place to park cash, moving it in and out as needed.

Tenants by the Entirety

Another common way for an entrepreneur to protect cash is to put it in what is called a tenants by the entirety account (TBE). Florida allows you to own any type of asset with your spouse as tenants by the entirety. Unlike joint tenancy with the rights of survivorship (JTWROS), tenants by the entireties makes the asset exempt from the creditor claims of one spouse. However, please note that it does not protect you from claims on both spouses. For example, if both spouses are guarantors on a loan, and the loan goes into default, tenants by the entireties will not protect both spouses. If just one spouse is a guarantor, then it will protect both. TBE is offered in many states other than Florida.

Confidence Booster Three: Protect Your Family

This is critical. People often put this low on their priority list because of the perceived cost of doing this type of planning. However, this is a mistake. You should by all means have an estate plan created or, if you have one, review it and bring it up to speed. It will increase your confidence as well as that of your family to know that if anything happens to you, they are protected. This area of the law, like many other areas of the law, is constantly changing.

Our number one recommendation to all of our entrepreneurial clients, in real estate or any other type of business, is to use a revocable living trust as the centerpiece for their plan. The living trust can provide privacy, protection, tax savings, and keep your family out of court. In my experience, only one out of ten trusts is utilized properly. Once again for more information, feel free to visit my website, thestrategiccounsel.net to download information on trusts.

Confidence Booster Four: Protect Your Business

In this wonderful day of creating your own entity (LLC or corporation) over the Internet, many business owners are able to avoid that horrible person called a lawyer. The experience of dealing with a lawyer can be traumatic, and financially painful. In my experience in hiring and using lawyers and working with lawyers, both as a developer investor and entrepreneur, I can say, "I feel your pain." However, most corporations and limited liability companies are playing "legal dress up." By that I mean that the corporate formalities, for both the corporations and limited liability companies, are not being followed. Why is this important? Because if you don't follow the corporate formalities, you can have your corporate entity disregarded for protection purposes. The corporation provides protection and tax benefits, but if you do not follow your state's annual requirements for corporate maintenance, a judge may allow a creditor to disregard the protection benefits of your corporation, and go through it and take your personal assets.

These are just a few strategies to structure and protect your real estate investments. Find an attorney who will take time to understand your goals, your current situation, and your exit plan to find the best strategies and legal tools for you. Have your plan routinely reviewed and updated. As your wealth grows, so should your planning. And don't forget that laws that can impact your plan are constantly changing. Always protect what it took you a lifetime to build.

> If money is your hope for independence,
> you will never have it. The only real security that a man
> can have in this world is a reserve of knowledge,
> experience and ability.
> —HENRY FORD

FIFTEEN

HOW DO I GROW?

Building Your Real Estate Empire

I hope that after reading this book you are excited about your future as a real estate investor and confident about your ability to achieve your dreams.

I know many of you may just be beginning your journey. You may have dreams of being a mega real estate investor. Some of you may already have successful careers you enjoy, and for you real estate is an investment vehicle, not a career. Many of you, like many of my students, may be working a day job and working hard to create a real estate empire so you can escape the corporate rat race. You dream of working for yourself, creating your own destiny, and having financial freedom to live the life of your dreams. Wherever you are in your journey, and however big or small your investment goals are, let me share some final keys to help you get to your destination.

AN ENTREPRENEURIAL LIFE

Whether you know it or not, by reading this book you just opened the door to a whole new world. This is the world of being an entrepreneur. You may not have meant to, and you may not have realized it yet, but you have planted a seed within your soul. That is the seed of determining your own destiny, and once it takes hold, you will never, ever be the same. Even if you procrastinate on your real estate goals, something deep inside you will nag at you to move forward and pursue your dreams.

When we speak of being an entrepreneur, being your own boss, making your own way, I can think of no better world to do so than in real estate. What other career does not require a college education or a huge capital investment?

More and more Americans are turning their backs on big business and throwing their hats into the entrepreneurial arena. As a successful entrepreneur myself, I can think of no better industry than real estate to begin creating for oneself that feeling of independence, control, passion, and financial freedom that owning rental property offers. There is no barrier to entry, no age requirement. Your personal background, race, color, religion, income level, and skill set are irrelevant. All may enter, if they choose to become the masters of their own destiny.

Years ago, in the 1960s and 1970s, people were encouraged to seek corporate jobs. Big companies represented long-term security, benefits, and a pension. Today, with corporate scandals and massive layoffs more and more commonplace, people are finding security in starting their own businesses. In chapter 1 we discussed the appeal of control in real estate investing versus the lack of control in the stock market. People are choosing to pursue their own careers rather than be at the mercy of corporate America. According to *Forbes*, 543,000 new businesses are created each month in the United States, and 52 percent of all small businesses are home-based. This makes starting your own business more popular than having a baby.

If you are reading this, chances are that you like the idea of being an entrepreneur and have chosen to enter this new world. I have shared with you in this book my experiences, successes and failures, my tips systems, checklists, and forms that have guided me to this point in my journey. My commitment to you in this book was to lay the foundation for you to create a dynamic business. And I applaud your commitment to begin your own journey to success.

THREE KEYS TO LONG-TERM GROWTH

Whether your dream is to own a multimillion-dollar real estate portfolio, or just to wisely invest your retirement funds, let me share with you three keys to long-term growth. These are the keys that allowed me to grow from a startup business with $100 in the bank to where I am today.

Treat Your Investing Like the Business It Is

First, recognize that your investing is a business. Even if you have a full-time career and investing is secondary to you, it's still a business. You are dealing with large amounts of money and, just as important, you have the responsibility of providing quality homes to your tenants. You aren't just dealing with dollars; you are dealing with people's lives. Each day I feel honored to have the ability to positively impact the lives of others, by treating them well and providing them with homes.

So if your investing is a business, treat it like one. Create a business plan, set goals, and work toward them continually and diligently. Even small steps move you forward. This is more, not less, important if you are doing this as a side business, because you have less time and energy to focus on it. You need clear, simplified goals to tackle. You don't have extra time to waste on things that will not help you achieve your goals.

Key elements of your business plan will be:

- Executive summary
- Business description
- Market strategies
- Competitive analysis
- Design and development plan
- Operations and management plans
- Financial components

From your plan, set goals and review them weekly.

> Nothing is particularly hard if you divide it into small jobs.
> —Henry Ford

Implement Systems

The second key is to implement systems. Remember the franchise approach we've talked about throughout this book? Since your time is precious, systems are key to your success. Even if you are the only one working in your business right now, develop an operations manual of your procedures. Write down step-by-step systems for each task you do. This will not only allow you to train someone else one day, but it will save you time from inventing the wheel each time you approach a task.

Find and Use Resources

The third key is to find and use resources. Resources might be educational tools, places you go to be inspired or learn more, or people you network with. Resources that help you grow come in a variety of forms. Remember always to continue your learning.

BRYAN'S TIP

There's a reason why some of the most talented people in the world—from athletes to business owners—hire private coaches. There is something about receiving personalized, one-on-one attention that will fast-track your success like nothing else. I have experienced this truth in my own life, and I am pleased to now offer personalized business coaching for real estate professionals through my site, www.landlording.com. If you've read everything in this book, yet you still want someone to walk you through the processes step-by-step, coaching may be for you. And I'll even give you a completely risk-free thirty-minute coaching session to find out.

Don't think coaching is for you? That's fine, too. I am committed to providing incredibly valuable resources at absolutely no cost to you, so feel free to browse around the site and check out the articles and free resources. I'm sure you'll quickly see that this is one instance where you get a lot more than what you pay for. In fact, based on the forms included in this book alone, you already have access to thousands of dollars' worth of resources that will save you from a very expensive meeting with your attorney.

The road to independence and entrepreneurial success will not be easy, and it won't be short. It will take dedication and perseverance. As a business owner, you will find yourself on a roller coaster of batting a thousand one day, then striking out the next, for you will play many roles and wear many hats. You will be forced out of your comfort zone. The first time I was asked to speak in public, my knees were literally knocking and I was terrible. Now, I have the privilege to teach others across the country how to get out of their comfort zones. Above all, being a business owner gives you confidence, for you are in control of your own future, but it keeps you amazingly humble at the same time. When I was starting out, I gave a speech one day and was given a standing ovation. People came up to me afterward with words of praise for how I inspired them and excited them about starting in real estate. My wife and I rushed from that seminar to spend the next six hours into the wee hours of the morning copying and assembling materials for a workshop I had to teach the next day. At the time we couldn't afford staff to prepare materials. One moment I was on top, the next moment the only thing I was on top of was the copy machine. I could only laugh at the "glamour" of being a business owner.

In the history of man we have had many ages, such as the Ice Age, the Stone Age, and the Information Age. These are each very significant periods of time that have greatly influenced us all. Each of these time periods was without a doubt shaped by mankind. We are now entering into what I consider a new age. An age of shifting power influenced by more costly consumer goods, stagnant wages, globalization, foreclosures, rising health care costs, and uncertainty in the financial markets. All of these various economic forces will affect various demographic groups differently. One group that will surely be impacted greatly will be the middle income demographic. Their need for affordable housing will be a major issue. These economic forces will forever change the landscape of real estate investing. New challenges will be faced, but the opportunities to grow wealth will be greater than ever before. For those investors who can learn to make the shift; those who learn to buy it, rent it, and profit; they will be ready to enter the new age . . . the Investor Age.

Everything we could wish for has already been given to us,
what we should ask for is the ability to see it.
—Anonymous

SIXTEEN

REAL ESTATE INVESTING FREQUENTLY ASKED QUESTIONS

Since publishing *Buy It, Rent It, Profit!* in 2009, I've received an incredible amount of feedback from readers around the country. It is an amazing feeling to know that I am helping so many people change their lives and the lives of their families by investing in real estate. But no matter how much information I provide, there's always a question that pops up that I haven't already addressed, so I am constantly updating my materials and presentations to be sure they're as inclusive and detailed as possible. I want everyone to know that being successful in real estate is completely doable, and if I can clear up any misconceptions or doubts along the way, I'm happy to do it.

Here, I've included some of the most common questions I've gotten over the years. I've been asked some of these so many times that I am willing to bet you were wondering the exact same thing. Read on for answers to the most pressing questions you haven't even asked me yet. And if for some reason you still have a question that's not included here, please hit me up online at **www.landlordacademy.com**. I try to answer as many questions as I can, but even if I don't get back to you, I may include your question in my next book!

Q: Why do you believe every investor should own rental property in their portfolio?
A: I like the idea of putting money into something that, if done correctly and with a simple approach, gives you all the control you need. You have control over the asset, and you have control over the tenant base. You have control over every asset of a real estate investment business. And we all know affordable housing is a huge issue in our nation, so being able to offer a product to a clientele, or being able to have supply for a huge demand, is what running a business is all about. Rental property is a product that people need. And there are tons of other benefits of owning rental property, including the ability to use rental income to offset the risk by decreasing debt and increasing value. When done right, owning rental property is one of the greatest income generators.

Q: You mention control, but no one can control the economy. Doesn't that impact a real estate investment business?

A: Yes and no. You have to look at economic cycles and understand where you're buying because you can mitigate a lot of issues depending on where you buy. So let's just say you're buying at the peak (which is of course impossible to predict with 100 percent certainty). At these times, we see a lot of product being sold at high prices with rental prices going up, which results in a rapid increase of property values. So when you buy at the peak, when the market is high, you do risk a decline, or a softening of the market. But you can still buy at the height of the market; just make sure you're able to cover those rents. This means you either want more liquid assets, or you want to put more money down (or both!).

As long as the market is conducive, and you're buying with prices right at, or below, market, and the job economy is stable with the ability to increase rent still there—then I would say those are all "go" signs, and you should definitely purchase rental property.

The first edition of this book sold well, even in the worst economy most of us have ever experienced in our lifetimes. There's a reason why: fundamentals. Sticking to the fundamentals of real estate investing will keep you afloat in any economy, no matter what happens. I bought property even when I knew prices were on the high side, because I followed the SEOTA method and I knew the net operating incomes of those particular properties were still attractive. But I always anticipated a downslide and softening of the rental rates, so when the market crashed, I was able to stay afloat.

The good news is that we are very unlikely to see something similar to the Great Recession again in our lifetime. So as long as you follow the fundamentals outlined in this book and pay attention to the economic cycles (if you buy high, be ready for a softening), you'll be fine.

Q: Is owning rental property difficult to manage when you have a full-time job or a family?

A: It comes down to, again, the fundamentals and what you buy, and it depends a lot on the asset class of what you buy. There are investors who own luxury high-rises, and their investments are on cruise control. If something breaks, they call in a plumber, or the maintenance men for the building, and the professionals take care of everything.

But when you buy certain asset classes, you've got to be careful. Typically, Class C (which is middle-income) and Class D (which is low-income) properties require much more hands-on care. You're dealing with a different demographic that leads to more wear and tear—instead of young professionals, you're dealing with a couple who has four or five kids. That's fine—young families need rental property, too, of course!—but you need to factor in these costs as you're evaluating your investment. And because the value of a Class C or Class D property is probably lower, the assets within the property aren't as valuable either, so you have appliances and other things that break down and require maintenance. And the reality is that with a middle- to lower-income demographic, you're also typically dealing with a lot more delinquencies, a lot more late payments, and a lot more tenant-landlord property management issues. (Though believe me, renting to so-called "wealthy" people does not necessarily guarantee that the rent will be paid on time; that's why you always need a safety cushion, no matter what asset class your property is!)

The thing is that Class C and Class D properties can be really affordable and easier for someone just starting out in real estate investing to get into. You just need to understand everything else that comes along with those properties. You're not actually buying property; you're buying tenants. So you have to consider the risk and the reward. If time is an issue for you, you may need to invest in a property—and tenants—that will require much less hand-holding.

Q: What are the most common mistakes that you see landlords make when first starting out with rental properties?
A: The biggest mistake I see is not approaching real estate investing like a business and losing sight of the fundamentals. Also, I see people who have a very misguided interpretation of what real estate investing is all about. There's too much of the "get-rich-quick" infomercial-type thinking influencing their decisions, and if you can't run a successful business, it's very difficult to be a real estate investor in this day and age.

Q: What are the most common mistakes you see landlords make when expanding their rental property portfolio?
A: The most common mistakes are probably owners not properly insuring their properties, and not having a good handle on the concept of creating corporate entities to acquire and expand their businesses. They don't include the real estate sales/brokerage, construction, and various other different extensions to their business that they need. And expanding too quickly can be a problem, too.

Q: How long does it normally take for the average new investor to reach his or her goals?
A: Everyone wants to know that, but it's actually a hard question to answer because there are a lot of moving parts to consider. I believe the biggest piece depends on the individuals themselves. When you start, you should have the end in mind, so you have to understand who you are and where you are in your career, your family situation, your goals, and so on. Are you young? Are you trying to build something? Are you a little older? Are you trying to cash out now?

So your success starts with you, as an individual. If your habits are bad, then the business's habits are going to be bad. If you're sick-minded, then the business is going to be sick. When you're starting a small business, the business is always a direct reflection of the owner. If you walk into a small business and the place is cluttered, I guarantee that the owner's house is the same way. So you've got to fix you before you can fix and grow your business. Then you move into economic seasons and how to properly navigate those seasons.

Q: What are the most common traits that you find in people who end up doing well in real estate investment?

A: Discipline and being passionate about what you're doing. These things are extremely important for longevity and for the business to actually get from point A to point B, because there are going to be more struggles than there will be successes. And if you're not prepared for that, then you probably should stay at that desk job, because owning a business is not easy.

There will be struggles. You'll struggle in the business, and you'll struggle in your personal life. So if you're not fundamentally and spiritually sound, if you're not taking care of yourself mentally and physically, if you're not a focused individual, if there's no passion behind what you do, more than likely your business is not going to be a long-term success. Now, in real estate, you don't necessarily have to be a long-term success. A lot of people just do real estate because they want a quick buck. So, again, that's why it's important to start with you, the individual, as you build your business.

Ultimately, the characteristics for being successful in real estate investing are the same characteristics necessary for success in any industry: discipline, focus, understanding fundamentals, and execution. Those are the staples.

ACKNOWLEDGMENTS

First, I must acknowledge the grace of God. I've been through a lot the last couple of years, and I know that it is only through His love and grace that I am still standing today. I also know that I can do nothing going forward without recognizing that.

I want to also acknowledge my beautiful wife, Dr. Lacy Chavis, and our daughter, Naomi Chavis. They are my inspiration and the reason I work as hard as I do.

I would like to thank the Tampa Housing Authority for helping us create one of the nation's first award-winning online training platforms. We are excited to use this program to help educate landlords everywhere.

Finally, thank you to my family, friends, and team members, as well as all of the people who played a role in my recovery. You are appreciated more than you will ever know.

APPENDIX

SEOTA AND DUE DILIGENCE FORMS

SEOTA CHECKLIST (FORM 1)

Target Area: _____

Preparation Date: _____

1. **Basic Area Information & Map**

2. **Building Permits (i.e., single family, multifamily, commercial)**

   # of Single Family _____   # of Multifamily _____   # of Commercial _____

3. **Employment**

   Largest Employment Class _____   Average Income _____

   Second Employment Class _____   Average Income _____

   Has employment been stable in the local area? _____

   Any impact from national employment anticipated? _____

   Comments: _____

4. **Average Household Size & Income**

   Average Household Size: _____   Average Household Income: _____

5. **Demographics & Psychographics**

   Annual Medium Income: _____

   Summary/Comments: _____

6. **Mortgage Interest Rates**

   Current Mortgage Interest Rates: _____

7. **Market Survey**

   Studio Average Rent: _____

   1 Bedroom Average Rent: _____

   2 Bedroom Average Rent: _____

8. **Occupancy Rates**

   Current Average Occupancy Rates: _____

MARKET SURVEY (FORM 2)

Date Completed:	Property 1	Property 2	Property 3
Rents Studio 1 bedroom/1 bathroom 2 bedroom/2 bathroom 3 bedroom/2 bathroom	(Note Square Footage and Rental Amount)	(Note Square Footage and Rental Amount)	(Note Square Footage and Rental Amount)
Fees & Deposits Deposit amount Is deposit refundable? Application fee			
Pets Pet fee Restrictions on pets			
Amenities Pool? Fitness center? Washer/dryer? W/D hookups? Other			
Occupancy When is unit available? How many?			
Any Specials?			

PROPERTY SNAPSHOT FORM (FORM 3)

Use this form to collect initial information on a property you would like to explore further.

Subject Property Address: _____

City: _____ County: _____

Area of Town: _____

Listing Realtor:_____ Phone #: _____

Single Family _____ Multifamily _____ (# of buildings: _____ # of Units: _____)

1 story _____ 2 story _____ 3 story _____

Type of Construction (circle): wood frame brick cement block stucco

Other: _____

Type of Roof (circle): flat pitched wooden shingles asphalt
rubber membrane fiberglass shingles

Amenities:

Garage: _____ Fence: _____ Pool: _____ Patio/Porch: _____

Other: _____

Condition of Structure: Poor Average Good

Repairs/Rehab: Minor Average Major

Occupied?: Yes No

Current Rent: _____ Market Rent: _____

Notable Problem Areas: _____

Notable Advantages: _____

Notes: _____

Any Nearby Rental Properties or Apartment Complexes for Comparison Due Diligence—Note Name and
Contact Number: _____

PROPERTY PROFILING CHECKLIST (FORM 4)

Use this form as a checklist of steps you can follow to collect more background information on a property.

_____ Complete Property Snapshot Form (Form 3).
Be sure you get subject property address and addresses of any surrounding similar properties for sale or apartment complexes.
_____ Take or request digital photos.

At home:
_____ Look online at the Property Appraisers Office and get owner name and property info. Print out.
_____ Run the owner's name to see how many properties he/she owns. Pay attention to when they purchased each. If several are recent, they could be cash poor. This also indicates how long they have been doing this and their level of experience.
_____ Run the owner's name on State Division of Corporation website (individual or corporation) and get corporate name and owner name. Print this out. See how many corporations they own, if they stay active for long, how recently they were started, and how many people are a part of them.
_____ If the owner owns a corporation, go back to the Property Appraisers Office website and see if they own any property under their corporation's name. All of this information helps you determine the type of investor you are dealing with and hints at their cash flow.
_____ Go to the website for, or call, the County Tax Collector and get amount of Property Tax: _____
_____ Call and get asking purchase price: _____
_____ Insert information into Property Profile Form (Form 5).
_____ Complete the Property Profile Form (Form 5).
_____ Go to the Property Appraisers Office and search for information on any surrounding properties for sale that you noted from the Property Appraisers Office.
_____ Conduct Market Survey (Form 2) on property.
_____ Compare the property you are profiling with the demographics and psychographics of the area.

At property:
_____ Tour property with someone with maintenance knowledge to get an estimate of what needs to be repaired or renovated. Use Subject Property Inspection Checklist (Form 6).
_____ (Take checklist) _____ (Take digital photos)

At home:
_____ Take your Subject Property Inspection Checklist (Form 6) and fill in your Repair Budget (Form 7) with estimated amounts to make any repairs or improvements.
_____ Use an amortization table to get your approximate mortgage payment if you were to purchase the property: _____
_____ CHECK IF THIS MAKES SENSE TO PURSUE. If the total of your repairs is already making the price too high, filter out this property and move on.
_____ Decide rent or selling price: _____
*THE LANDLORD ACADEMY™ offers a service to help you determine what rent you can command— see **landlordacademy.com**.

A PROFILE CONSISTS OF:

____   Profile w/ photo

____   Estimated Income & Expenses

____   Repair Budget (Form 7)

____   Subject Property Inspection Checklist (Form 6)

____   Market Survey (Form 2)

____   Map

____   "Comps" (other listings in area)

PROPERTY PROFILE FORM (FORM 5)

Use this form when you contact a property's seller or seller's representative to learn more about the asking price and conditions of sale.

Date: _____ Address: _____

Owner's Name: _____ Phone #: _____

Contact's Name (if different than owner): _____

Phone Number(s): _____ Fax #: _____

Email: _____

Area of Property: _____

How long has the property been for sale? _____

Why are you selling? _____

Is there a time limit in which you must sell? _____

Realty Company or Buy Owner? _____

Property Type (single, duplex, multi, etc.): _____

Sq. Footage _____ Price per Sq. Ft. _____ Bed/Bath _____

Lot Size _____ Garage: *Yes No* Pool: *Yes No* Fenced In: *Yes No*

Other: _____

Asking Price _____ Negotiable? _____ Owner Terms: Yes No

Down _____ Interest Rate _____ % Other Fees *(association, community)* _____

Lease Option? _____ Monthly Rent _____

How much toward purchase? _____

Is there a mortgage? *Yes No* How much? _____ Assumable? _____

Directions to Property: _____

NOTES: _____
_____

Next Action to Be Taken: _____

By Who? _____ By When? _____

SUBJECT PROPERTY INSPECTION CHECKLIST (FORM 6)

Use this form to physically inspect the condition of a property. (Can be used with tape recorder.)

Property Address: _____

Date: _____ Completed By: _____

Exterior of Home

	Foundation: Type: _____ Condition: _____ Comments:
	Roof: Type: _____ Shingles (missing pieces, cracking, damage) Framing (bowed, sagging ridge) Comments:
	Windows: Type: _____ Condition (broken glass, missing latches, missing screens) Comments:
	Trim: Condition (decaying wood, missing sections) Comments:
	Siding: Type: _____ Condition (decaying, cracked, dented, damaged) Repairs Required (replace or repair missing sections) Comments:
	Entrances: Condition of doors (fair, good, needs repair) Condition of steps (decaying, deteriorating brickwork, unsafe for use) Rails (yes/no) Comments:
	Porches: Location: _____ Condition (decaying or damages wood, sips of wood-boring insects, needs repair) Comments:
	Skylights: Damage (missing putty, cracked glass, decaying or damaged frame) Comments:

	Garage: Attached/Detached Condition (needs repair) Comments:
	Driveway: Condition (cracking, decaying, heaving, needs repair—minor, major) Comments:
	Landscaping: Overgrown shrubs (yes/no) Ivy on house (yes/no) Overhanging tree branches (yes/no) Location: _____ Comments:
	Fences: Types: _____ Condition (rusting, decaying) Comments:
	Other:

Mechanical Systems

	Plumbing: Drainage (poor, fair, good) Water pressure (adequate, inadequate) Leaks (yes/no) Septic or cess pool system works properly (yes/no) Use of lead waterlines or lead traps (yes/no) Sufficient amount of shutoff valves (yes/no) Working (yes/no) Comments:
	Hot Water: Type: _____ Condition of tank (leaking, corrosion, needs replacement) Type of fuel (electricity, oil, gas) Safety valves working (yes/no) Size of tank Sufficient hot water (yes/no) Location: _____ Comments:

	Electrical: Main disconnect (outside panel) working (yes/no) Aluminum wiring (yes/no) Comments:
	Air Conditioner: Condition (good, fair, needs repair) Size of unit: _____ Type (split, integral) Comments:
	Other:

Attic

	Installation: Condition (damaged, needs to be replaced) Comments:
	Framing: Condition (structurally sound, insect activity, decaying) Comments:
	Other:

Kitchen

	Stove: Type of fuel (electricity, gas, oil) Unit working (yes/no) Comments:
	Sink(s): Condition (poor, fair, good) Piping (damage, leaks, needs replacement) Comments:
	Ceilings: Condition Comments:
	Appliances: Condition Working (yes/no) Comments:

Walls: Needs repairs (yes/no) Location: _____ Comments:
Floors: Type Needs replacement (yes/no) Location: _____ Comments:
Cabinets and Counter Space: Cabinet type/color Adequate/Inadequate Needs repair (yes/no) Counter space type/color Adequate/Inadequate Needs repair (yes/no) Comments:
Other:

Bathrooms

Fixtures: Type Condition (poor, fair, good) Leaks (yes/no) Damaged or chipped fixtures (yes/no) Location: _____ Faucets dripping (yes/no) Comments:
Ceilings: In need of repairs (yes/no) Location: _____ Comments:
Water Pressure: Adequate/Needs Repair Comments:
Tile: Condition (missing, chipped, broken, falling off of walls) Comments:
Floors: Type (vinyl, tile) Condition (tile pulling up, needs replacement, deteriorating or decaying) Comments:

Walls: Condition (damaged walls from water, needs repair, loose plaster) Location for repairs: _____ Comments:	
Drainage: Normal/Sluggish Comments:	
Other:	

Interior Rooms

Walls: Condition (needs repair, missing sections, holes) Location for repairs: _____ Comments:	
Windows: Condition (needs repairs, needs screens, general tightening up) Location for repairs: _____ Comments:	
Closets: Sufficient size/Insufficient size Need more closets or closet space Comments:	
Ceilings: Condition (sagging plaster, water stains, cracks, damaged areas) Location for repairs: _____ Comments:	
Floors: Type (carpet, tile, wood) Condition (refinish, install new floor, replace carpeting) Location for repairs: _____ Comments:	
Doors: Condition (damaged, needs repair, missing) Location for repairs: _____ Comments:	
Electrical: Overhead lights/Need additional outlets Location for repairs: _____ Comments:	

OTHER/NOTES

REPAIR BUDGET (FORM 7)

After completing the Subject Property Inspection Checklist (Form 6), use this form to itemize and estimate cost of all items needed for repair.

	Price Per Item	# Items Needed	TOTAL PRICE
KITCHEN			
Kitchen Faucet			
Light Fixtures			
Miniblinds			
Garbage Disposal			
Stoves			
Refrigerators			
Sinks			
Cabinets			
LIVING ROOM			
Blinds			
Light Fixtures			
BEDROOM			
Blinds			
Light Fixtures			
Door Locks			
Passage Door			
BATHROOM			
Door Locks			
Wall Cabinet w/ Light Fixtures			
Toilets			
MISCELLANEOUS			
Electrical Outlet Plates			
Wall Switch			
Flooring (wood)			
Painting/Interior & Exterior			
Heating & A/C Units			
Maintenance Equipment/Tools			
Contract Labor			
Fire Extinguishers			
Window Glass			

Equipment Rental			
Electrical			
Plumbing			
TOTAL	$		$

DUE DILIGENCE ACTION LIST (FORM 8)

Use this form once you find a subject property you wish to make an offer on to ensure that every major area of consideration (legal, tax, physical condition, and financial) is inspected and meets your approval. This form is critical to keep you organized as you execute your due diligence on a property and make sure nothing is missed.

LETTER OF INTENT
- Review and sign off by (date) _____
- Review and sign off by legal team

Make sure:
- Due diligence will expire without obligation by buyer
- Deposit release requires written action
- Sufficient time is allowed for due diligence
- Sufficient time is allowed for financing
- Preapproval letter from lender
- Deposit goes hard on (date) _____

PURCHASE AGREEMENT
- Confirm investment commitment date
- Deposit goes hard on _____
- Sufficient time allowed for due diligence
- Sufficient time allowed for due financing
- Deposit release requires written action
- Due diligence will expire without obligation by the buyer
- Review and sign off by legal team
- Review and sign off by _____

FINANCING
- Select lender
- Send preliminary numbers to lender
- Calendar of any dates that were agreed to
- Prepare and send lender package
- Send all lender-required documents to appropriate personnel (i.e., rent rolls, etc.)
- Agree to and verify closing date and funding date

COMPARABLE PROPERTIES
- Complete economic rent comps
- Complete at least three market surveys along with shopping the target area

SALES COMPS
- Complete economic sales comps
- Tour sales comps of other like properties
- Check accuracy of market rents with third party sources (i.e., locator services)

MARKET SURVEY RENTAL INCOME CHECK

· Obtain the most current rent roll
· Verify rent-roll totals by running a tape
· Compare current rents in place match up with the deal sheet
· Verify market rents on the street match up with deal sheet
· Verify rents match up with the operating statements

LEASE AUDIT COMPLETED

· Check leases to make sure they match up with rent rolls provided
· Check deposits to make sure they match up with rent rolls and leases
· Check all move-out dates to make sure they match up to rent rolls
· Check tenant correspondence with current management and ownership to make sure no disputes
· Check leases for any side deals or concessions with tenants
· Check the cash deposits against the collected rents

ESCROW ACCOUNTS

· Check tenants' security deposits against owner's escrow account holding deposits
· Open escrow account for security deposits to be transferred before or at closing
· Check owner's reserves for replacement account

RENT GROWTH FORECAST AND MARKET SURVEY

· Verify by third party research
· Check reliable sources for rent growth
· Check to make sure that rent growth percent is used in financial projections for each year

VACANCY

· Check historic vacancy for the past three years
· Calculate financial projections vacancy based on market survey info

BAD DEBT

· Check history of bad debt
· Check to see if bad debt is included in cash flows

OTHER INCOME

· Receive reports showing other income generated by property
· Review other income for accuracy
Note: Do not evaluate nonrecurring items; do not evaluate forfeited deposits.

LAUNDRY CONTRACTS

· Check to see when they expire
· Check to see who they are with
· Check to see last time renewed
· Check what the vendor and landlord splits are

OPERATING EXPENSES

General
- Obtain copies of all service contracts from Seller
- Review and make sure cancelable in thirty days
- Obtain list copies of all insurance claims for past year from Seller
- Obtain list of pending litigation (if any)
- Obtain list of any government notices or code informant claims

ADVERTISEMENT COSTS
- Review all advertising contracts
- Make sure all contracts are cancelable in thirty days or less upon purchase

TOTAL PAYROLL COSTS
- Verify number of office personnel and payroll

GENERAL AND ADMINISTRATION COSTS
- Review equipment lease
- Verify all office leases are cancelable within thirty days
- Review supply list and pricing
- Review legal expenses (i.e., evictions)
- Review business permits and the renewal date of each
- Review pool permits
- Review janitorial costs

MANAGEMENT FEE COSTS
- Select property management company, if you are outsourcing management
- Agree to the fee you will pay company or if you are managing yourself, determine the fee you will pay yourself and add to financial projections
- Review pest control cost
- Review historicals for expense
- Examine any unusual items or indication of recurring items
- Include them in financial projections

LANDSCAPE COSTS
- Review historical costs
- Review general condition of existing landscape
- Check condition of irrigation system, clocks, and timers
- Budget fully for landscape improvements

APARTMENT TURNOVER COSTS
- Check historical turnover rate
- Check historical turnover cost per rental unit
- Factor turnover rate into operating costs
- Factor turnover costs per unit

- Evaluate any unusual turnover expenditures (i.e., wallpaper, stoves, etc.)
- Check maintenance checklist to see what items need to be budgeted for

REPAIR AND MAINTENANCE COST
- Review maintenance checklist
- Check historical maintenance costs
- Review any unusual items that showed up on the maintenance checklist
- Pull out nonrecurring capitalized items
- Evaluate any work orders unit by unit (should show up on maintenance checklist)

UTILITIES
Evaluated historical cost
Service providers:
- Water/Sewer
- Gas
- Electricity
- Trash
- Other
- Speak personally with utility providers re: forecast rate increases (include in financial projections)

PROPERTY TAX
- Recalculate property tax based on sales price

PROPERTY INSURANCE
- Get insurance bids
- Include new bid in financial projections
- Receive personal property insurance quote
- Obtain hurricane insurance (if needed)
- Include all new quotes in financial projections

RESERVES
- Check historical capital expenditures
- Evaluate recurring items of concern
- Create adequate reserve amounts

THIRD PARTY DUE DILIGENCE
- Perform physical inspection
- Complete maintenance check on each unit performed and report reviewed. Use Subject Property Inspection Checklist (Form 6)

FINAL APPROVAL CHECKLIST
- Complete tour property by all member managers and owners
- Match executive summary with deal summary
- Complete financial review by accounting

- Complete rent growth assumptions supported and sign off on
- Review refinance option for accuracy
- Review exit strategy tax adjustment
- Check deferred maintenance numbers for accuracy
- Review annual return

CLOSING DEAL DETAILS
- Check that the closing rent roll was received and approved
- Check tax calculation
- Confirm purchase price on statement is correct
- Confirm seller credits on statement are in order
- Confirm payment of closing cost consistent with contract
- Check to see if financing amount is correct
- Check payment for points
- Check other finance cost and approve
- Check legal costs and approve
- Verify total cash due from buyer
- Transfer tenants' escrow deposits to buyer's account

SAMPLE LETTER OF INTENT (FORM 9)

Apartment Investment Advisors, LLC
Address _____
Phone/Fax/Email _____

April 4, 2017

Re: Letter of Intent for (Property Address)

This Letter of Intent (hereinafter referred to as the "Letter of Intent") is intended to set forth the general terms and conditions under which APARTMENT INVESTMENT ADVISORS, LLC (the "Buyer"), or its assigns, successors, subsidiaries, etc., is proposing the acquisition, as stated below, of SAMPLE APARTMENTS, a 60-unit single-story residential apartment complex located at 3315 Main Street in Tampa, Florida 33609 (the "Property") from FLORIDA APARTMENTS, INC. (the "Seller"). If the terms and conditions set forth below are acceptable to the parties, the Buyer is prepared to promptly begin its due diligence review and preparation of definitive documentation, including a Purchase and Sale Agreement (the "Purchase and Sale Agreement") under the following terms and conditions:

1. Purchase Price: The proposed purchase price (the "Purchase Price") to be paid by Buyer shall be Three Million Eight Hundred Thousand Dollars ($3,800,000.00) for a one hundred percent (100%) interest in the Property. The Purchase Price is based upon information provided to date to Buyer by the Seller and is subject to both the Due Diligence Review (as defined herein) and a satisfactory inspection. This offer is based upon the accuracy of any information pertinent to the Property received by Buyer as of the date of this Letter of Intent; thus, any inaccuracy may affect and alter the proposed Purchase Price.

2. Inspection Period: The inspection period (the "Inspection Period") shall commence with the full execution and delivery of this Letter of Intent and terminate sixty (60) days thereafter. Buyer may, in its sole discretion and with or without cause and without penalty, terminate by giving Seller notice in writing at any time prior to the end of the Inspection Period. Should Buyer not terminate, then Seller shall furnish Buyer with those items in Paragraph 4 below within ten (10) days after the later of: (a) Buyer's acceptance of the Inspection Period; or (b) execution and delivery of the long-form purchase and sale agreement for the Property.

3. Deposit: An initial good-faith deposit of two hundred thousand dollars ($200,000.00) (the "Initial Deposit") shall be paid to North American Title as escrow agent by Buyer following the full execution and delivery of this Letter of Intent, pursuant to mutually agreeable escrow instructions, and upon the expiration of the Inspection Period. The terms of this Letter of Intent shall be incorporated into the Purchase and Sale Agreement (the "Purchase and Sale Agreement") to be drafted by Buyer and negotiated by the parties.

4. Seller's Duties: Seller shall pay for and obtain (where applicable) state stamps on the deed, cost of fee title insurance policy in the full amount of the purchase price, new staked survey certified to Buyer and Buyer's lender(s), real estate commission, its attorney's fees, and acceptable new termite inspection report. Seller shall furnish Buyer with a Phase I Environmental Audit acceptable to Buyer and its lender(s). Should said updated Phase I Environmental Report dictate the necessity of a Phase II Report, then Seller shall promptly furnish same to Buyer at Seller's expense. Should Seller not be able to deliver the property free and clear from any environmental problems, Buyer may terminate the Purchase and Sale Agreement.

5. Buyer shall pay for Buyer's financing costs (including mortgage assumption, intangible tax, and transfer fee, if applicable), its attorney's fees, and recording fees.

6. Buyer and Seller shall prorate taxes, insurance, utilities, assessments, and net rents as of the date of closing.

7. Security deposits and all funds in Common Area Maintenance (CAM) account held by Seller shall be transferred to Buyer at closing.

8. WITHIN THREE (3) BUSINESS DAYS AFTER THE FULL EXECUTION AND DELIVERY OF THIS LETTER OF INTENT, SELLER SHALL DELIVER TO BUYER AND/OR BUYER'S BROKER(S) THE FOLLOWING ITEMS, AS WELL AS SUCH OTHER INFORMATION AND DOCUMENTS AS BUYER MAY REASONABLY REQUEST DURING THE INSPECTION PERIOD:

   - Copies of or access to all tenant leases encumbering the Property.
   - Copies of or access to all contracts of employment or consultancy affecting the Property.
   - Copies of or access to all management, maintenance, service, and other agreements affecting the Property.
   - An up-to-date rent roll showing the rental due under each lease, security deposits held, prepaid rentals, and the status of each tenant's rental payments.
   - Copies of all plans and specifications, reports, etc., used in the construction of the Property, and "as built" plans if available.
   - Copies of all insurance policies applicable to the Property.
   - Operating statements for the year-to-date and two preceding years.
   - Memoranda covering the terms and conditions of any unwritten leases or contracts affecting the Property.
   - Copies of inspection reports, existing notices, and due dates for same from any governmental agency having jurisdiction for or an effect on the Property, including any additional notices which may be received prior to closing.
   - Copies of the last three years ad valorem tax bills, and current bill, if available.
   - Copies of all documents relating to litigation or other disputes affecting the Property.
   - A copy of all permits and certificates applicable to the Property, including Certificates of Occupancy.
   - Copies of all warranty agreements for real or personal property, including roof bonds.
   - Financial statements on all tenants in the Property, if any.
   - Tenant delinquency reports for the past two years, if any.
   - Schedule of personal property to be transferred with the Property.
   - Declarations certifying there are no tenant delinquencies (a) as of this Letter of Intent and (b) as of the date of closing.
   - Copy of the Common Area Maintenance budget and ledger showing all payments and disbursements.
   - All pertinent information of Seller's existing financing, if assumable.
   - Copies of Seller's existing appraisals and environmental audits, if any.

9. The Purchase and Sale Agreement shall contain standard "prevailing party" language.

10. Seller shall be solely responsible for: (a) payment of any commissions with respect to leases on the Property through the closing date and for future contingent commissions for lease renewals of option periods applicable to said leases; and (b) completion, at Seller's or tenant's sole cost, for all tenant improvement work for pending or signed leases on the Property.

11. Financing shall be obtained to the satisfaction of the Buyer. **This offer is specifically conditioned, in part, upon Buyer's obtaining financing, on terms and conditions acceptable to Buyer in its sole discretion and judgment.**

12. If Buyer does not terminate during the Inspection Period, then Seller shall deliver those items described in Paragraph 4, all acceptable to Buyer in its sole discretion, within ten (10) days following the expiration of the Inspection Period.

13. Closing shall be thirty (30) days after the last item in Paragraph 4 is delivered and Buyer has obtained the financing described in Paragraph 11 (with all of the foregoing to be acceptable to Buyer in its sole discretion). Both parties confirm that time is of the essence and agree to make every effort to expedite a closing.

14. Seller shall hold Buyer harmless against all claims by brokers and agents for any real estate commissions due in this transaction.

15. Seller shall deliver to Buyer, within ten (10) days of full execution of the Purchase and Sale Agreement, an estoppel certificate, in a form and with content reasonably acceptable to Buyer, signed by each tenant in the Property.

16. In the event of Buyer's default after full execution of the Purchase and Sale Agreement and acceptance of the Property by Buyer following the Inspection Period and upon the securing of adequate and acceptable financing by Buyer, the Initial Deposit shall be forfeited by Buyer as Seller's sole remedy. In the event of Seller's default after full execution of the Purchase and Sale Agreement and acceptance of the Property by Buyer following the Inspection Period, with the exception of any change in financing by Buyer's Lender, Buyer shall have the option of: (a) having the Initial Deposit returned, including reasonable costs, expenses, and attorney's fees; or (b) pursuing specific performance of the Purchase and Sale Agreement. The Buyer's deposit will be refundable, if at any point, should Lender change any aspect of the financing of this transaction.

17. Seller shall not enter into any agreements (including any contracts of sale of the Property, or any letter of intent in connection therewith), lease amendment or extensions until the Purchase and Sale Agreement is fully executed or negotiations terminated. Should Seller enter into any such agreements without Buyer's prior written approval or should Seller not be able to deliver estoppel certificates from the tenants acceptable to Buyer and its lender, Buyer may, at its option and in its sole discretion, terminate this Letter of Intent and/or the Purchase and Sale Agreement and have any binder money paid returned.

18. Either party hereto shall have the right to treat the Property as part of a tax-deferred like-kind exchange under Section 1031 of the Internal Revenue Code and, to that end, shall have the right to assign or otherwise alter this Letter of Intent in order to accomplish that objective; provided, however, that the net economic effect (including exposure to liability) shall be essentially the same as under the original Letter of Intent.

19. Seller and Buyer shall keep the terms of and existence of this Letter of Intent strictly confidential and shall not disclose any of its terms or its existence to any third party other than to their respective brokers, consultants, attorneys, accountants, lenders, and engineers.

20. The last signature date below shall be deemed the effective date of this Letter of Intent.

While this Letter of Intent is nonbinding, it is the intent of both parties to negotiate and execute within thirty (30) days of execution of this Letter of Intent a binding and definitive long-form Purchase and Sale Agreement along the above lines and with other terms and conditions customary for this type of transaction and mutually acceptable to both parties. The terms of this Letter of Intent shall be incorporated into the Purchase and Sale Agreement. If the general terms as outlined above are acceptable, please indicate by signing one copy of this Letter of Intent and returning it to the undersigned Buyer.

Agreed to and accepted:

BUYER   SELLER

By: _____   By: _____
Apartment Investment Advisors, LLC   Florida Apartments, Inc.

Date: _____   Date: _____

APPLICANT QUALIFYING AND APPROVAL OF PROSPECT CHECKLIST (FORM 10)

This form is used when you are leasing rental units to make sure all important steps are completed.

____ Complete Phone Card (Form 11) or Guest Card (Form 12)
____ Review Statement of Qualifying Criteria (Form 13)
____ Schedule a meeting with prospective tenant at property
____ Show rental property
____ Complete Rental Application *completely* (Form 14)
____ Collect application fee
____ Screen tenant (**landlordacademy.com**)
____ Determine if approved:

If yes:
____ Collect security deposit
____ Review Move-In Cost Sheet (Form 15)
____ Schedule move-in meeting
____ Complete lease (Form 20 or 21)
____ Complete addendums if needed
____ Complete Rules and Regulations Form (Form 22 or 23)

If yes, but raising deposit amount:
____ Have tenant sign letter requiring increase in deposit

If not approved:
____ Send Tenant Rejection Letter (Form 17)

PHONE CARD (FORM 11)

This form is used by you when taking phone call inquiries about your rental property. It is used to collect all contact information.

Date: _____

Name: _____

Address: _____

Telephone: (H) _____ (W)_____ (C)_____

Type of rental home desired: _____

How many will live in home: _____

Price range: _____

Date needed: _____

Pets: _____

Why moving: _____

Comments: _____

How did you hear about us?

❏ Referral

❏ Newspaper   ❏ Flyer/brochure

❏ For Rent sign   ❏ Locator service

❏ Yellow pages

Other: _____

Appointment scheduled: _____

GUEST CARD (FORM 12)

This form is to be completed by prospective tenants you meet face to face. It is used to collect all contact information.

Date: _____

Name: _____

Address: _____

Telephone: (H) _____ (W)_____ (C)_____

Type of rental home desired: _____

How many will live in home: _____

Price range: _____

Date needed: _____

Pets: _____

Why moving: _____

Comments: _____

How did you hear about us?

❏ Referral

❏ Newspaper   ❏ Flyer/brochure

❏ For Rent sign   ❏ Locator service

❏ Yellow pages

Other: _____

Appointment scheduled: _____

STATEMENT OF QUALIFYING CRITERIA (FORM 13)

This form should be reviewed with a prospective tenant to inform them of the qualifications they must meet to be approved for rental by you.

Thank you for visiting and applying.

To assure our neighbors of a well-maintained community, as well as enjoyable neighbors, we require that all prospective residents meet the following qualifying criteria when completing the rental application:

Applicant must be employed or have verification of income. We require monthly gross income to be at least three times the monthly rental rate. If income from employment is the primary source of income, a minimum of six months at the same place of employment must be verified. Self-employment will require the applicant's previous year's tax return as income verification. Income other than wages from employment such as tips, commissions, school subsidies, or allowances from parents will require notarized verification. An applicant that is not currently employed must provide proof of funds (current bank statement), which will equal the full term of the lease agreement.

Applicant must have a minimum of one-year verifiable rental history. Verifiable rental history for a period of at least 12 months, in which all the lease terms have been satisfactorily fulfilled, is required. Negative rental history, eviction, or outstanding monies owed to a previous landlord are unacceptable. If applicant owned a home, applicant must furnish all mortgage information. If applicant has no prior verifiable rental history, an additional security deposit up to a full month's rent will be required.

Applicant must physically reside in the apartment for which he/she is applying. Applicant must live in the rental unit and must disclose all persons who will be occupying the unit. All persons under the age of 21 are subject to background checks prior to occupancy. All persons 18 years of age or older must be a leaseholder and qualify for the unit with the applicant.

Credit history for a two-year period prior to this application will be evaluated. Lack of credit history as well as discharged bankruptcies is acceptable. Negative credit history, other than not fulfilling terms of a lease contract, will be considered provided there are more positive accounts than negative accounts. More than 30% of applicant's credit accounts showing negative remarks is unacceptable.

A criminal background check will be done on all applicants and any occupant 18 years of age or older. No felony convictions within the past five years will be accepted. No misdemeanor convictions against persons or property, prostitution, or drug-related offenses will be accepted.

If rental property is a single-family dwelling or single unit, landlord reserves the right to ask for a security deposit equal to one month's rent and first and last month's rent in advance.

If you are inquiring about a rental unit, occupancy limits have been established per unit size. Maximum number of persons allowed is as follows with no more than three unrelated adults per rental or duplex in either a two- or three-bedroom floor plan:

Sample Occupancy Criteria—be sure to check local and state guidelines for occupancy standards

Studio/Efficiency—no more than 2 persons
One Bedroom—no more than 2 persons
Two Bedroom—no more than 4 persons
Three Bedroom—no more than 6 persons

In order to view a rental home you must show a form of identification. Your driver's license or an alternate second form of identification will be photocopied. Please have identification with you.

We do business in accordance with the Federal Fair Housing Law. We do not discriminate against any person because of race, color, religion, sex, national origin, familial status, or disability.

I have read and understand the above qualifying criteria.
Note: False information given on an application will be grounds for rejection of the application.

Applicant _____ Date _____

Applicant _____ Date _____

RENTAL APPLICATION (FORM 14)

This application should be completed by a prospective tenant who wishes to apply for rental. It must be fully completed and signed by all applicants.

Rental Address _____ Unit Type _____

Rent Rate $ _____ Deposit $ _____ Desired Move-in Date _____

Applicant's Last Name	First Middle	Birth Date	Driver's License & State	Social Security #
☐ Unmarried ☐ Married ☐ Separated	Spouse's Name	Birth Date	Driver's License & State	Social Security #
Expected Move-in Date	# of Persons to Occupy Unit	Full Name(s) of Each Occupant		
Do You Have Pets? Yes No	How Many?	Type & Size (Keeping of pets requires a pet deposit and owner's consent)		

RESIDENCE HISTORY

Present Address City State Zip	How long? Yrs Mths	Area Code & Phone #	☐ Rent ☐ Own
Name & Address of Present Landlord or Mortgage Co.	Area Code & Phone #		Monthly Pmt. $
Previous Residence Address City State Zip	Previous Landlord	Area Code & Phone #	How long? Monthly Pmt.

Have you ever been filed on for an eviction? YES NO

EMPLOYMENT HISTORY PAST YEAR

Applicant Employed By	Supervisor's Name		How long? Yrs Mths
Address City State Zip	Phone	Position Held/Occupation	Salary $ Per
Previously Employed By	Supervisor's Name		How long? Yrs Mths
Address City State Zip	Phone	Position Held/Occupation	Salary $ Per
Previously Employed By	Supervisor's Name		How long? Yrs Mths
Address City State Zip	Phone	Position Held/Occupation	Salary $ Per

CREDIT AND LOAN REFERENCES

No. of Vehicles on Property	Do you have any recreational vehicles, vans, boats, motorcycles? If so specify:	
Auto No. 1—Type	License	State
Financed Through	Account No.	Monthly Payment
Auto No. 2—Type	License	State
Financed Through	Account No.	Monthly Payment

Loans & Charge Accounts Including Department Stores, Credit Cards, etc.				
Owed To	Account #	Address Zip	Total Debt	Payments
				$ per
				$ per
				$ per

BANK REFERENCES

Name of Bank or Savings & Loan	Account #	Address	City	State	Zip

Family Physician	Address City State Zip	Area Code & Phone #
In Case of Emergency, Call	Relationship	Address City State Zip	Area Code & Phone #

Applicant hereby authorizes verification of any and all information set forth on this Application, including release of information by any bank or savings and loan, credit reporting agencies, employer (present and former), and any Lender. Applicant hereby specifically authorizes Management to perform a credit check and criminal background check to verify information on this Application. All such information hereon, and released as authorized above, will be kept confidential. APPLICANT REPRESENTS THAT THE INFORMATION SET FORTH ON THIS APPLICATION IS TRUE AND COMPLETE. Material misrepresentations on the Application will constitute a default under the Lease or Rental Agreement between the parties.

CREDIT CHECK CHARGE—Applicant has submitted the sum of $ _____ which is nonrefundable payment for a credit check and processing charge, receipt of which is acknowledged by Management. Such sum is not a rental payment or deposit amount. In the event this application is approved or disapproved, this sum will be retained by Management to cover the cost of processing application as furnished by applicant. This application must be signed before it can be processed by Management.

GOOD FAITH DEPOSITS—I hereby deposit $ _____ with Management as a good faith deposit in connection with this rental application. If my application is accepted, I understand this deposit can be applied toward payment of my security deposit of $ _____ when I take possession of the rental unit. If for any reason Management decides to decline my application, the Management will refund this good faith deposit to me in full. I understand I may cancel this application by written notice within 72 hours and receive a full refund of this good faith deposit within 30 days of the cancellation. If I cancel after 72 hours or refuse to occupy the premises on the agreed upon date, I understand this good faith deposit will be held until Management can determine if it has incurred any expenses or rent loss due to my cancellation. These costs will be deducted from this good faith deposit and the balance will be refunded to me.

Applicant's Signature _____ Applicant's Signature _____

RELEASE OF GOOD FAITH DEPOSIT—I authorize Management to release my good faith deposit of $ _____ on rental unit and apply it toward a security deposit of $ _____.

Applicant's Signature _____ Applicant's Signature _____

MOVE-IN COST SHEET (FORM 15)

This form should be completed by you for a tenant who is approved for move in. It itemizes all costs the tenant must be prepared to pay at move in so they can bring proper funds.

WELCOME TO YOUR NEW HOME

Dear _____,

The management/owner of your new rental home extends a warm welcome to you. We hope your residency will be enjoyable.

Your new address is: _____

Your move-in date is: _____

If your move-in date is after the 24th of the month, pay the pro-rated rent on move-in day, as well as the next month's rent. It is pertinent that the lease be signed by all parties on or before the move-in date. The application fees, security deposit, all rent due, and any other move-in costs must be paid by cashier's check or money order.

Lease agreement to be for the period from _____ to _____

Market Rent:	$ _____
Concession:	$ _____
Monthly Base Rent:	$ _____
Charges due are as follows:	
Pro-rate Rent (Based on a 30-day month)	$ _____
Full Rent for First Month	$ _____
Security Deposit	$ _____
Nonrefundable Pet Fee	$ _____
Pet Deposit	$ _____
Pet Rent	$ _____
Application Fee(s)	$ _____
Other	$ _____
TOTAL RENT, FEES, DEPOSITS REQUIRED	$ _____
LESS AMOUNT PAID WITH APPLICATION	$ _____
TOTAL BALANCE DUE PRIOR TO MOVE IN	$ _____

Please contact the following utility companies BEFORE you move in and arrange for service in your name:

Electric Service: _____ Phone #: _____

Telephone: _____ Phone #: _____

Cable: _____ Phone #: _____

Please note that proof of utility transfer will be required at the time of move in.

APPLICANT(S) understands the above acknowledged rental deposit will be applied against the required amount due as indicated above, and that no representations, promises, or agreements as to occupancy, lease, or date of possession have been made. **APPLICANT(S)** also understands that the rental application submitted with this deposit is not to be construed as a lease or rental agreement.

OWNER reserves the right to reject **APPLICANT(S)'s** rental application any time prior to execution and delivery of the lease agreement. In the event of rejection, any sums deposited (with the exception of nonrefundable application fees) shall be refunded. If **APPLICANT(S)** withdraws application prior to execution of a lease agreement, the deposit will be forfeited unless written cancellation is received within seventy-two (72) hours from the date and time indicated below. **If OWNER** for any reason cannot deliver possession of the premises to **APPLICANT(S)** at the commencement of the term, all deposits paid to Owner shall be refunded to **APPLICANT(S),** releasing Owner from all liability.

_____

Applicant Signature

_____   _____

Applicant Signature   Rental Unit Address

_____   _____

Date/Time   Owner/Agent

APPLICATION APPROVAL CHECKLIST (FORM 16)

Complete the following steps to determine if an application is approved or not.

1. Determine your criteria for approval. What is the minimum income, credit score, and rental history you are going to require of your tenant? Use the Statement of Qualifying Criteria (Form 13) as a list of criteria to consider.
2. Screen your applicant. Go to **landlordacademy.com** to use our comprehensive tenant screening services. Our packages include credit check, criminal background check, eviction checks, and more.
3. Compare your applicant's results to your qualifying criteria and determine the application:

   approved _____   not approved _____

If an application is not approved:

____   Send applicant Tenant Rejection Letter (Form 17)
       This must be done to comply with the Fair Credit Reporting Act.

If an application is a marginal risk, you can increase deposit or require first and last months rent to limit your risk.

____   Notify the applicant of the adjustment. Be sure to put in writing why you increased the deposit and have the tenant sign. You can use Form 17 to note this change.

If an applicant is approved:

____   Notify the prospect. Ask them to leave a security deposit if they haven't already and sign the lease.
____   Schedule a move-in day, including a move-in meeting. Schedule this meeting to occur at the rental property, as you will need to complete a Move-In/Move-Out Inspection Report (Form 24).

TENANT REJECTION LETTER (FORM 17)

This form must be provided to an applicant who is denied rental or who is required to pay an additional deposit amount. This form is required by the Fair Credit Reporting Act.

To: _____   Date: _____

Address: _____

We regret to inform you that your application for residency has the following adverse action:

___ Your application for rental has been declined.

___ We are requesting a larger security deposit for approval.

    Total deposit required $_____

___ You must provide us qualified lease guarantor for approval.

The reason for this is based on one or more of the following reasons:

___ Residence History	___ Credit History
___ Employment Information	___ Public Criminal Records
___ Insufficient Income	___ Public Eviction Records

___ Other _____

___ Information that resulted in adverse action was received from a person or company other than a consumer reporting agency. You have the right to make a written request to us within 60 days for a disclosure of the nature of this information.

___ Information that resulted in adverse action was obtained from the following consumer reporting agency:

_____

The consumer reporting agency did not make the decision and is not able to explain why it was made. According to the Fair Credit Reporting Act, Public Law 91-508, you have the right to review all consumer reporting information used in the evaluation of your application, and you also have the right to dispute any information on file. If you would like to receive a free copy of the information used in the decision, contact the agency within 60 days. Include your full name, date of birth, Social Security number, current and former address, daytime and evening phone numbers. You have the right to dispute directly with the consumer reporting agency the accuracy or completeness of the information in your file. The agency must then, within a reasonable period of time, reinvestigate and modify or remove any inaccurate information. There is no charge for this service. If reinvestigation does not resolve the dispute to your satisfaction, you have the right to prepare a consumer statement of up to 100 words explaining your position, which will be kept in your credit file.

Sincerely yours,

_____

Printed Name of Owner/Agent

Hand delivered on (date): _____   by (name): _____

or

Mailed on (date): _____   by (name): _____

Keep a copy of this notice with the applicant's file for 2 years.

LEASE ADDENDUM—PET (FORM 18)

This lease addendum should be completed if a tenant has a pet.

This is an addendum to the following described lease.

Rental Unit Address: _____

Lease Date: _____ Unit Number (If Any): _____

Resident Name(s): _____

If there is more than one resident, "resident" includes all residents.

The lease is modified to allow resident to keep the below described pet in the rental unit under the conditions which follow.

1. Pet description

    Species: _____ Breed or type: _____

    Weight: _____ lbs. Height: _____ inches

    Color(s): _____ Age(s): _____

    Pet Name(s): _____

2. Resident must pay one or more of the following as indicated:

    ___ Additional security deposit of $_____ increasing the total lease security deposit to $_____.

    ___ Non-refundable fee of $_____.

    Additional monthly rent of $_____ increasing total rent to $_____.

3. Whenever pet is outside resident's rental unit it must be controlled by resident with a leash.

4. If pet disturbs or annoys neighbors or persons on the property, resident may be required to remove pet from the premises upon 7 days' notice.

Date Executed: _____ Date Executed: _____

Resident Signature(s): Landlord or Property Manager Signature:

_____ _____

_____

MOVE-IN MEETING CHECKLIST (FORM 19)

Use the checklist below to complete all the actions necessary to ensure a smooth, successful move in of your new tenant.

Prior to your move-in meeting:

____ Complete Lease filling in all blanks (Form 20 or 21)

____ Complete any Addendums filling in all blanks *(example: Lease Addendum—Pet,* Form 18)

At move-in meeting:

____ Review Lease and have tenant sign if it is not already signed

____ Review any Addendums and have tenant sign

____ Review Rules and Regulations Form (Form 22 or 23)

____ Collect security deposit if you haven't already

____ Collect first month's rent *(certified check or money order)*

       If you are requiring last month's rent, collect that also

____ Collect any other fees due, such as a pet deposit or pet fee

____ Conduct inspection of unit using the Move-In/Move-Out Inspection Report (Form 24)

____ Give tenant keys

After the move-in meeting:

____ File documents in tenant's file

____ Calendar a "check in" with your tenant for one week away

____ Contact all utility companies to confirm accounts are transferred from your name to tenant's name

SAMPLE RESIDENTIAL POWER LEASE (FORM 20)

Rental Unit Address:		Community Name (If Any):		Initial Lease Term (see paragraph 3) Beginning: Ending:	
Monthly Rent	Prorated Rent	Security Deposit	Administrative Fee	Pet Fee	Prepared by:
$	$	$	$	$	

Resident(s) Name(s):   Full Name(s) of Child(ren):   Date(s) of Birth:

_____

_____

_____

_____

_____

Additional Agreement(s):

This is a lease between the above named Resident(s) and the below named Owner for the rental dwelling described above. It (and any contemporaneously executed additional agreements) is the entire agreement between Resident(s) and Owner and may be modified only in writing. As used in this lease "you" means the Resident or Residents whose names appear above. If there is more than one Resident, you are jointly and severally liable for any liability to us. "We," "our," or "us" means the Owner. "Premises" means the entire rental property. **UPON EXECUTION OF THIS LEASE, YOU ACKNOWLEDGE THAT YOU HAVE READ AND AGREE TO ALL OF ITS PROVISIONS.**

BY SIGNING THIS RENTAL AGREEMENT YOU AGREE THAT UPON SURRENDER OR ABANDONMENT, WE SHALL NOT BE LIABLE OR RESPONSIBLE FOR THE STORAGE OR DISPOSITION OF YOUR PERSONAL PROPERTY.

_____   _____
Resident Signature   Owner Name

_____   _____
Date   Managing Agent Name

_____   _____
Resident Signature   Owner/Agent Signature

_____   _____
Date   Date

_____   _____
Witness   Witness

_____   _____
Date   Date

Rental Unit Address: _____

1. SECURITY DEPOSIT:

A. Your security deposit will be held as indicated below:

____ Deposited in a separate: ____ interest bearing ____ non-interest bearing account with _____ (bank name and address). You will receive 75% of any interest paid on your deposit but not more than 5% per year.

____ Commingled with our other funds. You will receive interest on your deposit at the rate of 5% per year.

B. Your security deposit is security for your full performance of this lease and may not be applied by you to any money which you owe to us.

C. (a) Upon the vacating of the premises for termination of the lease, if the Landlord does not intend to impose a claim on the security deposit, the Landlord shall have 15 days to return the security deposit together with interest if otherwise required, or the landlord shall have 30 days to give the tenant written notice by certified mail to the tenant's last known mailing address of his or her intention to impose a claim on the deposit and the reason for imposing the claim. The notice shall contain a statement in substantially the following form:

This is a notice of my intentions to impose claim for damages in the amount of _____ upon your security deposit, due to _____. You are hereby notified that you must object in writing to this deduction from your security deposit within 15 days from the time you received this notice or I will be authorized to deduct my claim from your security deposit. Your objection must be sent to _____. If the landlord fails to give the required notice within the 30-day period, he or she forfeits the right to impose a claim upon the security deposit.

(b) Unless the tenant objects to the imposition of the landlord's claim or the amount thereof within 15 days after receipt of the landlord's notice of intention to impose a claim, the landlord may then deduct the amount of his or her claim and shall remit the balance of the deposit to the tenant within 30 days after the date of the notice of intention to impose claim for damages.

(c) If either party institutes an action in a court of competent jurisdiction to adjudicate the party's right to the security deposit, the prevailing party is entitled to receive his or her court cost plus a reasonable fee for his or her attorney. The court shall advocate the cause on the calendar.

(d) Compliance with this section by an individual or business entity authorized to conduct business in this state, including licensed real estate brokers and salespersons, shall constitute compliance with all other relevant law pertaining to security deposits held pursuant to a rental agreement or other landlord-tenant relationship. Enforcement personnel shall look solely to this section to determine compliance. This section prevails over any conflicting provisions in state law, and shall operate to permit licensed real estate brokers to disburse security deposits and deposit money without having to comply with the notice and settlement procedures.

2. RENT: You agree to pay the monthly rent indicated above at _____ on or before the 1st day of each month without deduction or set off. If prorated rent is indicated, it is the amount due for the partial first month of this lease. Time is of the essence. Rent payments must be made by one check or money order even if there is more than one Resident. Payment may not be made by third party checks nor in cash. **Payment after the 5th day of the month must be by money order and include a onetime late charge of $50.00 paid in full,** all as additional rent. However, we reserve the right to refuse payment after expiration of our demand for rent or possession. If your check is dishonored by your bank, you must pay us a service charge of $50.00 plus any other charges provided by law and plus any accrued late charge(s). If one of your checks is dishonored, you may be required to pay, at our option, future rent by money order. We are not required to redeposit a dishonored check. You must pay any taxes due on your payments. Any payment due under this lease is rent. We may apply any payment to any outstanding balance regardless of any notation on or with the payment.

3. RENEWAL: This lease will continue for one year after the Initial Lease Term unless either you or we give the other **at least 30 days' written notice** of termination before the end of the initial term. During the continuation term, either you or we may terminate the lease at the end of a calendar month by giving the other not less than 60 days' written notice. We may increase the rent at the end of the initial term or during the continuation term by giving you not less than 70 days' notice before the beginning of a calendar month.

4. UTILITIES: Water and sewer service are provided to you. However, you may be required to pay for this service. If you are required to pay, you will be given an invoice each month. You must pay the amount of the invoice according to its terms as additional rent. You must obtain and pay for all other utilities. We are not liable for interruption or malfunction in service. You may not occupy your rental unit without electric service except during brief interruptions beyond your control.

5. OCCUPANCY: Only those persons whose names appear on the lease may occupy your rental unit without our prior written consent except guests for no more than 7 consecutive or 14 total days. The rental unit may be used solely for private housing. You may not assign this lease or sublet any portion of your rental unit. If you will be absent for more than 14 days, you must notify us in writing.

6. PETS: No pets may enter or be kept in your rental unit or on the premises without our written consent.

7. CRIMINAL ACTIVITY: If you or your invitee engages in criminal activity on the premises or near enough to adversely affect it or other residents such activity will be a default for which this lease may be immediately terminated.

8. REMEDIES: You and we have all remedies provided by law. If you vacate before the end of your lease (even if due to eviction) you must still pay rent for the entire lease less any net rent which we receive from rerenting your rental unit. We have no duty to rerent. The prevailing party in any dispute arising out of this lease will be entitled to recover reasonable collection costs including attorney fees from the nonprevailing party.

9. NOTICES: Any notices from us to you will be deemed delivered when mailed to you at your rental unit by first class mail; or personally handed to you or anyone in your rental unit; or left at your rental unit in your absence. Delivery of one copy of a notice is sufficient for all residents. Any notice from you to us will be deemed delivered when received at our office, by certified mail, return receipt requested, or personally delivered to our office staff during normal business hours.

10. RIGHT TO ENTER: You consent to our entering your rental unit during reasonable hours for any inspections (by us or prospective buyers or renters), maintenance and repairs, pest control, for delivering notices, and for other purposes as provided by law.

11. REPAIR AND MAINTENANCE: You acknowledge that you have inspected the rental unit and are fully satisfied and accept it in its "as is" condition, except as otherwise agreed by you and us in writing. You must maintain your rental unit in a clean and sanitary condition including prompt removal of trash and garbage and placing it in a collection point container. We will maintain air-conditioning and heating equipment, plumbing fixtures and facilities, electrical systems, and appliances provided by us, unless noted otherwise in this lease agreement. Any damage to your rental unit or the premises, except for normal wear, caused by you or your invitees will be corrected, repaired, or replaced at your expense. **You must immediately notify us in writing of any needed maintenance or repair. You must inspect your smoke detector at least once a month to determine if it is working properly and notify us of any deficiency. You must change the air-conditioning and heating filter monthly, or more often if required.**

12. MOLD: You must take steps to limit the growth of mold in your rental unit. This includes operating your heating and air-conditioning system as appropriate to reduce humidity, using appropriate ventilation, limiting evaporation of water, promptly removing any visible mold, and immediately reporting to us any leaks or other water intrusion into your rental unit or any visible mold that you cannot remove.

13. ALTERATION: You may not make alterations or additions, nor install or maintain in the rental unit, or any part of the premises, any fixtures, large appliances, devices, or signs without our written consent. Any alterations, additions, or fixtures which are made or installed will remain a part of the rental unit unless we specifically agree otherwise.

14. LIABILITY: We will not be liable for any damages, loss, or injury to persons or property occurring within your apartment or upon the premises. Although there may be entrance and exit gates for the rental unit, they do not significantly limit access to the property by anyone. There will be times when they do not work due to malfunction or damage. In addition, access is not restricted by a wall or fence. You are responsible for obtaining your own casualty and liability insurance. With respect to your family or invitees, you agree to hold us harmless and indemnify us from liability. **WE STRONGLY RECOMMEND THAT YOU SECURE INSURANCE TO PROTECT YOURSELF AND YOUR PROPERTY.** Your successors, heirs, beneficiaries, and personal representatives are bound by the provisions of this lease.

15. SECURITY: We do not provide and have no duty to provide security services to protect you, others, or property. You must look solely to the public police for such protection. We will not be liable for failure to provide security services or for the criminal or wrongful acts of others. If, from time to time, we provide any security service, these services are only for the protection of our property and will not constitute a waiver of, or in any manner modify, this disclaimer. They may be modified or discontinued at any time without notice.

16. CONDO/HOA ASSOCIATION PROPERTIES LEASE LANGUAGE: If the leased premises are included in a condominium association or homeowners association, you agree to abide by its bylaws, rules, and regulations including as they may be amended and that failure to do so is a violation of this lease.

17. DAMAGE: If we determine that your rental unit should not be occupied because of damage or risk to property, health, or safety we may, at our option, terminate this lease. If it is unoccupiable due the fault of you, your family, or invitee, you will be liable for any monetary loss to us including rent. Nothing may be used or kept in or about your rental unit which would in any way increase our insurance cost, be a violation of law, or otherwise be a hazard.

18. WAIVERS: Our acceptance of rent after knowledge of a breach of this lease by you is not a waiver of our rights nor an election not to proceed under the provisions of this lease or the law. Our rights and remedies under this lease are cumulative; the use of one or more shall not exclude or waive our right to other remedies. Your rights under this lease are subordinate to any present or future mortgages on the premises. We may assign our interest in this lease. You and we waive any right to demand a jury trial concerning the litigation of any matters arising between us.

19. POSSESSION: If the rental unit is not ready for your occupancy on the beginning date of this lease, the beginning date may be extended up to 30 days or the lease may be voided at our option. We shall not be liable for any loss caused by such delay or termination.

20. APPLICATION: If any information given by you in your application is false or not complete, we may, at our option, terminate this lease. You must notify us promptly in writing of any changes in the information provided to us in your application.

21. RADON GAS: Radon is a naturally occurring radioactive gas that, when it has accumulated in a building in sufficient quantities, may present health risks to persons who are exposed to it over time. Levels of radon that exceed federal and state guidelines have been found in buildings in our state. Additional information regarding radon and radon testing may be obtained from your county health department.

22. CREDIT REPORTS: We have the right to obtain credit and any other reports on you which we may deem appropriate until all of your obligations under this lease are fulfilled. Upon your written request, we will inform you of the name and address of each agency from which a credit report is obtained. We have the right to report to others our credit and other experience with you.

23. PARKING: No more than one automobile or noncommercial small truck is allowed for each rental unit **and for each visitor (as long as adequate parking space remains),** without our written consent. No other vehicles or things may be parked or placed on the premises without our written consent **(except for loading or unloading)** including motorcycles, trucks, boats, trailer, motorhomes, and storage containers. All vehicles must be currently licensed with the license displayed as required by law; be in good operating condition; be in compliance with all requirements to operate on public streets including insurance; and not be unsightly (within our sole discretion).

Vehicles must be parked only within the boundary of designated parking space. Anything in violation of the foregoing may be removed without notice at the owner's or your expense. We are not liable for any claim arising as a result of removal. It is your responsibility to advise your invitees of these requirements and to determine that they have complied. You agree to indemnify and hold us harmless for any claims by your invitees for the removal of their property for violation of these requirements and to pay immediately as additional rent any amount due pursuant to such claim. No vehicle maintenance or repairs or similar activities may be performed on the premises. Signs may not be displayed on or from vehicles.

24. POLICIES: You must observe the policies below and any other reasonable policies which may be given to you now or later by us.

(a) No "garage" or other sales may be conducted by you on the premises.

(b) Solicitation by you or others is not allowed on the premises.

(c) Locks may not be altered nor may new locks, knockers, or other door or window attachments be installed without our prior written consent.

(d) No noise, music or other sounds, or conduct or attire (or lack of) is permitted at any time in such manner as to disturb or annoy other persons. Certain attire may be prohibited such as "T-back" swimsuits.

(e) No spikes, adhesives, screws, hooks or nails, or the like may be driven into or applied to the walls or other surfaces without our prior written consent except that small nails may be used for hanging wall decorations. You are responsible for the cost of repairing any holes.

(f) No water-filled furniture is permitted except water beds. Water beds are not permitted unless we are first protected as a loss payee on an insurance policy approved by us.

(g) Any draperies or other window covering must be white or lined in white so that only white may be seen from outside your rental unit.

(h) Water may not be wasted. Water hoses may be used only with automatic shutoff nozzles. Washing of vehicles may be restricted to designated areas and times. Outside water use may be prohibited. Water leaks must be promptly reported to us.

(i) Patios, balconies, and entrances may not be used to store belongings. Only appropriate potted plants and other outdoor furniture are permitted on patios and balconies. We may further limit what is placed in outside areas. Only electric grills may be kept or used on the premises.

LANDLORD/RESIDENT RESPONSIBILITY
SINGLE-FAMILY DWELLING

1. Utilities. Utilities shall be paid for by the party indicated on the following chart:

Utility Expense	LANDLORD	RESIDENT
Electricity		
Gas		
Water		
Garbage		
Other		

When electricity, gas, or water is to be furnished by landlord, resident agrees not to use any supplemental heating or air-conditioning units, washing machine, dryer, dishwasher, or other appliance other than those provided by landlord and listed in Section 2. No appliances without landlord's written approval.

2. Appliances. Appliance furnished to resident by landlord:

Appliance	YES	NO
Refrigerator		
Stove		
Air Conditioner		
Dishwasher		
Washer		
Dryer		
Garbage Disposal		

3. Pool. Pool will be maintained by: LANDLORD   RESIDENT
   Resident agrees to maintain pool by:

   _____

   _____

   _____

   _____

   _____ (Resident initial) Resident agrees to said conditions.
   _____ (Resident initial) Not applicable.

4. Grounds. Grounds will be maintained by: LANDLORD   RESIDENT
   Resident agrees to maintain grounds by:

   _____

   _____

   _____

   _____

   _____ (Resident initial) Resident agrees to said conditions.
   _____ (Resident initial) Not applicable.

5. Pest Control. Pest Control will be provided by: LANDLORD   RESIDENT
   Resident agrees to provide pest control by:

   _____

   _____

   _____

   _____

   _____ (Resident initial) Resident agrees to said conditions.
   _____ (Resident initial) Not applicable.

6. Repairs. Repairs will be provided by: LANDLORD   RESIDENT
   Resident agrees to provide repairs under the following conditions:

   _____

   _____

   _____

   _____

Maintenance requests, except in emergencies, must be made in writing or left on voice message at address
_____ (provided by landlord) or phone number _____ (provided by landlord).

_____ (Resident initial) Resident agrees to said conditions.

_____ (Resident initial) Not applicable.

7. Policies. Additionally resident agrees to:

_____

_____

_____

_____

_____ (Resident initial) Resident agrees to said conditions.

_____ (Resident initial) Not applicable.

SAMPLE APARTMENT POWER LEASE (FORM 21)

Apartment Address:		Community Name:		Initial Lease Term (see paragraph 3) Beginning: Ending:	
Monthly Rent $	Prorated Rent $	Security Deposit $	Administrative Fee $	Pet Fee $	Prepared by:

Resident(s) Name(s):   Full Name(s) of Child(ren):   Date(s) of Birth:

_____

_____

_____

_____

_____

Additional Agreement(s):

_____

This is a lease between the above named Resident(s) and the below named Owner for the apartment dwelling described above. It (and any contemporaneously executed additional agreements) is the entire agreement between Resident(s) and Owner and may be modified only in writing. As used in this lease "you" means the Resident or Residents whose names appear above. If there is more than one Resident, you are jointly and severally liable for any liability to us. "We," "our," or "us" means the Owner. "Premises" means the entire apartment community. **UPON EXECUTION OF THIS LEASE, YOU ACKNOWLEDGE THAT YOU HAVE READ AND AGREE TO ALL OF ITS PROVISIONS.**

BY SIGNING THIS RENTAL AGREEMENT YOU AGREE THAT UPON SURRENDER OR ABANDONMENT, WE SHALL NOT BE LIABLE OR RESPONSIBLE FOR THE STORAGE OR DISPOSITION OF YOUR PERSONAL PROPERTY.

_____   _____
Resident Signature   Owner Name

_____   _____
Date   Managing Agent Name

_____   _____
Resident Signature   Owner/Agent Signature

_____   _____
Date   Date

_____   _____
Witness   Witness

_____   _____
Date   Date

Rental Unit Address: _____

1. SECURITY DEPOSIT:

A. Your security deposit will be held as indicated below:

_____ Deposited in a separate: _____ interest bearing _____ non-interest bearing account with _____ (bank name and address). You will receive 75% of any interest paid on your deposit but not more than 5% per year.

_____ Commingled with our other funds. You will receive interest on your deposit at the rate of 5% per year.

B. Your security deposit is security for your full performance of this lease and may not be applied by you to any money which you owe to us.

C. (a) Upon the vacating of the premises for termination of the lease, if the Landlord does not intend to impose a claim on the security deposit, the Landlord shall have 15 days to return the security deposit together with interest if otherwise required, or the landlord shall have 30 days to give the tenant written notice by certified mail to the tenant's last known mailing address of his or her intention to impose a claim on the deposit and the reason for imposing the claim. The notice shall contain a statement in substantially the following form:

This is a notice of my intentions to impose claim for damages in the amount of _____ upon your security deposit, due to _____. You are hereby notified that you must object in writing to this deduction from your security deposit within 15 days from the time you received this notice or I will be authorized to deduct my claim from your security deposit. Your objection must be sent to _____. If the landlord fails to give the required notice within the 30-day period, he or she forfeits the right to impose a claim upon the security deposit.

(b) Unless the tenant objects to the imposition of the landlord's claim or the amount thereof within 15 days after receipt of the landlord's notice of intention to impose a claim, the landlord may then deduct the amount of his or her claim and shall remit the balance of the deposit to the tenant within 30 days after the date of the notice of intention to impose claim for damages.

(c) If either party institutes an action in a court of competent jurisdiction to adjudicate the party's right to the security deposit, the prevailing party is entitled to receive his or her court cost plus a reasonable fee for his or her attorney. The court shall advocate the cause on the calendar.

(d) Compliance with this section by an individual or business entity authorized to conduct business in this state, including licensed real estate brokers and salespersons, shall constitute compliance with all other relevant law pertaining to security deposits held pursuant to a rental agreement or other landlord-tenant relationship. Enforcement personnel shall look solely to this section to determine compliance. This section prevails over any conflicting provisions in state law, and shall operate to permit licensed real estate brokers to disburse security deposits and deposit money without having to comply with the notice and settlement procedures.

2. RENT: You agree to pay the monthly rent indicated above at the community office on or before the 1st day of each month without deduction or set off. If prorated rent is indicated, it is the amount due for the partial first month of this lease. Time is of the essence. Rent payments must be made by one check or money order even if there is more than one Resident. Payment may not be made by third party checks nor in cash. **Payment after the 5th day of the month must be by money order and include a onetime late charge of $50.00 paid in full,** all as additional rent. However, we reserve the right to refuse payment after expiration of our demand for rent or possession. If your check is dishonored by your bank, you must pay us a service charge of $50.00 plus any other charges provided by law and plus any accrued late charge(s). If one of your check is dishonored, you may be required to pay, at our option, future rent by money order. We are not required to redeposit a dishonored check. You must pay any taxes due on your payments. Any payment due under this lease is rent. We may apply any payment to any outstanding balance regardless of any notation on or with the payment.

3. RENEWAL: This lease will continue for one year after the Initial Lease Term unless either you or we give the other **at least 30 days' written notice** of termination before the end of the initial term. During the continuation term, either you or we may terminate the lease at the end of a calendar month by giving the other not less than 60 days' written notice. We may increase the rent at the end of the initial term or during the continuation term by giving you not less than 70 days' notice before the beginning of a calendar month.

4. UTILITIES: Water and sewer service are provided to you. However, you may be required to pay for this service. If you are required to pay, you will be given an invoice each month. You must pay the amount of the invoice according to its terms as additional rent. You must obtain and pay for all other utilities. We are not liable for interruption or malfunction in service. You may not occupy your apartment without electric service except during brief interruptions beyond your control.

5. OCCUPANCY: Only those persons whose names appear on the lease may occupy your apartment without our prior written consent except guests for no more than 7 consecutive or 14 total days. The apartment may be used solely for private housing. You may not assign this lease or sublet any portion of your apartment. If you will be absent for more than 14 days, you must notify us in writing.

6. PETS: No pets may enter or be kept in your apartment or on the premises without our written consent.

7. CRIMINAL ACTIVITY: If you or your invitee engages in criminal activity on the premises or near enough to adversely affect it or other residents such activity will be a default for which this lease may be immediately terminated.

8. REMEDIES: You and we have all remedies provided by law. If you vacate before the end of your lease (even if due to eviction) you must still pay rent for the entire lease less any net rent which we receive from rerenting your apartment. We have no duty to rerent. The prevailing party in any dispute arising out of this lease will be entitled to recover reasonable collection costs including attorney fees from the nonprevailing party.

9. NOTICES: Any notices from us to you will be deemed delivered when mailed to you at your apartment by first class mail; or personally handed to you or anyone in your apartment; or left at your apartment in your absence. Delivery of one copy of a notice is sufficient for all residents. Any notice from you to us will be deemed delivered when received at our office, by certified mail, return receipt requested, or personally delivered to our office staff during normal business hours.

10. RIGHT TO ENTER: You consent to our entering your apartment during reasonable hours for any inspections (by us or prospective buyers or renters), maintenance and repairs, pest control, for delivering notices, and for other purposes as provided by law.

11. REPAIR AND MAINTENANCE: You acknowledge that you have inspected the apartment and are fully satisfied and accept it in its "as is" condition, except as otherwise agreed by you and us in writing. You must maintain your apartment in a clean and sanitary condition including prompt removal of trash and garbage and placing it in a collection point container which we provide. We will maintain air-conditioning and heating equipment, plumbing fixtures and facilities, electrical systems, and appliances provided by us. Any damage to your apartment or the premises, except for normal wear, caused by you or your invitees will be corrected, repaired, or replaced at your expense. **You must immediately notify us in writing of any needed maintenance or repair. You must inspect your smoke detector at least once a month to determine if it is working properly and notify us of any deficiency. You must change the air-conditioning and heating filter monthly, or more often if required.** We supply filters at no cost to you.

12. MOLD: You must take steps to limit the growth of mold in your apartment. This includes operating your heating and air-conditioning system as appropriate to reduce humidity, using appropriate ventilation, limiting evaporation of water, promptly removing any visible mold, and immediately reporting to us any leaks or other water intrusion into your apartment or any visible mold that you cannot remove.

13. ALTERATION: You may not make alterations or additions, nor install or maintain in the apartment, or any part of the premises, any fixtures, large appliances, devices, or signs without our written consent. Any alterations, additions, or fixtures which are made or installed will remain a part of the apartment unless we specifically agree otherwise.

14. LIABILITY: We will not be liable for any damages, loss, or injury to persons or property occurring within your apartment or upon the premises. Although there are entrance and exit gates for the apartment community, they do not significantly limit access to the property by anyone. There will be times when they do not work due to malfunction or damage. In addition, access is not restricted by a wall or fence. You are responsible for obtaining your own casualty and liability insurance. With respect to your family or invitees, you agree to hold us harmless and indemnify us from liability. **WE STRONGLY RECOMMEND THAT YOU SECURE INSURANCE TO PROTECT YOURSELF AND YOUR PROPERTY.** Your successors, heirs, beneficiaries, and personal representatives are bound by the provisions of this lease.

15. SECURITY: We do not provide and have no duty to provide security services to protect you, others, or property. You must look solely to the public police for such protection. We will not be liable for failure to provide security services or for the criminal or wrongful acts of others. If, from time to time, we provide any security service, these services are only for the protection of our property and will not constitute a waiver of, or in any manner modify, this disclaimer. They may be modified or discontinued at any time without notice.

16. CONDO/HOA ASSOCIATION PROPERTIES LEASE LANGUAGE: If the lease premises are included in a condominium association or homeowners association, you agree to abide by its bylaws, rules, and regulations including as they may be amended and that failure to do so is a violation of this lease.

17. DAMAGE: If we determine that your apartment should not be occupied because of damage or risk to property, health, or safety we may, at our option, terminate this lease. If it is unoccupiable due the fault of you, your family, or invitee, you will be liable for any monetary loss to us including rent. Nothing may be used or kept in or about your apartment which would in any way increase our insurance cost, be a violation of law, or otherwise be a hazard.

18. WAIVERS: Our acceptance of rent after knowledge of a breach of this lease by you is not a waiver of our rights nor an election not to proceed under the provisions of this lease or the law. Our rights and remedies under this lease are cumulative; the use of one or more shall not exclude or waive our right to other remedies. Your rights under this lease are subordinate to any present or future mortgages on the premises. We may assign our interest in this lease. You and we waive any right to demand a jury trial concerning the litigation of any matters arising between us.

19. POSSESSION: If the apartment is not ready for your occupancy on the beginning date of this lease, the beginning date may be extended up to 30 days or the lease may be voided at our option. We shall not be liable for any loss caused by such delay or termination.

20. APPLICATION: If any information given by you in your application is false or not complete, we may, at our option, terminate this lease. You must notify us promptly in writing of any changes in the information provided to us in your application.

21. RADON GAS: Radon is a naturally occurring radioactive gas that, when it has accumulated in a building in sufficient quantities, may present health risks to persons who are exposed to it over time. Levels of radon that exceed federal and state guidelines have been found in buildings in our state. Additional information regarding radon and radon testing may be obtained from your county health department.

22. CREDIT REPORTS: We have the right to obtain credit and any other reports on you which we may deem appropriate until all of your obligations under this lease are fulfilled. Upon your written request, we will inform you of the name and address of each agency from which a credit report is obtained. We have the right to report to others our credit and other experience with you.

23. PARKING: No more than one automobile or noncommercial small truck is allowed for each apartment **and for each visitor (as long as adequate parking space remains for residents)**, without our written consent. No other vehicles or things may be parked or placed on the premises without our written consent (**except for loading or unloading**) including motorcycles, trucks, boats, trailer, motorhomes, and storage container. All vehicles must be currently licensed with the license displayed as required by law; be in good operating condition; be in compliance with all requirements to operate on public streets including insurance; and not be unsightly (within our sole discretion). Vehicles must be parked only within the boundary of a single designated parking space. Anything in violation of the foregoing may be removed without notice at the owner's or your expense. We are not liable for any claim arising as a result of removal. It is your responsibility to advise your invitees of these requirements and to determine that they have complied. You agree to indemnify and hold us harmless for any claims by your invitees for the removal of their property for violation of these requirements and to pay immediately as additional rent any amount due pursuant to such claim. We may impose additional parking requirements including limiting the number of vehicles which your or your invitees may park on the premises, requiring the use of parking decals and/or assigning parking spaces. No vehicle maintenance or repairs or similar activities may be performed on the premises. Signs may not be displayed on or from vehicles.

24. POLICIES: You must observe the policies below and any other reasonable policies which may be given to you now or later by us.

(a) No "garage" or other sales may be conducted by you on the premises.

(b) Solicitation by you or others is not allowed on the premises.

(c) Locks may not be altered nor may new locks, knockers, or other door or window attachments be installed without our prior written consent.

(d) No noise, music or other sounds, or conduct or attire (or lack of) is permitted at any time in such manner as to disturb or annoy other persons. Certain attire may be prohibited such as "T-back" swimsuits.

(e) No spikes, adhesives, screws, hooks or nails, or the like may be driven into or applied to the walls or other surfaces without our prior written consent except that small nails may be used for hanging wall decorations. You are responsible for the cost of repairing any holes.

(f) No water-filled furniture is permitted except water beds. Water beds are not permitted unless we are first protected as a loss payee on an insurance policy approved by us.

(g) Any draperies or other window covering must be white or lined in white so that only white may be seen from outside your apartment.

(h) Water may not be wasted. Water hoses may be used only with automatic shutoff nozzles. Washing of vehicles may be restricted to designated areas and times. Outside water use may be prohibited. Water leaks must be promptly reported to us.

(i) Patios, balconies, hallways, and entrances may not be used to store belongings. Only appropriate potted plants and other outdoor furniture are permitted on patios and balconies. We may further limit what is placed in outside areas. Only electric grills may be kept or used on the premises.

RULES AND REGULATIONS ADDENDUM FOR SINGLE-FAMILY RENTAL (FORM 22)

This form should be signed in addition to your lease. Use this Rules and Regulations for a single-family rental. Use Rules and Regulations Form 23 for a multifamily rental.

THIS ADDENDUM IS HEREBY MADE A PART OF THAT CERTAIN LEASE AGREEMENT DATED _____, 20_____, EXECUTED BY _____ ("Resident").

The following Rules and Regulations have been established by the Owner/Management and are considered an addendum to your Lease Agreement. Failure to comply with said Rules and Regulations may, at the discretion of Owner/Management, be grounds for termination of the Lease Agreement.

1. RENTAL PAYMENT: Rent is due on the first day of each month. Rent received after 5:00 p.m. on the fifth (5th) must include the late fee specified in the Lease Agreement. Checks which do not include the late fee as required will not be accepted. All late payment checks and charges must be paid by cashier's check, certified check, or money order. After you tender two (2) NSF checks during the term of the lease agreement, personal checks will no longer be accepted and all monies due must be paid by cashier's check, certified check, or money order. Please mail or deliver your rental payment to: _____.

2. MAINTENANCE REQUESTS: Maintenance requests should be made by phone or in writing to the business office. Maintenance hours are weekdays from _____ a.m. to _____ p.m. In case of an emergency, call the office and you will be given an emergency number to call. Emergencies include fire, flood, electrical shortage, and sewer backups. Your maintenance request cannot be fulfilled if pets are left unattended. It is not our policy to make appointments for maintenance work.

3. LOCKS: You are prohibited from adding, changing, or in any way altering locks installed on the doors of the residence.

4. ENTRANCES, HALLWAYS, WALKS, AND LAWNS: Entrances, doorways, walks, and lawns should not be obstructed or used for any purpose other than entering and exiting.

5. PERSONAL PROPERTY: Due to legal limitations, it is not possible for us to insure your personal property. It will be necessary for you to obtain rental dweller's coverage at your expense from a local insurance agent to cover any possible loss of personal property.

6. PARKING AREAS: Our driveway, lawn, or parking area is not to be used for abandoned or inoperable vehicles. The determination of whether a vehicle is abandoned or inoperable shall be within the discretion of Management, but a vehicle will be deemed to be inoperable if not "street legal." All vehicles must be periodically moved to prevent buildup of dirt and debris. Automobiles should not be parked on the grass. Vehicles not conforming to these rules may be towed away at the owner's expense.

7. PEST CONTROL: Residence is sprayed on a regular basis. If you have a special problem with pests, notify the management and the exterminator will pay special attention on his next visit. You are asked to assist our pest control by maintaining a high standard of good housekeeping. It you have a pet and it becomes necessary to spray for fleas, you must pay an additional charge.

8. LAWN AND LANDSCAPING UPKEEP: The Owner maintains a high degree of lawn maintenance. Owner/Management requests that you help in maintaining our high standards.

9. TRASH: Please ensure that your trash is placed in a trash can with a lid when placed anywhere outside of the rental unit.

10. GUESTS: You are responsible and liable for the conduct of your family, invitees, licensees, and guests. Acts of

these persons in violation of the Lease Agreement, or one of these or future rules and regulations, may be deemed by Management to be a breach by you which may result in termination of the Lease Agreement.

11. MOTORCYCLES, MINIBIKES, ETC.: Except for automobiles and noncommercial small trucks, no vehicles (including motorcycles, trucks, boats or boat trailers, campers, travel trailers, and motorhomes) may be parked on the premises without our prior written consent. All vehicles must be currently licensed with the license displayed as required by law, be in good operating condition, be in compliance with all requirements to operate in public areas including any insurance requirements, and not be unsightly (within our sole discretion). Vehicles must be parked only within spaces provided for parking. No vehicle may be parked in front of Dumpsters, blocking other vehicles, on the grass, outside the boundaries of a single designated parking space or driveway, or in entrances or exits. Any violations of the foregoing rules will subject the vehicle to being towed without notice at the owner's expense. We are not liable for any damage arising as a result of towing. You acknowledge that it is your responsibility to advise your invitees of these vehicle policies, and you further agree to determine in each case that they have complied therewith. You agree to indemnify and hold us harmless for any claims by your invitees for the towing of their vehicles for violation of these policies; you agree to pay for said towing and other charges related thereto as additional rent to be paid immediately. We may impose additional parking regulations including limiting the number of vehicles which you or your invitees may park on the premises. No vehicle maintenance or repairs or similar activities may be performed on the premises.

12. PLUMBING: A charge will be made for unclogging plumbing equipment, in cases where malfunctions are caused by the introduction of improper objects therein, such as toys, cloth objects, grease, and other foreign matter. The cost of repair or replacement of other equipment or furnishings of the Owner will be borne by you.

13. LOCKOUTS: It you find it necessary to have authorized personnel unlock the rental unit after hours you will be charged a fee payable at time of entry. If this service is not available it will be necessary to call a locksmith and you will be responsible for locksmith fees.

14. DRAPERIES: Window treatments must have white linings or a shade. Bed linens, towels, tinfoil, flags, reflector film, etc., are not acceptable. You are requested to comply within ten (10) days of move in.

15. TELEPHONE HOOKUPS: Telephones may only be placed at previously wired locations provided by the telephone company. Additional drilling, cutting, or boring for wires is not permitted without written permission from Owner/Management.

16. WATER BEDS: Water beds are allowed subject to Owner/Management's prior written approval.

17. STORAGE: No goods or materials of any kind or description which are combustible or would increase fire risk shall be placed in storage areas. Storage in such areas shall be at your risk and Owner/Management shall not be responsible for any loss or damages. Heating/air-conditioning or water heater closets are not to be used for storage purposes.

18. ANTENNAS: Radio, television, CB, or other types of aerials or antennas should not be placed or erected by you on the roof or exterior of any building.

19. DISTURBING NOISES: Your family, invitees, licensees, and guests shall have due regard for the comfort and enjoyment of your neighbors. Your Residence is your home, free from interruption by Owner/Management, unless you or your guests disturb your neighbors. Televisions, stereo units, radios, and musical instruments are not to be played at such a volume or time that will annoy neighbors.

20. PATIOS: All balconies or patios must be kept clean and clear of storage items. Hanging of clothes, garments, or rugs over railing of balconies or patios will not be permitted. Patios or balconies should not be used for anything except patio furniture, flower boxes, and plants. They are not to be used for storage under any circumstances. For safety, please do not place plants on balcony railings.

21. PETS: No pets allowed except with the permission of Owner/Management and the execution of a Pet Adden-

dum. An additional fee will be required, a portion of which is nonrefundable. The entire fee may be applied against damages to the residence in the event of default by you under the Lease Agreement.

22. ALTERATIONS: No alterations allowed without Owner/Management's prior written approval.

To avoid misunderstandings regarding the **SECURITY DEPOSITS** that are made at the time you sign your Lease Agreement, the following information is provided:

RELEASE OF THE SECURITY DEPOSIT IS SUBJECT TO THE FOLLOWING PROVISIONS:

1. Full term of lease has expired, and all persons have vacated the Residence.
2. **A written notice** of Intent to Vacate effective the end of the calendar month must be given by the 1st of the calendar month prior to said vacating.
3. No damage to property beyond normal wear and tear.
4. Entire Rental Unit including range, refrigerator, bathroom, closets, and cupboards are clean. Refrigerator to be defrosted.
5. No unpaid legal charges, delinquent rents, or late fees.
6. **All** keys must be returned.
7. **All** debris, rubbish, and discards placed in proper rubbish containers.
8. Forwarding address left with Owner/Management.
9 Move-In/Move-Out Inspection Report must be completed when you move in and signed by the Owner/Property Manager and you. This form must also be completed and signed by both parties when you move out.

QUESTIONS AND ANSWERS ON SECURITY DEPOSIT POLICY:

Q. What charges are made if the prerequisite conditions are not complied with?

A. The costs of labor and materials for cleaning and repairs will be deducted. Also, any delinquent payments including late charges will be deducted.

Q. How is the Security Deposit returned?

A. By a check mailed to your forwarding address. The check is jointly payable and addressed to all persons who sign the Lease Agreement. No pick ups from the landlord or management.

Q. Can the Security Deposit be applied to any rent still outstanding during the lease term?

A. No. All rents must be paid separate and apart from the Security Deposit.

ADDITIONAL RULES AND REGULATIONS (if any):

_____

INITIALS (if any additional rules and regulations)

I/we hereby acknowledge that I/we have read the foregoing Rules and Regulations and hereby agree to abide by each and every one.

_____   _____
Date   Resident

_____   _____
Date   Resident

RULES AND REGULATIONS ADDENDUM FOR MULTIFAMILY RENTAL (FORM 23)

This form should be signed in addition to your lease. Use this Rules and Regulations for a multiunit rental. Use Rules and Regulations Form 22 for a single-family rental.

THIS ADDENDUM IS HEREBY MADE A PART OF THAT CERTAIN LEASE AGREEMENT DATED _____, 20_____, EXECUTED BY _____ ("Resident").

The following Rules and Regulations have been established by the Owner/Management and are considered an addendum to your Lease Agreement. Failure to comply with said Rules and Regulations may, at the discretion of Owner/Management, be grounds for termination of the Lease Agreement.

1. RENTAL PAYMENT: Rent is due on the first day of each month. Rent received after 5:00 p.m. on the fifth (5th) must include the late fee specified in the Lease Agreement. Checks which do not include the late fee as required will not be accepted. All late payment checks and charges must be paid by cashier's check, certified check, or money order. After you tender two (2) NSF checks during the term of the lease agreement, personal checks will no longer be accepted and all monies due must be paid by cashier's check, certified check, or money order. Please mail or deliver your rental payment to the business office.

2. MAINTENANCE REQUESTS: Maintenance requests should be made by phone or in writing to the business office. Maintenance hours are weekdays from _____ a.m. to _____ p.m. In case of an emergency, call the office and you will be given an emergency number to call. Emergencies include fire, flood, electrical shortage, and sewer backups. Your maintenance request cannot be fulfilled if pets are left unattended. It is not our policy to make appointments for maintenance work.

3. LOCKS: You are prohibited from adding, changing, or in any way altering locks installed on the doors of the residence.

4. ENTRANCES, HALLWAYS, WALKS, AND LAWNS: Entrances, hallways, walks, lawns, and other public areas should not be obstructed or used for any purpose other than entering and exiting.

5. PERSONAL PROPERTY: Due to legal limitations, it is not possible for us to insure your personal property. It will be necessary for you to obtain rental dweller's coverage at your expense from a local insurance agent to cover any possible loss of personal property.

6. DELIVERY OF PACKAGES OR FURNITURE: Our employees are prohibited from receiving packages for anyone. Please make your own arrangements for such items. If you are expecting delivery of furniture, appliances or repairs to these items, you may leave a key at the office for the serviceman, but you must sign a release of responsibility for theft or damages. We will not be able to accompany any serviceman to your residence.

7. SPEED LIMIT: The maximum speed limit throughout the Community is 10 m.p.h. Please drive carefully and watch out for children.

8. PARKING FACILITIES: Our parking lots are not to be used for abandoned or inoperable vehicles. The determination of whether a vehicle is abandoned or inoperable shall be within the discretion of Management, but a vehicle will be deemed to be inoperable if not "street legal." All vehicles must be periodically moved to prevent buildup of dirt and debris. Automobiles should not be parked on the grass. Recreational vehicles and trailers may only be parked in certain areas, which are clearly marked for recreational purposes. Vehicles not conforming to these rules may be towed away at the owner's expense.

9. PEST CONTROL: Residence units are sprayed on a regular basis. If you have a special problem with pests, notify the office and the exterminator will pay special attention on his next visit. You are asked to assist our pest control by maintaining a high standard of good housekeeping. It you have a pet and it becomes necessary to spray for fleas, you must pay an additional charge.

10. GROUNDS UPKEEP: The Owner maintains a high degree of grounds maintenance. Owner/Management requests that you help in maintaining our high standards.

11. DUMPSTERS: There are Dumpsters conveniently located throughout the Rental Community. Please ensure that your trash is placed in plastic bags and securely tied before placing it in the Dumpster, not beside it. You must break down boxes before placing them in Dumpsters.

12. GUESTS: You are responsible and liable for the conduct of your family, invitees, licensees, and guests. Acts of these persons in violation of the Lease Agreement, or one of these or future rules and regulations, may be deemed by Management to be a breach by you which may result in termination of the Lease Agreement.

13. POOL: Pool Regulations are posted at pool area. Children under age _____ must be accompanied by an adult. Older children may use the pool without supervision as long as they have parental permission and behave in a responsible manner.

14. MOTORCYCLES, MINIBIKES, ETC.: All state regulations that apply on the street will apply in the Rental Community. All vehicles, including motorcycles and minibikes, must be properly licensed, and all operators must be licensed as well. No one underage is allowed to operate a motor vehicle of any type on the grounds of the Rental Community at any time. All motorcycles and minibikes must be parked in the parking lot, and may not be placed in the rental unit.

15. PLUMBING: A charge will be made for unclogging plumbing equipment, in cases where malfunctions are caused by the introduction of improper objects therein, such as toys, cloth objects, grease, and other foreign matter. The cost of repair or replacement of other equipment or furnishings of the Owner will be borne by you.

16. LOCKOUTS: It you find it necessary to have authorized personnel unlock the rental unit after hours you will be charged a fee of $_____ payable at time of entry. If this service is not available at the Rental Community it will be necessary to call a locksmith and you will be responsible for locksmith fees.

17. DRAPERIES: Window treatments must have white linings or a white shade. Bed linens, towels, tinfoil, flags, reflector film, etc., are not acceptable. You are requested to comply within ten (10) days of move-in.

18. TELEPHONE HOOKUPS: Telephones may only be placed at previously wired locations provided by the telephone company. Additional drilling, cutting, or boring for wires is not permitted without written permission from Owner/Management.

19. WATER BEDS: Water beds are allowed subject to Owner/Management's prior written approval.

20. STORAGE: No goods or materials of any kind or description which are combustible or would increase fire risk shall be placed in storage areas. Storage in such areas shall be at your risk and Owner/Management shall not be responsible for any loss or damages. Heating/air-conditioning or water heater closets are not to be used for storage purposes.

21. RECREATION: You agree to abide by rules and regulations established for use of recreational and service facilities provided by Owner/Management.

22. ANTENNAS: Radio, television, CB, or other types of aerials or antennas should not be placed or erected by you on the roof or exterior of any building.

23. DISTURBING NOISES: Your family, invitees, licensees, and guests shall have due regard for the comfort and enjoyment of all other residents in the Rental Community. Your Residence is your home, free from interruption by Owner/Management, unless you or your guests disturb other residents of the Community. Televisions, stereo units, radios, and musical instruments are not to be played at such a volume or time that will annoy persons in other residences.

24. SIGNS: You should not display any signs, exterior lights, or markings on the rental unit. No awnings or other projections should be attached by you to the outside of the building of which the rental unit is a part.

25. PATIOS: All balconies or patios must be kept clean and clear of storage items. Hanging of clothes, garments, or rugs over railing of balconies or patios will not be permitted. Patios or balconies should not be used for any-

thing except patio furniture, flower boxes, and plants. They are not to be used for storage under any circumstances. For safety, please do not place plants on balcony railings.

26. PETS: No pets allowed except with the permission of Owner/Management and the execution of a Pet Addendum. An additional fee will be required, a portion of which is nonrefundable. The entire fee may be applied against damages to the residence in the event of default by you under the Lease Agreement.

27. LAUNDRY ROOM: If the Rental Community provides laundry facilities, please remove clothing from machines promptly. Do not use tints or dyes. Report any malfunction of machines to the office.

28. ALTERATIONS: No apartment alterations allowed without Owner/Management's prior written approval.

To avoid misunderstandings regarding the **SECURITY DEPOSITS** that are made at the time you sign your Lease Agreement, the following information is provided:

RELEASE OF THE SECURITY DEPOSIT IS SUBJECT TO THE FOLLOWING PROVISIONS:

1 Full term of lease has expired and all persons have vacated the Residence.

2. **A written notice** of Intent to Vacate effective the end of the calendar month must be given by the 1st of the calendar month prior to said vacating.

3. No damage to property beyond normal wear and tear.

4. Entire Rental Unit including range, refrigerator, bathroom, closets, and cupboards are clean. Refrigerator to be defrosted.

5. No unpaid legal charges, delinquent rents, or late fees.

6. **All** keys must be returned.

7. **All** debris, rubbish, and discards placed in proper rubbish containers.

8. Forwarding address left with Owner/Management.

9. Move-In/Move-Out Inspection Report must be completed when you move in and signed by the Owner/Property Manager and you. This form must also be completed and signed by both parties when you move out.

QUESTIONS AND ANSWERS ON SECURITY DEPOSIT POLICY:

Q. What charges are made if the prerequisite conditions are not complied with?

A. The costs of labor and materials for cleaning and repairs will be deducted. Also, any delinquent payments including late charges will be deducted.

Q. How is the Security Deposit returned?

A. By a check mailed to your forwarding address. The check is jointly payable and addressed to all persons who sign the Lease Agreement. No pick ups from the office.

Q. Can the Security Deposit be applied to any rent still outstanding during the lease term?

A. No. All rents must be paid separate and apart from the Security Deposit.

ADDITIONAL RULES AND REGULATIONS (if any):

————————

INITIALS (if any additional rules and regulations)

I/we hereby acknowledge that I/we have read the foregoing Rules and Regulations and hereby agree to abide by each and every one.

_____   _____
Date   Resident

_____   _____
Date   Resident

MOVE-IN/MOVE-OUT INSPECTION REPORT (FORM 24)

Resident(s) Name: _____ Date: _____

Address: _____ Unit #: _____

PRE/AT OCCUPANCY ITEM	ND=No Damage Condition (unless noted otherwise in exception column)	Note Exception to Condition	POST OCCUPANCY Move-Out Condition	Cost per item to clean or replace	#	Total Cost
Kitchen:						
Floors	Clean, ND			10		
Walls/Ceiling	Paint Good			10		
Counters	Paint Good			10		
Cabinets/Drawers	Clean, ND			10		
Stove/Oven	Clean, ND			25		
Drip Pans	Clean, ND			5		
Hood, Filter Fan	Clean, ND			25		
Refrigerator	Clean, ND			15		
Dishwasher	Clean, Working, ND			50		
Sink & Stopper	Clean, Working, ND			10		
Lights	Clean, Working			10		
Windows/Track, Screens	Clean, No Breaks			15		
Other						
Living & Dining Area:						
Floor/Carpet	Clean, ND or spots			50		
Carpet Rips/Tears/Burns	Clean, ND			25		
Vacuuming Only	Clean, ND			10		
Walls/Ceiling	Paint Good			20		
Lights, Dimmer Switch	Clean, Working			12		
Heating, AC	Clean, Working			10		
Blinds	Clean, Working			30		

		1	2	3	1	2	3			
Windows/Tracks, Screens	Clean, ND							15		
Fireplace	Clean, ND							2		
Ceiling Fans	Clean, ND							10		
Bedroom:		1	2	3	1	2	3			
Floor/Carpet	Clean, ND							20		
Carpet Rips/Tears/Burns	Clean, ND							25		
Vacuuming Only	Clean, ND							10		
Walls/Ceiling	Paint Good, ND							20		
Lights, Dimmer Switch	Clean, Working, ND							15		
Blinds	Clean, ND							25		
Windows/Tracks, Screens	Clean, No Breaks							15		
Closets	Clean, ND							5		
Other										
Bathroom:		1		2	1		2			
Floor	Clean, ND							10		
Walls/Ceiling	Paint Good, ND							10		
Sink	Clean, ND							5		
Vanity/Counter	Clean, ND							10		
Vent Fan	Clean, Working							10		
Lights	Clean, Working							5		
Tile/Grout	Clean, ND							15		
Bath/Shower Enclosure	Clean, ND							10		
Toilet	Clean, ND							10		
Towel Bar/Soap Dish/ Mirror	Clean, ND							15		
Windows/Tracks, Screens	Clean, No Breaks							5		
Halls:										
Walls/Ceiling	Paint Good, ND							10		
Cabinets/Closet	Clean, ND							10		
Floors/Carpet	Clean, ND							15		

Patio/Balcony:						
Floor/Door Cleaning	Clean, ND			10		
Patio Door Replacement	Clean, ND			125		
Storage Area	Clean, ND			5		
Misc. Other:						
Fire Ext./Smoke Detector	Clean, Working, ND			25		
Drywall Repair	Clean, ND			25		
Trash Removed				10		
Doors-Interior Replace	Clean, ND			95		
Doors-Exterior Replace	Clean, ND			105		
Other						
Pet Deodorization				40		
			TOTAL			

Comments: _____   Comments: _____

_____   _____

_____   _____

Resident has inspected the Rental Unit prior to occupancy and accepts same as noted above. Resident understands that upon vacating the rental unit cleaning will be charged as set forth above and he or she will be responsible for damage as provided in the Rental Agreement.

Resident has inspected the Rental Unit subsequent to vacation and concurs in the above except as noted.

Dated: _____, 20 _____   Dated: _____, 20 _____

_____   _____
Resident   Resident

_____   _____
Resident   Resident

_____   _____
Owner/Management   Owner/Management

NOTICE TO PAY RENT OR DELIVER POSSESSION (FORM 25)

To be issued when tenant is late on rent.

TO: _____   DATE: _____

_____

_____

YOU ARE HEREBY NOTIFIED THAT YOU ARE INDEBTED TO US IN THE SUM OF: $ _____
FOR THE RENT AND USE OF THE ABOVE REFERENCED PREMISE IN _____ COUNTY,
STATE OF _____, NOW OCCUPIED BY YOU AND THAT WE DEMAND PAYMENT OF SAID
RENT OR THAT YOU SURRENDER POSSESSION OF THE SAID PREMISES WITHIN THREE (3) DAYS (EX-
CLUDING SATURDAYS, SUNDAYS, AND LEGAL HOLIDAYS, FROM THE DATE OF DELIVERY OF THIS
NOTICE:

ON OR BEFORE THE _____ DAY OF _____ 20___.

YOUR FAILURE TO COMPLY WITH THIS NOTICE MAY RESULT IN EVICTION PROCEEDINGS BEING
INSTITUTED AGAINST YOU. WE WILL RETAKE POSSESSION FOR YOUR ACCOUNT IN THE EVENT YOU
VACATE OR ARE EVICTED. YOU WILL BE HELD LIABLE FOR PAST DUE RENT, AND, FUTURE RENT DUE
UNDER THE FULL TERM OF YOUR RENTAL AGREEMENT MINUS ANY RENT RECEIVED FROM RE-
RENTING THE PREMISES, ANY CHARGES DUE UNDER THE TERMS OF YOUR RENTAL AGREEMENT,
DAMAGES TO THE PREMISES, ATTORNEYS' FEES AND COURT COSTS.

_____
Owner/Agent Signature and Printed Name

_____
Property/Company Name

_____
Property/Company Address

_____
Telephone Number

CERTIFICATE OF SERVICE

I hereby certify that a copy of the above notice was:
_____ delivered to _____ by hand
_____ posted on the premises described above in the tenant's absence
on _____, 20___.
By:

_____
Owner/Agent

LEASE VIOLATION NOTICE WITH OPTION TO CURE (FORM 26)

Sample completed form—to be issued when tenant breaks a rule of the lease and you wish to give them 7 days to correct the problem and remain in your rental unit.

TO: _Arianna McDowall_   DATE: _06/05/15_

    3333 Celtic Drive

    Tampa, Florida 33615

YOU ARE NOTIFIED THAT YOU HAVE VIOLATED YOUR RENTAL AGREEMENT AND/OR THE LAW AS FOLLOWS:

Presence of a pet without approval by management or execution or a Pet Addendum

DEMAND IS HEREBY MADE THAT YOU REMEDY THE NONCOMPLIANCE(S) WITHIN SEVEN (7) DAYS OF RECEIPT OF THIS NOTICE OR YOUR RENTAL AGREEMENT SHALL BE DEEMED TERMINATED AND YOU SHALL VACATE THE PREMISES UPON SUCH TERMINATION. IF THIS SAME CONDUCT OR CONDUCT OF A SIMILAR NATURE IS REPEATED WITHIN TWELVE (12) MONTHS, YOUR TENANCY IS SUBJECT TO TERMINATION WITHOUT YOUR BEING GIVEN AN OPPORTUNITY TO CURE THE NONCOMPLIANCE(S).

WE WILL RETAKE POSSESSION FOR YOUR ACCOUNT IN THE EVENT YOU VACATE OR ARE EVICTED. YOU WILL BE HELD LIABLE FOR PAST DUE RENT, AND, FUTURE RENT DUE UNDER THE FULL TERM OF YOUR RENTAL AGREEMENT MINUS ANY RENT RECEIVED FROM RERENTING THE PREMISES, ANY CHARGES DUE UNDER THE TERMS OF YOUR RENTAL AGREEMENT, DAMAGES TO THE PREMISES, ATTORNEYS' FEES, AND COURT COSTS.

Jim Landlord
Owner/Agent Signature and Printed Name
Happy Apartment Management
Property/Company Name
1044 Wisdom Lane, Tampa, FL 33615
Property/Company Address
_813-100-1514_
Telephone Number

CERTIFICATE OF SERVICE

I hereby certify that a copy of the above notice was:

_____ delivered to _____ by hand

_X_ posted on the premises described above in the tenant's absence

On _June 5_____, 201_5_.

By:

_Jim Landlord_____
Owner/Agent

LEASE VIOLATION NOTICE WITH OPTION TO CURE (FORM 26)

To be issued when tenant breaks a rule of the lease and you wish to give them 7 days to correct the problem and remain in your rental unit.

TO: _____   DATE: _____

_____

_____

YOU ARE NOTIFIED THAT YOU HAVE VIOLATED YOUR RENTAL AGREEMENT AND/OR THE LAW AS FOLLOWS:

_____

DEMAND IS HEREBY MADE THAT YOU REMEDY THE NONCOMPLIANCE(S) WITHIN SEVEN (7) DAYS OF RECEIPT OF THIS NOTICE OR YOUR RENTAL AGREEMENT SHALL BE DEEMED TERMINATED AND YOU SHALL VACATE THE PREMISES UPON SUCH TERMINATION. IF THIS SAME CONDUCT OR CONDUCT OF A SIMILAR NATURE IS REPEATED WITHIN TWELVE (12) MONTHS, YOUR TENANCY IS SUBJECT TO TERMINATION WITHOUT YOUR BEING GIVEN AN OPPORTUNITY TO CURE THE NONCOMPLIANCE(S).

WE WILL RETAKE POSSESSION FOR YOUR ACCOUNT IN THE EVENT YOU VACATE OR ARE EVICTED. YOU WILL BE HELD LIABLE FOR PAST DUE RENT, AND, FUTURE RENT DUE UNDER THE FULL TERM OF YOUR RENTAL AGREEMENT MINUS ANY RENT RECEIVED FROM RERENTING THE PREMISES, ANY CHARGES DUE UNDER THE TERMS OF YOUR RENTAL AGREEMENT, DAMAGES TO THE PREMISES, ATTORNEYS' FEES, AND COURT COSTS.

_____

Owner/Agent Signature and Printed Name

_____

Property/Company Name

_____

Property/Company Address

_____

Telephone Number

CERTIFICATE OF SERVICE

I hereby certify that a copy of the above notice was:

_____ delivered to _____ by hand

_____ posted on the premises described above in the tenant's absence

on _____, 20___.

By:

_____

Owner/Agent

LEASE VIOLATION NOTICE TO TERMINATE/VACATE (FORM 27)

Sample notice—to be issued when tenant severely or continually breaks a rule of the lease and you are terminating their lease and requiring them to vacate the unit within 7 days.

TO: _Aislinn McDowall_   DATE: _06/05/15_

    333 Celtic Drive

    Tampa, Florida 33615

YOU ARE ADVISED THAT YOUR TENANCY IS TERMINATED EFFECTIVE IMMEDIATELY. YOU SHALL HAVE SEVEN (7) DAYS FROM DELIVERY OF THIS NOTICE TO VACATE THE PREMISES. THIS ACTION IS TAKEN BECAUSE:

Discovery of drug paraphernalia in premises

WE WILL RETAKE POSSESSION FOR YOUR ACCOUNT IN THE EVENT YOU VACATE OR ARE EVICTED. YOU WILL BE HELD LIABLE FOR PAST DUE RENT, AND FUTURE RENT DUE UNDER THE FULL TERM OF YOUR RENTAL AGREEMENT MINUS ANY RENT RECEIVED FROM RERENTING THE PREMISES, ANY CHARGES DUE UNDER THE TERMS OF YOUR RENTAL AGREEMENT, DAMAGES TO THE PREMISES, AT-TORNEYS' FEES, AND COURT COSTS.

Jim Landlord
Owner/Agent Signature and Printed Name
Happy Apartment Management
Property/Company Name
1044 Wisdom Lane, Tampa, FL 33615
Property/Company Address
_813-100-1514_
Telephone Number

CERTIFICATE OF SERVICE

I hereby certify that a copy of the above notice was:

_____ delivered to _____ by hand

__X__ posted on the premises described above in the tenant's absence

On _June 6_____, 201_5_ .

By:

____Jim Landlord_____

Owner/Agent

LEASE VIOLATION NOTICE TO TERMINATE/VACATE (FORM 27)

To be issued when tenant severely or continually breaks a rule of the lease and you are terminating their lease and requiring them to vacate the unit within 7 days.

TO: _____ DATE: _____

_____

_____

YOU ARE ADVISED THAT YOUR TENANCY IS TERMINATED EFFECTIVE IMMEDIATELY. YOU SHALL HAVE SEVEN (7) DAYS FROM DELIVERY OF THIS NOTICE TO VACATE THE PREMISES. THIS ACTION IS TAKEN BECAUSE:

_____

WE WILL RETAKE POSSESSION FOR YOUR ACCOUNT IN THE EVENT YOU VACATE OR ARE EVICTED. YOU WILL BE HELD LIABLE FOR PAST DUE RENT, AND FUTURE RENT DUE UNDER THE FULL TERM OF YOUR RENTAL AGREEMENT MINUS ANY RENT RECEIVED FROM RERENTING THE PREMISES, ANY CHARGES DUE UNDER THE TERMS OF YOUR RENTAL AGREEMENT, DAMAGES TO THE PREMISES, ATTORNEYS' FEES, AND COURT COSTS.

_____

Owner/Agent Signature and Printed Name

_____

Property/Company Name

_____

Property/Company Address

_____

Telephone Number

CERTIFICATE OF SERVICE

I hereby certify that a copy of the above notice was:

_____ delivered to _____ by hand

_____ posted on the premises described above in the tenant's absence

on _____, 20___.

By:

_____

Owner/Agent

DISTURBANCE NOTICE (FORM 28)

To be issued when tenant causes a disturbance.

TO: _____   DATE: _____
_____
_____

YOU UNREASONABLY DISTURBED YOUR NEIGHBORS BY: _____
_____
_____
_____
_____
_____

IF YOU UNREASONABLY DISTURB YOUR NEIGHBORS AGAIN DURING THE NEXT 12 MONTHS, YOUR LEASE MAY BE TERMINATED AND YOU MAY BE REQUIRED TO VACATE YOUR UNIT WITHIN 7 DAYS OF TERMINATION. IF YOUR LEASE IS TERMINATED, WE WILL RETAKE POSSESSION OF YOUR UNIT. YOU WILL STILL BE LIABLE FOR RENT AND LATE CHARGES UNTIL THE LEASE EXPIRES, LESS ANY RENT WE RECEIVE FROM RERENTING THE PREMISES. IF SUIT IS FILED YOU ALSO WILL BE LIABLE FOR OUR SUIT COSTS INCLUDING ATTORNEYS' FEES.

_____
Owner/Agent Signature and Printed Name

_____
Property/Company Name

_____
Property/Company Address

_____
Telephone Number

CERTIFICATE OF SERVICE

I hereby certify that a copy of the above notice was:

_____ delivered to _____ by hand

_____ posted on the premises described above in the tenant's absence

on _____, 20____.

By:

_____
Owner/Agent

DISHONORED CHECK NOTICE (FORM 29)

To be issued when tenant's check is returned for nonsufficient funds.

_____, 20____
(date)

_____
(name of check writer)

_____
(rental unit street address & number)

_____
(city, county, state, zip)

You are hereby notified that a check, numbered _____, in the face amount of $ _____, issued by you on (date) _____, drawn upon _____ (name of bank), and payable to _____, has been dishonored. You have 7 days from receipt of this notice to tender payment of the full amount of such check plus a service charge of $25, if the face value does not exceed $50; $30, if the face value exceeds $50 but does not exceed $300; $40, if the face value exceeds $300; or an amount of up to 5 percent of the face amount of the check, whichever is greater, the total amount due being $ _____ and _____ cents. Unless the amount is paid in full within the time specified above, the holder of such check may turn over the dishonored check and all other available information relating to this incident to the state attorney for criminal prosecution. You may be additionally liable in a civil action for triple the amount of the check, but in no case less than $50, together with the amount of the check, a service charge, court costs, reasonable attorney fees, and incurred bank fees, if payment is not made within 30 days.

_____
(signature)

_____
(name and title)

_____
(community name, if any)

_____
(street address)

_____
(city, state)

_____
(telephone number)

Sent certified mail # _____ on _____.

Mailed by:

_____
(signature of person who mailed it)

WORK ORDER (FORM 30)

Use this form to take down information when a tenant calls and needs a repair made.

Date & Time	
Resident Name	
Address	

Type of Work to Be Performed

Tools Needed to Complete Work

Maintenance Tech or Contractor's Name or Company Name

Price of labor/parts	# of hours or parts	Total Cost
	TOTAL COSTS	

Work Performed By:	Date:

Notes:

Complete Section Below, Tear Off, and Leave in Unit

NOTICE OF ENTRY TO RESIDENCE

Date:	Time Entered:
Reason for Entering: Maintenance:	Time Left:
Work Completed By:	
Work Performed:	
Notes:	

PREVENTIVE MAINTENANCE CHECKLIST (FORM 31)

Use this form to maintain good repair of your unit.

Date: _____   Inspected by: _____

Address: _____

Pets: _____ Yes _____ No

Unit Condition: _____ Good _____ Fair _____ Poor

Category	Check Where Available	Condition			Work Completed/ Notes
		Good	Fair	Poor	
PLUMBING					
Leaks/Drips:					
#1 Bath Fixtures					
#2 Bath Fixtures					
#3 Bath Fixtures					
Heating/AC:					
Change Filter					
Thermostat Operation					
APPLIANCES					
Gas Water Heater					
Gas Heater Venting					
Electric Water Heater					
Refrigerator Coils					
GAS FURNACE					
Venting/Heat Exchanger					
Burners					
Evaporator Motor					
FIRE SAFETY					
Check Smoke Alarm					
Hard Wired					
Battery					
Fire Extinguisher (pressure gauge)					
SAFETY					
Check Sliding Door Locks					
Charlie Bar					
Pin					
Additional Locks					

Windows/Locks					
Check Handrails					
Patio					
Balcony					
Alarm System					

Additional Comments: _____

_____

_____

_____

RENEWAL NOTICE (FORM 32)

Send this form to your tenant at least 30 days prior to the end of the lease term if you wish to renew their lease.

Date: _____

To: _____

_____

_____

This letter is to advise you that in accordance with paragraph _____ of your lease agreement, I am giving you official notice that your lease is due to expire on _____. **Please be advised your new monthly rent amount shall be $_____ a month.** Please be informed it is imperative you come to _____ during the hours of _____ on the days of _____ as soon as possible to have a new lease signed. In the event you choose not to renew your lease, this is your official notice that I will not allow you to remain as a month-to-month resident. You will be required to vacate the premises on the _____ day of _____, 20___. If you fail to turn in your keys, you will be considered a holdover resident and charged accordingly.

_____

Owner/Agent

CERTIFICATE OF SERVICE

I hereby certify that a copy of the above notice was:

_____ delivered to _____ by hand

_____ posted on the premises described above in the tenant's absence

on _____, 20___.

By:

_____

Owner/Agent

NONRENEWAL NOTICE (FORM 33)

Send this form to your tenant at least 30 days prior to the end of the lease term if you are not renewing their lease.

Date: _____

To: _____

_____

_____

This letter is to advise you that in accordance with paragraph _____ of your lease agreement, I am giving you official notice that your lease is due to expire on _____. **Please be advised I will not be renewing your lease agreement, nor will you be given the opportunity to remain as a month-to-month resident.** *You must make all arrangements to vacate the premises on the _____ day of _____ , 20 ___.* If you fail to turn in your keys and do not vacate by the above referenced date, I shall have no alternative but to advise my attorney's office to proceed in regaining possession of your unit. Please be advised that the landlord is entitled to demand double your monthly rent for as long as you remain a holdover resident.

_____

Owner/Agent

CERTIFICATE OF SERVICE

I hereby certify that a copy of the above notice was:

_____ delivered to _____ by hand

_____ posted on the premises described above in the tenant's absence

on _____, 20___.

By:

_____

Owner/Agent

NOTICE OF INTENTION TO IMPOSE CLAIM ON SECURITY DEPOSIT (FORM 34)

Send this form to your tenant after they vacate your unit to notify them you are deducting charges from their security deposit.

TO: _____ DATE: _____

_____

_____

THIS IS A NOTICE OF THE LANDLORD'S INTENTION TO IMPOSE A CLAIM FOR DAMAGES UPON YOUR SECURITY DEPOSIT AS INDICATED BELOW. YOU ARE HEREBY NOTIFIED THAT YOU MUST OBJECT IN WRITING TO THIS DEDUCTION FROM YOUR SECURITY DEPOSIT WITHIN FIFTEEN (15) DAYS FROM THE TIME YOU RECEIVE THIS NOTICE, OR THE LANDLORD WILL BE AUTHORIZED TO DEDUCT ITS CLAIM FROM YOUR SECURITY DEPOSIT. YOUR OBJECTION MUST BE SENT TO THE LANDLORD AT THE ADDRESS SHOWN BELOW.

_____

_____

_____

Amount of Security Deposit $ _____

Interest if due $ _____

Total security deposit and interest (if due) $ _____

Less damages and rent:

_____ $ _____

DAMAGES

_____ $ _____

RENT

Total damages and rent due $ _____

Total due to: ( ) landlord

            ( ) tenant $ _____

Sent certified mail # _____ on _____, 20___.

Mailed by: _____

Note: This notice does not waive or limit any of landlord's rights to damages or amounts due which may exceed security deposit or amounts listed on this form.

NOTICE OF TERMINATION OF MONTH-TO-MONTH TENANCY (FORM 35)

Send this form to any month-to-month tenant when you wish to notify them they have 30 days to vacate.

Date: _____

To: _____ and all others in possession

_____

_____

You are a month-to-month tenant in the above described premises, your rental period beginning on the _____ of each month.

You are hereby notified that your landlord is terminating your tenancy, and that you are required to vacate the premises and surrender same to your landlord or his agent on the _____ day of _____, 20___, this notice being served upon you not less than 15 days prior to the end of the applicable rental period.

As an alternative to the aforementioned, the management of _____ will discuss your options in remaining as a resident. It is imperative that you contact the management immediately to discuss the situation.

_____

Owner/Agent

CERTIFICATE OF SERVICE

I hereby certify that a copy of the above notice was:

_____ delivered to _____ by hand

_____ posted on the premises described above in the tenant's absence

on _____, 20___.

By:

_____

Owner/Agent

NOTICE OF RESIDENT MANAGER'S/OWNER'S INTENT TO ENTER (FORM 36)

Send this form to any tenant to notify them you need to enter their unit.

Date: _____

To: _____

_____

_____

Please be advised that the manager/owner of _____ will be entering your residence on the _____ day of _____, 20___, in order to _____

_____ .

_____

Owner/Agent

CERTIFICATE OF SERVICE

I hereby certify that a copy of the above notice was:

_____ delivered to _____ by hand

_____ posted on the premises described above in the tenant's absence

on _____, 20___.

By:

_____

Owner/Agent

KEY RELEASE FORM (FORM 37)

If a tenant ever asks you to let someone enter their unit, like a service person, have them complete and sign this form authorizing you to allow someone access to the key to their unit.

Date: _____

Address: _____

_____

_____

I, _____, hereby authorize _____ to release a key to my residence on _____, 20____ in order to _____

_____ .

I understand that _____ is not responsible for the actions of to whom the key is released.

_____   _____
Resident   Owner/Agent

_____
Resident

_____
Date

IMPORTANT NOTICE REGARDING PATIOS AND WALKWAYS (FORM 38)

Send this form to tenants when they need to be reminded to clean their patio or walkway.

Date: _____

Dear Tenant:

We are excited to announce we will be improving our community by pressure washing the sidewalks, patios, balconies, and walkways. To avoid damage, please remove **ALL ITEMS** from the sidewalks, patios, balconies, and walkways other than patio furniture. Patio furniture consists of patio chairs or tables. All toys, grills, and other items must be removed no later than (**date**) _____. Any item not removed may be discarded.

Once the cleaning is complete, only patio furniture, doormats, and potted plants will be allowed to be placed on the sidewalks, patios, balconies, and walkways to comply with Code Policy.

Thank you for your support as we continue to improve our community.

Sincerely,
Management Team

INTRODUCTION OF NEW MANAGEMENT TO TENANT (FORM 39)

Send this form to all tenants when you take over management of a property to introduce yourself and your team.

Date: _____

Re: Management Services

Dear Tenant:

We are excited to announce that our company will begin handling the management of your unit beginning on _____. Providing quality housing and great service is important to our company. We look forward to helping provide you a wonderful place to call home.

Beginning with rent for the month of _____, please make checks or money orders payable to _____ and <u>continue to place in the rent drop box/mail to</u> _____. You can also give rent payments to the new on-site management that will be introduced to you soon. If you have not yet paid _____'s rent, please follow this new procedure as well.

The new number to contact for **Maintenance** needs is _____.

We will be personally delivering a new lease within a week to you. This lease provides you with important information, like where your security deposit is now being held and how to contact us. The lease does not increase your rent, nor does it extend the length of your original lease term. It simply updates relevant matters now that we will be assisting you with your housing needs.

We are also enclosing photos of our team so you can recognize us next time we meet.

We look forward to working with you.

Sincerely,
Management Team

IMPORTANT NOTICE EVICTION PROCEEDINGS (FORM 40)

Send this form to any tenant you are filing for eviction on.

Date: _____

To: _____

_____

_____

Please be advised you have been turned over to our attorney and are currently under eviction proceedings <u>for nonpayment of rent</u>. You must contact our office at _____ to make arrangements to move out and return your keys.

Eviction proceedings will continue and proper measures will be taken to regain possession of your dwelling should you fail to follow these instructions.

_____
Owner/Manager

_____
Property/Company Name

_____
Property/Company Address

_____
Telephone Number

CERTIFICATE OF SERVICE

I hereby certify that a copy of the above notice was:

_____ delivered to _____ by hand

_____ posted on the premises described above in the tenant's absence

on _____, 20___.

By:

_____
Owner/Agent

INDEX

Page numbers in *italics* refer to forms.

prepayment, 90, 97

prequalifying, 90–92

preventive maintenance, 32

Preventive Maintenance Checklist, 181, *280–81*

prime rate, 89

procrastination, 26

professionalism, 28, 109, 115

promise to pay, 154

property evaluation, 20

property inspections, *see* inspections

property inspectors, 96

property insurance, 10, 78, 82, 128

property management, 20, 86, 105–6, 115, 150, 177

    see also landlording

property management software program, 150

property-management systems, 6

Property Profile Form, *221*

Property Profiling Checklist, *219–20*

property setup sheet, 59, 60, 61

Property Snapshot Form, 50, *51, 218*

property taxes, 10, 53, 78, 82

psychographics, 43, 44, 45, 56, 57, 108

public housing, 74

purchase agreement, 79

purchase price, 71

reading people, 63–64

Reagan, Ronald, 98

real estate:

    cyclical nature of, 10, 11

    different segments of, 19

    leverage in, 7

real estate investing:

    advantages of, 15

    five controls of, 12–13

frequently asked questions in, 208–11

    keys to growth in, 205–7

real estate terms, 57

RealtyTrac.com, 101

recourse loans, 97

refrigerators, 185

regulations, *see* rules and regulations

renewal, of leases, 135–36

Renewal Notice, 166–67, *282*

renovations, 31–32

Rental Application Form, *242*

rental investing, 4, 16

    Da Vinci Code of, 56

rental market rates, 43, 45–46

rental market surveys, 74, 102

rental property, 208–9

    advantages of long-term, 18–19

    amenities in, 45

    asset classes in, 41–42

    evaluating financial makeup of, 58–59

    financing for, *see* financing

    finding target area for, 44–49

    getting a good deal in, 30–32

    negotiating for, 63–84

    reevaluating financial makeup of, 51–56

    resilience of, 17–18

    SEOTA method of evaluating, 39–62

    see also landlording; landlords

rental units:

    equipping of, 108

    showing of, 115

    staging of, 113

rent growth forecast, 74

rent rolls, 75, 98

rent rolls/schedule, 72

rent-roll trick, 98

Bryan M. Chavis is the founder of The Landlord Academy™ and author and creator of "The Land-lording 101 Operations Manual"™, "The Rental Investor's Guide"™, and training material for the Certified Property Management Specialist™ designation, recognized by the Florida Real Estate Commission for continuing education. Bryan speaks throughout the United States on behalf of the National Apartment Association, teaching their Certified Apartment Manager courses to individuals and groups. Bryan also started Apartment Investment Advisors (AIA), a multifamily investment company, and was named one of the top forty up-and-coming entrepreneurs under the age of forty by the *Gulf Coast Business Review*.

Bryan overcame major obstacles to achieve his goal of becoming a successful entrepreneur. At the age of five, he was diagnosed with a severe learning disability, including dyslexia and attention deficit disorder. In grade school, Bryan's teachers put his desk inside a used refrigerator box with a hole cut out in the front—his parents were told it was the only way their hyperactive son could remain in school. But Bryan refused to allow his disability to control him or his future. Through hard work and determination, he went on to become one of the most successful property managers and real estate investors in the southeastern United States, developing intuitive and user-friendly landlording systems that work for *any* user. Today, his landlord training materials are taught in colleges and seminars throughout North America.

Bryan is a cofounder of the Winky Wright Landlord Academy Celebrity Charity Golf Tournament, along with Winky Wright, the WBA and WBC super welterweight boxing champion of the world. One of Bryan's favorite quotes is "Your actions can be no wiser than your thoughts, and your thinking no wiser than your understanding."